The Ballad and the Folk

The Ballad and the Folk

David Buchan

TUCKWELL PRESS

First published 1972
by Routledge & Kegan Paul Ltd
This edition published in 1997 by
Tuckwell Press
The Mill House
Phantassie
East Linton
East Lothian EH40 3DG
Scotland

ISBN 1 898410 67 4

The publishers gratefully acknowledge
financial assistance from

THE SCOTTISH ARTS COUNCIL

towards the publication of this volume

Printed and bound by
Cromwell Press, Melksham, Wiltshire

For Moyra, Rhona and Gavin

Contents

Contents

Foreword

Following David Buchan's premature death in October 1994 at his home in St John's, Newfoundland, it was hardly surprising that the British and Scottish national newspapers carried lengthy obituaries, for he was a scholar of internationally recognised worth. Born (1939), bred, and educated in Aberdeen, at whose University he gained both an Honours degree in English and a Doctorate, he had taught for a number of years in North America before returning in 1968 to the new Scottish University of Stirling where he was Lecturer, later Senior Lecturer, in English Studies and the convenor and only lecturer for the Folklife Studies component of the English Studies with Folklife Studies degree programme. During this period he published *The Ballad and the Folk* (1972).

In 1979 he was appointed Professor of Folklore and Head of Department at Memorial University of Newfoundland, where he remained—apart from visiting professorships to Binghampton, Guelph, Aberdeen and Sheffield—for the rest of his life. In early 1994 he was appointed by unanimous decision to the newly-created Chair of Scottish Ethnology at the University of Aberdeen (only the second such Chair to be established in the United Kingdom) despite his having made clear to the committee that he was suffering from a recurrence of cancer. He had hoped for sufficient time to establish the Chair and its research Institute on a firm footing, but soon afterwards fell gravely ill and selflessly relinquished his post in order that a successor might be swiftly sought.

Throughout his distinguished and productive career, David was noted for the thoroughness of his work, for his imaginative handling of complex and difficult problems, and for his generosity and kindness to colleagues and students alike. Although his lectures and publications were to be extremely wide-ranging, from six-teenth-century Scottish ballads to Glasgow prison humour and from urban legends to medical folklore, the work that initially made him famous (or, to some, notorious) was his *tour de force* on the balladry and society of the North-East of Scotland, the significantly titled *The*

Ballad and the Folk. Although it was (unbelievably) eventually allowed to go out of print, it has remained in the current domain of ballad scholarship and must be one of the most commonly quoted works in the field. David was, however, adamant that any republication should be a simple reprint of the original work without amendment or further commentary, and this present edition honours that request.

This book took up the cudgels of the oral-formulaic approach to balladry initiated by the publication of Albert Lord's *The Singer of Tales* in 1960, and as William McCarthy describes in his masterly treatment of it in *The Ballad Matrix* (1990), it '...synthesises much that is best in the two not always contiguous fields of folklore and oral tradition'. I do not want, however, to dwell on this well-known aspect of the book: his (then) unique thesis that the great, classical ballads can only be fully understood in relation to their performance (and performers) *and* in relation to the society—including its history, geography and sociology—which sustained them, in this case that of the North-East of Scotland from the mid-eighteenth century to the present day. Such ideas have now become commonplace, but what put them into his mind when he first developed his hypothesis in the early 1960s?

David Buchan was born into an unusual part of the world. The North-East of Scotland, until very recently largely a farming area with its 'capital' in Aberdeen, is geographically isolated, bounded by the sea to the north and east, and by hills and mountains to the south and west. Its people like to think of themselves as restrained—almost withdrawn—cautious and undemonstrative. Yet it has contained, at least since the seventeenth century, a thriving traditional singing and musical culture which transcends local, national and even international boundaries. When, for example, Professor Child began his initial search in Britain for 'great' ballads he was directed to this area, and was not to be disappointed for it was to provide him with one-third of both his Scottish and his 'A' texts. (It should be noted in passing that almost half of the eight volumes of 3,500 folksongs amassed by Gavin Greig and James Bruce Duncan in the decade before the Great War of 1914–18 from the supposedly dour, reserved, undemonstrative denizens of this area are devoted to the category of 'Love Songs'.)

Like all Aberdonians David had strong family connections with the hinterland, especially in his case with the fishing and seafaring community. This community has thrived along the North-East coast for well over two hundred years, reaching a peak before the Great War. It largely inhabits its own world of the narrow coastal strip and relates to similar communities around the coasts of the British Isles and Ireland. Its villages and towns have supplied seamen for coastal fishing, the Arctic hunt for the whale, deep-sea fishing and long-distance sailing, both sail and steam. For centuries it has looked outwards in its trade to Scandinavia and the Baltic, Germany and Russia, and much of the rest of Europe. Its people tend to be deeply religious with a strong singing tradition which has been heavily influenced by revivalist evangelism.

David himself was brought up in, and ultimately rebelled from, the Church of Scotland, a Protestant, Presbyterian religion owing more to Calvin than Luther. Its fiercely democratic Church insists on personal effort to gain a personal salvation; it has, furthermore, a highly influential singing tradition whose hymns and psalms draw on four centuries of international compositions and settings, many of them folksongs. To the end of his days David would sing these hymns in unlikely places: in the car, in the shower—a special favourite being 'Onward! Christian Soldiers' by the English folksong collector, Sabine Baring-Gould.

He attended local schools, including a spell during the 1939–45 War in the fishing village of Findochty (where my uncle was Headmaster) before entering Robert Gordon's College in Aberdeen at the age of eleven, where we first met. 'Gordon's' was a remarkable institution. It had been founded in 1732 by Robert Gordon, who had amassed a fortune during his life as a trader in Danzig. A bachelor, he bequeathed his fortune to establish a school 'for the education of poor boys; that the knowledge of letters and lawful employments may flourish and be advanced to all succeeding generations'. In the 1950s, unlike most other similar foundations which had evolved into upmarket exclusive private schools, Gordon's remained true to its founder's intentions, and provided a good general education to a wide social mix of boys (women in any shape or form were specifically forbidden in the Foundation Charter), many of whom were supported financially by College bursaries. Every Founder's Day, speakers from all over the world strove (with degrees of success) to vary the theme of how Gordon's international endeavours amongst the Hanseatic traders combined with his love of the North-East to produce such a generous outcome.

Robert Gordon had come from a cadet branch of the great Gordon clan, originally one of the Anglo-Norman families invited into the region some seven centuries before to help keep the King's peace— and who had indulged in almost constant warfare with their neighbours thereafter—inspiring, incidentally, many of the historical Child ballads David was later to study. There was an Army cadet unit of the Gordon Highlanders at the school, but David's interests lay in two other directions—outdoor sport and Scouting, and drama. Through Scouting he developed a great love for the mountains that lie only a few miles outside the city, especially the Cairngorms to the far west, the highest wilderness in Scotland. This Arctic plateau of great beauty is prone to rapid, violent weather changes; in pre-helicopter days, the consequences of immobilisation or poor navigation in that shelterless area were invariably lethal. Nevertheless they drew him constantly; his mind was seldom far from them and his early poetry celebrates their violent beauty. Rugby was also a constant pleasure and he played both for his school and for the former pupils' teams. The sport has a notorious singing tradition whose obvious folk roots have never been properly examined; from this he probably developed his permanent affinity for bawdry.

In English and drama the school possessed three highly influential masters. 'Doc' (John) Forrest lectured to a standard few University staff could meet, while the charismatic Brian Ludwig, newly arrived at the school from the North African Campaign of the 1939–45 war, injected an astonishing vigour and vitality into the Dramatic Society and other public performances, putting on a wide range of plays from Shakespeare to Edgar Wallace. David responded enthusiastically, but it was the enthralling John Foster who introduced him to the extraordinarily lively amateur theatre scene in the city, especially the British Empire Shakespeare Society. 'Frosty' was a superb Shakespearean actor in his own right and had made many radio broadcasts. He would sweep aside the school syllabus to expound on Shakespeare's works, acting out his examples and theories before bemused classes. David joined as many societies as he could, and began to think of little else but acting.

His schooldays were not long after a debilitating war (food rationing still existed) which had followed years of depression and hardship in Britain, and David's family naturally wanted a secure profession for their son. Acting was regarded as a highly chancy career and not to be thought of. David temporised by reading

Honours English at Aberdeen University, where he not only continued his city theatre group connections but joined in the several University dramatic societies as well. During this period he wrote at least three plays, lacking in sophistication, perhaps, but imbued with a directness and passion remembered to this day. His work suffered as a result and he gained only a Second-Class Honours degree in English in 1960.

Towards the end of his course, however, he had faced up to the fact that he could not disappoint his parents by pursuing professional acting, and reluctantly turned towards a career in English, preferably University teaching, which would give him, he thought, the free time and opportunity to indulge his passion for drama and playwriting. Without a First-Class degree he could not undertake advanced studies at centres such as Oxford, but he had sufficiently impressed his teachers at Aberdeen for him to be awarded a postgraduate research fellowship from 1960 to 1964 (with one year's spell in the middle, and one at the end, as an Instructor of English at the University of Victoria—where he spent every spare moment on drama).

In one way it was surprising that he was encouraged to work on ballads, for although they were regarded as 'literature' of a sort, ethnological studies were (and still are) looked down upon by the British academic community. On the other hand the Folk Music Revival was under way, and centres such as the School of Scottish Studies at Edinburgh were demonstrating that Scottish balladry had great research potential; he also had a farsighted mentor in John Lothian. David came across two impressive collections of folksong in the University Archives. These were carefully preserved and jealously guarded, and initially he had difficulty in persuading the Librarian, Dr Douglas Simpson, to allow them to be handled by a mere student.

The Glenbuchat MSS consisted of four volumes of some sixty Child ballads collected by a local parish minister in the early nineteenth century. As David's work on these progressed, a highly impressed Dr Simpson persuaded the University Library Committee to give David permission to edit and publish the manuscripts—a very remarkable concession. Although David worked away steadily at the project, at the time of his death it was incomplete, as it lacked the final version of a grand contextualising chapter. (Almost every year, though, the editing had provided him with a good reason to return to Aberdeenshire in order to accumulate another painstaking piece of research on the Glenbuchat papers; perhaps he had never really wanted to finish.)

But also on the Library shelves was the already mentioned Greig-Duncan Folk Song Collection, one of the largest and most comprehensive ever made, consisting of some 3500 texts, 3100 tunes—and 108 Child ballads. Only the Child ballads had ever been published, in a posthumous 1925 volume edited by Alexander Keith, who had given it the significant title of *Last Leaves of Traditional Ballads and Ballad Airs Collected in Aberdeenshire by the Late Gavin Greig*. In a letter written to me four weeks before his death on 12 October 1994, David spoke of those early days:

> When I started out on my doctoral research in 1960 my initial research area was the Greig-Duncan MSS (or the Gavin Greig MSS, as they were then habitually referred to). My choice was warmly supported by Professor John Lothian who was acutely aware that the University had a responsibility to encourage work on this priceless collection in the University Archives. As a young and green postgraduate student I paid a visit to the editor of *Last Leaves*, hoping for some practical advice and collegial encouragement. At Eigie Farm, near Balmedie, I was most hospitably received by Alex Keith and Mrs Keith (who inspired no little awe, I remember, by her steady ladylike consumption of Capstan Full Strength cigarettes). When, however, we came to the purpose of the visit and I declared the subject of my proposed research, cold water was poured on it from a great height. I was informed by Alex Keith that nothing more remained to be said about the Gavin Greig manuscripts, the songs having been covered by Greig in the *Buchan Observer* volumes and the last word on the ballads having been delivered by *Last Leaves*. 'I wouldna bother. It's aa been deen', he concluded. Acculturated in Northeast reductiveness though I was, this ex cathedra pronouncement left me dumfoonert. It must also have stirred in me a certain Northeast thrawnness, for once I became aware (quite early) that the entire collection was too huge for one tyro researcher to encompass in one three-year project, and for thesis purposes required delimitation, I focussed my attention on the ballads on which the last word had been delivered and, sparked initially by the pronounced differences in texture between the ballad texts in *Last Leaves* and the eighteenth century ballad texts of Anna Brown, determined on contextualising the *Last Leaves* ballads by showing the evolutionary place in the development of the region's ballad tradition, hoping, in rather utopian fashion, that this might also serve as a kind of paradigm for the development of the entire folksong tradition of the Northeast, and thereby provide a general

context for all the songs in the Greig-Duncan collection. This work resulted eventually in *The Ballad and the Folk*. So I personally have a great deal to thank Alex Keith for; had it not been for his sweeping negation, and my contermashious reaction to it, I might never have been impelled along the research track I was to find so stimulating and culturally revealing.

Such were the beginnings, and in any other person they could have led on to a lifetime of worthy but pedestrian textual scholarship. With David it was to be different, for he saw the Greig-Duncan ballads as *records of performances* in a geographical region he loved and knew well. With his knowledge of the theatre he saw also that the singer, the song, the performance and the audience were inextricably bound together, all mutually interdependent. To understand one part, you had to understand all the others. From his background in drama he derived a unique approach not only to the question of social contextualisation of the ballads but also to the question of creativity and recreativity in performance which was to involve him in so much controversy and debate. From the very beginning the way was quite clear to him as described in the last verse of a poem written in his final student year, entitled 'Curtain Up':

The curtains hiss open...
Beyond, a sea of faces
Awaiting the world you
Are about to create.

Ian A. Olson
Aberdeen

Preface and Acknowledgments

This book is an exercise in an interdisciplinary discipline which is firmly established in many countries but has been rather neglected in Britain. The discipline is known variously: in Scandinavia as *Folkliv*, in Central Europe as *Volkskunde*, and in North America as Folklore. Since 'folklore' in Britain connotes mostly triviality and untruth, a happier term for the subject is Folklife Studies, although its practitioners retain the name of folklorists. Folklorists are concerned with traditional culture, that is, the culture maintained and transmitted by word-of-mouth and by custom and practice rather than by printed document. The literary folklorist, it follows, is concerned with the literature created and transmitted by traditional means within that culture. He is also concerned with the relationship between the literature and the social and cultural context: especially with how the literature in quality, substance, and style is determined by the conditions of the society that produces it. In the following pages I have attempted to show the social context of a ballad tradition and its effects on the literature, and, conversely, the functions of the literature in the social context.

The correlation of literature and society is particularly necessary in the field of oral literature, a once vague area that has been given new definition by the groundbreaking studies of Milman Parry and Albert Lord. Working in a new field like oral literature, however, poses certain problems, and not the least of these is the lack of adequate terminology. Inevitably, one is forced into minting terms; I have tried to avoid an undue barbarity in the neologisms, but ask for sufferance. There are, again inevitably, other topics on which I crave the sufferance of that declining species, the gentle reader. Since this volume is long enough as it stands, it does no more than touch on two subjects which ideally require fair-sized books to themselves. One is ballad music (though I hope the comments in chapter 20 may provoke an ethnomusicologist into investigation), and the other is the relationship between Scandinavian and Scottish (especially Northeast) balladry. A work not referred to in the text because it appeared after the relevant parts of the manuscript were completed is T. C. Smout's *A History of the Scottish People 1560–1830*; this excellent book is now the standard work on the subject.

I am very grateful to a number of people and institutions for their ready co-operation in allowing me to publish excerpted material. The quotations from the Will Walker Collectanea are printed by permission of the Corporation of the City of Aberdeen; from the Will Walker MSS. by permission of Aberdeen University Library; from *Ballads* and *Curious Tracts, Scotland* by permission of the Trustees of the British Museum; from Peter Buchan: A Collection of 17 letters, Francis James Child MSS., James Gibb MS., Letters and Papers Relating to the Harris MS., Robert Jamieson-Brown MS., George R. Kinloch MSS., Alexander Laing of Brechin MS., William Motherwell MSS., William Motherwell: A Ballad Note-Book 1826–27, North Country Ballads (Abbotsford MS.), Robert Pitcairn MSS., William Tytler-Brown MS. by permission of the Harvard College Library; from H. M. and N. K. Chadwick, *The Growth of Literature*, by permission of Cambridge University Press; from Albert B. Lord, *The Singer of Tales*, by permission of Harvard University Press; and from Henry Hamilton, *Selections from the Monymusk Papers 1713–1755*, by permission of the Council of the Scottish History Society.

The *ur*-version of the book that follows was a thesis accepted for the Aberdeen Ph.D., and I would like to thank the University of Aberdeen for the award of the Gordon Bottomley Fellowship, and to record my debt of gratitude to the late Professor John M. Lothian and to Dr James Michie. I am grateful also to the staffs of various libraries, especially those of King's College, University of Aberdeen, and the Houghton Library, Harvard University. Above all, I am grateful to my wife, whose ability to exercise both critical intelligence and domestic tolerance has given me a pristine appreciation of that unfashionable word, helpmate.

Two final notes: parts of chapters 4 and 17 originally appeared in *Journal of the Folklore Institute* and *Ariel* and I thank their editors for permission to use them here; numerals in brackets after a ballad title refer to that ballad-story's number in the standard collection, F. J. Child, *The English and Scottish Ballads*.

Abbreviations

Abbreviations employed in the notes:

AUR	*Aberdeen University Review*
FSNE	*Folk-Song of the North-East*, 2 vols (Peterhead, 1909, 1914). 1 vol. (Hatboro, Penn., 1963)
PMLA	*Publications of the Modern Language Association*
SHR	*Scottish Historical Review*
SS	*Scottish Studies*
TBC	*Transactions of the Buchan Field Club* (1887–1908) *Transactions of the Buchan Club* (1908–)

Abbreviations employed in the diagrams:

H = He, Hero, Leading Male Character
S = She, Heroine, Leading Female Character
S^2 = Other Woman, and (103) Second Heroine
H^2 = (103) Second Hero

M	= Mother		F	= Father
Br	= Brother		Sr	= Sister
Sn	= Son		b	= boy
K	= King		Q	= Queen
V	= Villain		V^2	= Second Villain
P	= Porter		BB	= Belly Blin
bw	= bowerwoman			

Capitals indicate one of the three major interacting characters; lower case indicates a narrative agent.

Chapter 1

Introduction

Ballads are awkward things. Few literary genres give so much pleasure to so many kinds of people and yet pose such refractory problems for the scholar and critic. These tales of marvel, love and butchery, told in a style strikingly distinct from that of most poetry, appeal to a diverse audience, but yet provoke questions which have never been satisfactorily answered. The most fundamental of these are, 'What is a ballad?' and 'Who were the folk who sang the ballads?' The problems involved in answering these questions, problems of authorship, definition, terminology, and classification, make up what one critic has called the 'ballad enigma'.[1] This book is an attempt to unriddle the enigma. Through an examination of the ballads and the folk of one particular regional tradition it tries to answer the basic questions about 'the' ballad and 'the' folk.

The only commonly accepted answer to the question, 'What is a ballad?' is 'A folksong that tells a story', where folksong means a song that has been transmitted by word-of-mouth rather than by print.[2] The use of the laborious 'by word-of-mouth' instead of the more obvious term 'orally' is intentional because the word 'oral' raises the most formidable, and the most significant, of the subject's terminological problems. This key word is, unfortunately, ambiguous, and much confusion has arisen from its ambiguity. It is used specifically, to refer to the tradition of non-literate societies, and it is also used generally to refer to that tradition *and* the word-of-mouth tradition of literate societies. Even from an *a priori* position one would suspect what actually is the case, that the tradition and transmission of a nonliterate society differ significantly from the tradition and transmission of a literate society. Anthropologists have recognized this by drawing a distinction between *primitive literature* and *folk literature*, the

1

latter denoting word-of-mouth material affected by literate influences, and the former word-of-mouth material relatively unaffected by literate influences. Just as the use of 'folk' in this instance illustrates how confused is the available terminology, so do the ambiguities inherent in 'oral'. Henceforth 'oral' will be employed only in the specific sense—to refer to nonliterate tradition—and 'verbal' will be employed for the word-of-mouth tradition of a literate culture. The necessity for distinguishing between oral tradition and verbal tradition has been dramatically emphasized in recent years by a number of works which have opened up for study the virtually unknown field of oral literature.

The three works which have done most to intensify our awareness of oral literature are the Chadwicks' *The Growth of Literature*, Albert B. Lord's *The Singer of Tales*, and more tangentially, Marshall McLuhan's *The Gutenberg Galaxy*.[3] The Chadwicks chart the oral literature of many peoples; Lord elucidates the nature of oral composition and the patterns of oral narrative poetry; and McLuhan, who describes his book as complementary to Lord's, explores the modification of oral consciousness brought about by the introduction of printing. Of these three it is Lord's work which is of most direct concern here. *The Singer of Tales* is a complete expression of the ideas on oral literature first adumbrated in the pioneering articles of Milman Parry. Prompted initially by the complexities of the Homeric question, Parry and Lord investigated the living oral tradition of Yugoslavia and, in doing so, revealed the workings of the oral technique of composition and its effects upon oral poetic form. Their writings have produced far-reaching reverberations. The most important extension of their work has appeared, appropriately enough, in Homeric scholarship, where Cedric Whitman builds a literary critique on oral data in his *Homer and the Heroic Tradition*; but the general application of their findings to a broad range of literatures, from Anglo-Saxon to medieval Greek, has provoked reconsiderations not only of individual literary traditions but also of our preconceptions about literature and literary composition.[4]

Balladry, it has been said often enough, is a genre of oral literature. But whereas 'oral' in the phrase 'oral literature' is normally used in the specific sense, most references to balladry as oral literature have used it in the general sense. By analysing the processes of transmission in a nonliterate culture Lord, however, has provided the means whereby one can see whether balladry is in fact a genre of oral literature in the specific sense. If ballads were oral literature, were originally composed and transmitted by nonliterate people, then many of the ballad riddles would be solved. But surely, the objection may come, this approach will not hold good for British balladry: hasn't Britain had a literate culture since the late Middle Ages? The reply is that only parts of British society had a literate culture. Lord shows that, 'While the presence of writing in a society *can* have an effect on oral tradition, it does not *necessarily* have an effect at all'. The written tradition of the Southern Slavs 'had no influence on the form of the oral tradition until the nineteenth and twentieth centuries. The two existed side by side, not, of course, within the same group, but certainly within the same district'.[5] Even though a society may have literate members who are acquainted with book-learning, oral trans-mission can, and does, flourish in the unlettered groups within that society. Even though the England and the Scotland of the ballads' recorded history had strong written traditions, many groups of people in these countries were, for most of that time, nonliterate, and it is in these groups that oral transmission would have flourished. This emphasizes how important it is when dealing with traditional material to correlate, as nearly as possible, a society and its literature—in this case, the folk and their ballads. Many years ago Louise Pound denounced in uncompromising terms the standard wrong approach to 'the folk':[6]

> Surely theorists and dictionary makers should know by
> this time that there is no mysterious national 'folk',
> 'the masses', the 'common people' of the old folklorists.
> . . . all oral tradition is necessarily regional or group lore,
> a generalisation too often overlooked. There is never any
> one folk from the point of view of folklore, but instead
> many folk groups, as many as there are regional cultures
> or occupations or racial groups within a region.

This dictum Entwistle applies to British balladry when he tentatively outlines the various regional traditions with their separate folks and separate balladries: 'I suspect that the phrase "English and Scottish" is too simple and that southern England, the Midlands, the Borders, the Scottish Lowlands, and Aberdeen-shire have each their own balladries with distinctive content and timetable.'[7] One of these regions, then, must provide the tradition whose folk and balladry will be the objects of scrutiny.

For answers to the central questions posed earlier—'What is a ballad?' and 'Who are the folk?'—the ideal region would be one which has a strong ballad tradition and which was affected by large-scale literacy so recently that the ballads, the folk, and the processes of transmission can be studied in both oral and post-oral states. There is, in fact, one region in Britain which comes as close to fitting this description as is practically possible. That region is the Northeast of Scotland. The area, which consists mainly of Aberdeenshire, possesses a rich ballad tradition and was substantially affected by literacy only in the later eighteenth century. Its recorded ballads include some that a singer learned by 1759 and some that were composed this century. The recorded tradition of this region, therefore, covers the tail-end of the nonliterate period and all of the literate period. The following account of this regional tradition has two parallel aims, one specifically literary—to investigate the ballad as oral literature—and one broadly ethnographic—to set the regional tradition in its social context. The initial chapters examine a nonliterate society to discover what factors besides nonliteracy helped foster its ballad tradition; the middle chapters analyse the processes of composition and transmission in the oral ballad; and the later chapters consider the changes which removed nonliteracy, altered social patterns, and seriously affected the ballad tradition.

THE REGIONAL TRADITION

Northeast balladry constitutes the richest regional tradition in Britain. The warrant for this assertion lies in both the quantity and the quality of the area's ballads: the tradition has more recorded ballads than any other and it includes what good authority has judged the 'best' ballads. Using the near-definitive Child collection as a yardstick, William Walker once showed[8] that one-third of Child's Scottish texts and almost one-third of his A-texts come from Aberdeenshire; and after Child's collection there appeared Alexander Keith's edition of Gavin Greig's *Last Leaves*, which contains 107 versions of ballad-stories found in Child, as many as have been recorded to date in North America. 'Last Leaves', as it turns out, is a misnomer, for the field is still being gleaned. In the last two decades the Fellows of the School of Scottish Studies have collected from the northeast several thousands of folksongs, among which are a fair number of ballads. And recently there have come to light the Glenbuchat MSS., a collection which contains fifty-eight Child ballads gathered in Aberdeenshire before 1818.[9] The tally of the region's collectors and collections that forms the Appendix testifies even further to the sheer bulk of the northeastern tradition.

But quantity alone is not everything. More and more it becomes obvious that the place of the individual singer within a tradition is of the utmost importance, and that the study of a tradition should begin with the individual singer and then work concentrically outwards.[10] The Northeast is fortunate in having a singer with a sizeable recorded corpus for each of the significant stages of the tradition's evolution. One of these singers is Mrs Brown, of whose ballads Child declares there are none 'superior in kind', an opinion corroborated by Kittredge, Gerould and Bronson.[11] And in a letter to Will Walker, Child stresses the quality of northeastern ballads in general: 'The original derivation of many of the ballads cannot be determined, but that the best Scottish ballads are from the North there can be no doubt.'[12] In Child, as in most other nineteenth-century scholars, the vague 'North' refers, not to the Celtic Highlands as one might expect, but to the Northeast.

To lay special emphasis upon the contribution of the northeast to British balladry might appear to be tilting at windmills, but it is necessary, for the Border fallacy still lingers on. It was reaffirmed as recently as 1961: 'Undeniably, the stronghold of British balladry since the sixteenth century has been the Lowlands of Scotland and the North of England.'[13] The Borders have a strong regional tradition characterized by a distinctive group of stirring ballad-stories—the Riding Ballads of the Border—but in neither quality nor quantity does this tradition equal that of the Northeast. The tendency to preface automatically

'Ballads' with 'Border' gained its initial and probably later impetus from the popular acclaim which greeted the many editions of Sir Walter Scott's *Minstrelsy of the Scottish Border*. This book, it was naturally assumed, represented a large number of ballads, the 'Abbotsford Collection', gathered by Sir Walter in the Borders. Despite the romantic accounts of his 'raids into Liddesdale', however, Scott does not appear to have been much of a field-collector himself; he preferred to garner texts from people who were.[14] Many of his ballad correspondents came from the Northeast, and through them Scott had access to most of the northeastern ballads then collected. The Abbotsford Collection contained at one time or another substantial recordings from Mrs Brown, the Old Lady, and James Nicol, and individual ballads gathered by Hugh Irvine of Drum, James Skene of Rubislaw, and Williamson Burnet of Monboddo in the Mearns. Mrs Brown's contribution to the *Minstrelsy of the Scottish Border* is large enough to invalidate Scott's title: 'Mrs Brown's material was to affect the whole character of the *Minstrelsy* . . . The Romantic section of the *Minstrelsy*, which is largely indebted to Mrs Brown, is perhaps that part of the work which is best known today.'[15] Ironically, then, many of the Scott ballads that helped establish the Borders as the pre-eminent ballad area come from the Northeast. The peculiar notions entertained about Scottish geography in one quite reputable ballad handbook perhaps exemplify how the fallacy, once accepted, was fostered. The author of the handbook goes astray, not by ignoring the other ballad regions of Scotland, but by assuming they all belong to 'the Borders'. Illustrating the book with a 'Border' scene of Perthshire, and her arguments with excerpts from 'Border' ballads indigenous to the Northeast, the writer claims that the atmosphere of the Border ballads derives from the borderers' having 'England to the south and the wild Highland clans to the north as enemies'.[16] This neat division of Scotland into 'Highlands' and 'Borders' would not be very well received in Edinburgh or Glasgow, as it is, of course, merrily oblivious to the existence of the entire Central Lowlands, where today live four-fifths of Scotland's population.

The northeastern tradition possesses a few general features which, although not of direct relevance to the topics in hand, are worthy of note. Almost two-thirds of the Anglo-Scottish ballad-stories in Child have been recorded in the Northeast tradition; some of these stories have been found only in the Northeast, and others are distinct Northeast oikotypes. The tradition includes two substantial and interesting groups of ballad-stories, the local–historical and the supernatural. While the first group demonstrates how the tradition was deeply rooted in local life, the second indicates how it was open to external influences, for the supernatural ballad-stories display close affinities with those of Scandinavia. In this they reflect a general characteristic of the region's balladry.

Since the days of Child and Grundtvig the relationship between British and Scandinavian balladry has received much attention—too much attention for our overall perspective, say some critics.[17] Still, there exists no definitive account of the relations between these balladries, a peculiar lack when one considers that the Scandinavian tradition is undeniably the British tradition's nearest sibling. While Britain has the national tradition most closely allied to the Scandinavian, the Northeast has the most closely allied regional tradition. The affinity is hardly surprising because, from the twelfth century onwards, the burgh of Aberdeen was an important commercial centre which traded with the continent rather than the rest of Britain. The provisions regarding merchants' losses that appear in the 1266 Treaty of Perth signed by Scotland and Norway would indicate a thriving trade between Aberdeen, then the major port north of Berwick, and at least one part of Scandinavia by the middle of the thirteenth century. Trade between the countries helped produce the steady political interaction that gave rise to a few royal marriages and, on one occasion, the events of 'Sir Patrick Spens' (58). And in post-medieval times the large number of Northeast mercenaries in the Scandinavian armies would undoubtedly have stimulated the exchange of material between traditions. The individual ballads show many correspondences:[18]

> of all the British ballads those of Aberdeenshire are most
> reminiscent of Scandinavian versions. The resemblances
> between Peter Buchan's Aberdeenshire gleanings and
> Danish ballads were so frequent and striking that a
> translator of the latter, three-quarters of a century ago,
> was moved to accuse Buchan of stealing from the Danish

versions. Of modern parallels a single example will suffice. Of Child's twenty-seven versions of 'Binorie' ('The Twa Sisters') two are from Aberdeenshire. These two and one other in his collection make the elder sister 'dun' and the younger a blonde, as in most of the Norse versions. Eleven Aberdeenshire versions recovered since Child's death have the same characteristic. Again, in none of Child's records does the drowning sister refuse to give up her lover to her rival and murderess: some of the Norse forms contain this refusal; and it occurs—for the first time in the British ballad—in four of the eleven recent Aberdeenshire texts.

Introductions to individual ballads throughout *Last Leaves* contain further evidence of the close relationship between northeastern and Scandinavian ballads.

Northeast balladry also has links with the folk-culture of the neighbouring Gaels. Although this relationship, like the former, is worth fuller study, certain facts stand out. In Gaelic folksong there is a marked absence of the classical ballad themes, and where they do appear, the objectivity that is such a dominant characteristic of most European balladry is missing. Instead of the ballads Celtic society had its heroic Ossianic poetry, a genre notably dissimilar to Anglo-Scottish balladry in both content and style.[19] There is little likelihood here of the kind of interaction that produced the correspondences between the northeastern and Scandinavian ballads. One should, however, bear in mind that much of British folklore might have a Celtic base, and that the Northeast, being a Celtic territory for centuries and later a border region, might well have a strongly Celtic base for its folklore.[20]

Although the texts have few correspondences, the tunes show some striking similarities. In *Last Leaves* Keith rather misleadingly says only that 'the weird lament and the temperamental fervour of the Celtic music are alike absent' from the folk-music of Aberdeenshire.[21] This is true enough, but ignores what Greig himself emphatically points out, that Northeast folk-music in general owes a considerable debt to Gaelic folk-music. The Anglo-Saxon and Anglo-Norman incomers of early medieval times adopted as their own a great deal of their

8

predecessors' melody. The evidence for this is the high proportion of Northeast tunes constructed on the basis of a Celtic form of the melodic quatrain, and the way in which the cadences of the northeastern folk-tunes are modelled on Gaelic prototypes. This body of folk-melody was presumably taken over from the twelfth to the fourteenth centuries, but even after that time the Gaelic influence was reinforced by the Northeast's assimilation of individual Gaelic tunes.[22] There is an interesting parallel between what happened to Gaelic culture in the Northeast and what happened to it in North America. There also, apart from such isolated enclaves as Cape Breton Island and Nova Scotia, the music was in large measure adopted while the bulk of the culture atrophied.[23]

Northeast tradition, then, has been uniquely individualized, in its texts by Scandinavian influences and in its tunes by Celtic influences. One prominent feature of the region itself also lends a distinctive cast and colouring to its ballads—its native dialect. This expressive speech, known locally as 'the Doric', is today the Scottish dialect most stubbornly resisting anglicization. Still capable of baffling the untutored ear, it provided many puzzles for Child last century, as his Glossary's preface indicates; in it he thanks no fewer than fourteen northeasterners for their linguistic help. What he had to contend with is made clear in the comments of one of these helpers, Thomas Davidson:[24]

> The combination of two words into one . . . is not rare
> in Scotch, nor is the reverse process. For example, the
> word 'hypochondriac' is turned into 'keepach and dreeach',
> and the two parts often used separately. 'I'm unco keepach'
> and 'I'm unco dreeach' are common expressions among
> old people. Imagine an etymologist, ignorant of the facts,
> trying to discover the etymology of 'keepach' or of 'dreeach'.

This dialect, the main sub-dialect of Northern Scots, is a composite speech whose basic Anglo-Saxon is enriched by graftings from the Scandinavian, French, Dutch and Gaelic languages. Just as its composition mirrors forces affecting local history, its vocabulary and idiom portray certain characteristics of the local folk. Northeastern speech, says David Murison succinctly, 'reflects the people, superficially somewhat grim, blunt, sardonic and non-committal, and yet beneath the surface durable, self-reliant

9

and sentimental in the better sense of the word'.[25] These comments on the folk and their language, when considered in the light of the dominant ballad tones, illustrate how the north-eastern folk have stamped their personality on their ballads, and how they have made the ballad a vehicle for the expression of a regional ethos and identity. The dialect's history also provides one important guideline for the study of local ballads. Since Scots drove out Gaelic and firmly established itself through most of the region only between the twelfth and fourteenth centuries, the mid-fourteenth century must mark the early chronological boundary for the first period of the regional tradition, just as the latter half of the eighteenth century, and the advent of general literacy, marks the later boundary.

Part I

The Oral Tradition:
the Folk

Chapter 2

The Land and the People

The Northeast has been described as 'the cold shoulder' of Britain.[1] Neither its climate nor its soil is naturally hospitable, but generations of stubborn farming folk have forced it into productivity by dint of the northeastern cure for most of life's ills—hard work. Though the Laigh of Moray to the west and the Howe of the Mearns to the south may, for folklore purposes, be taken as secondary areas of influence, the region itself consists of the counties of Aberdeen and Banff and the northern part of Kincardineshire. Topographically, these shires vary greatly as they stretch westwards from flat, treeless Buchan through the uplands of Strathbogie and the Garioch to mountainous Mar and the highest land-mass in Britain, the Cairngorms. Bounded by these mountains to the west, the sea to the north and east, and the Grampians or the Mounth to the south, the Northeast is a distinct geographical entity.

Historically, the most important feature of Northeast geography has been the southern boundary, the Mounth. From the seventh century onwards, it served as a political or administrative dividing line. Once the frontier between the North and South Picts, in early medieval times it helped shape the administrative division of Scotland into Lothian, Galloway, Scotland 'south of the Mounth' and Scotland 'north of the Mounth'.[2] The poet John Barbour, a fourteenth-century Archdeacon of Aberdeen, found it quite natural to refer to his country as the land 'benorth the Mounth'. In the sixteenth century one ecclesiastic, Bishop Leslie, described the Mounth in this fashion:[3]

> In the bordirs of Marr and Mernes the gret hill named Grampie, sa meikle renouned in the alde Romane histories, begins nocht far frome the cost besyd Abirdin, extending

13

> throuch the mid-cuntries, sum tymes braider, sum tymes
> narower, evin to the West Sey, ay quhil it cum to
> Dunbartane, ye and til Argyle.

Another ecclesiastic, John Major, declared that these 'Alps of
Scotland' were 'impassable by horsemen'.[4] These comments
clearly indicate how the Mounth was then regarded: it was the
eastern part of a mountain barrier that in effect bisected Scotland.
As roads were not materially improved during the next two
hundred years, the Mounth remained a large obstacle to travellers
until the late eighteenth century. Inevitably, the comparative
isolation brought about by the Mounth's existence fostered the
growth of a regional culture; cut off from the Lowlands, the
Northeast developed its own lore, customs, and dialect. But it
did not remain a backwater. Although the Mounth curbed large-
scale social and commercial intercourse with the Lowlands, it
helped turn the Northeast's attention to the continent. Consequently, while relative isolation enabled the regional culture
to grow in its own ways, interaction with continental cultures
prevented its succumbing to provincial stagnation. What the
Northeast lost through lack of contact with southern Scotland it
more than gained through contact with the continent, as this
interaction helped create a rich diversity in the local folk-culture.

The Northeast's remoteness encouraged the development of a
regional type of personality. Rather curiously, the foreigner's
comic stereotype of the Scotsman corresponds very closely to the
Scotsman's comic stereotype of the northeasterner. Scotsmen,
says the foreigner, are canny; northeasterners, says the Scotsman,
are the canniest. Scotsmen are dour; northeasterners are the
dourest. Scotsmen are mean; Aberdonians are the closest-fisted.
Scotsmen are natural-born lawyers; Aberdeen lawyers outdo all
in professional rapacity.[5] The northeasterner, it would appear
from the stereotypes, is the Scotsman writ large.

Yet the local folk differ somewhat from other Scotsmen in
their ethnic composition. Around 2000 B.C. the region was settled
by a race from Holland, known from a distinctive burial habit
as the 'beaker people'. Analysis of their skeletons this century
has demonstrated close physical correspondences between the
beaker people and the contemporary rural population.[6] Although
this basic strain in the ethnic make-up of the Northeast is not

14

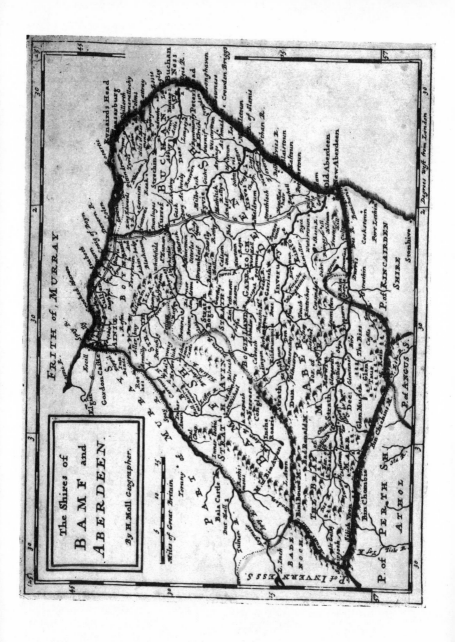

The Shires of
B A M F and
A B E R D E E N.

By H. Moll Geographer.

Miles of Great Britain

found in concentration anywhere else in Scotland, the other strains are; only the proportions of the mixture differ. The Picts and the Celts were the next people after the beaker folk to colonize the region on a large scale, and their domination covered a thousand years, until the twelfth century. From then till the fourteenth century, the Celts were gradually absorbed or pushed westward into the mountains by the Anglo-Saxon and Anglo-Norman incomers. Many of the English settlers arrived at the instigation of David I (1124–53) whose policy it was to encourage foreign traders to settle in newly-established burghs. His inducements also attracted many Flemings to the east coast and particularly to Aberdeenshire; so, for a second time, the region received an important influx of people from the north-western lowlands of Europe.[7]

These varied ethnic elements have combined to produce in the northeastern folk a distinctive breed. Their essential characteristics are well caught in this account of the Northeast farmer; he is:[8]

> canny and not in the least given to gushing. He has an
> extreme dislike to superlatives in conversation, and prefers
> to state his opinion in moderate language. The Nor'East
> is and always was the centre of Moderatism. In all things
> it prefers, with Aristotle, wise men, the *via media*. None
> the less it is sincere. But its sincerity and truthfulness are
> thoroughly consistent with a character that is cautious and
> a temperament inclined to the phlegmatic.

To these traits that reflect the northeasterners' kinship with the Netherlanders were allied strong social propensities: 'They are in general fond of going to markets and public places of resort; and they mix together frequently in society, especially in the winter months'.[9] The innate 'Moderatism' of outlook that characterizes the northeasterner shows clearly in his attitude to religion during the post-Reformation centuries. The Northeast accepted the Reformation late and with singularly little enthusiasm. For long the most solidly Catholic part of Lowland Scotland, the Northeast gradually adapted itself in the reigns of James I and Charles I to Episcopacy, which was found particularly congenial to its moderate spirit. So congenial was it in fact that there grew up in Aberdeen an Episcopalian culture, whose scholars, 'the Aberdeen Doctors', had a European reputation.

When, in the eighteenth century, Episcopalianism became dangerously associated with Jacobitism, its popularity waned and it was replaced in the Northeast by a very moderate kind of Presbyterianism.[10] It would appear that the folk, like their pagan ballads, were more concerned with the hard facts of living than with the abstract luxuries of dogma.

The people of the Northeast are rarely thought of as highly 'imaginative'. Up to the nineteenth century the region produced few writers and almost no written lyric poetry, and this was not due simply to the smallness of the literate community.[11] The imaginative energies of the northeasterner have normally been expended on the more practical arts of living or channelled into areas where passion is an encumbrance—mathematics, the sciences, philosophy—which is what one would expect from a race not given to overt displays of emotion. Yet the immediate forebears of such Scottish writers as Fergusson and Burns hailed from Aberdeenshire and Kincardine; northeastern genius, it seems, requires one or two generations' time in the south to thaw out. After literacy, of course, the region produced a fair number of good writers, most notably Lewis Grassic Gibbon.

Though phlegmatic and ostensibly unemotional, the north-easterner has a strong sense of the dramatic; in pre-Reformation times Aberdeen was the Scottish burgh most renowned for its plays and pageants.[12] And the hallmark of the old northeastern ballads is that they are dramatic, the best of them integrating lyric emotion and narrative event within powerfully dramatic wholes. Here, perhaps, is one key to a psychological under-standing of why the Northeast folk liked their ballads. Not a demonstrative race, they found their aesthetic form in the ballad, where emotions were objectified in near-ritualized terms and subordinated to the dramatic recounting of factual event. In this society the ballads served a cathartic function, for they provided a dramatic yet disciplined outlet to the emotions denied regular expression by the dour, canny, undemonstrative, northeastern folk.

Chapter 3

The Agricultural Society

Recent folklore scholarship has stressed the necessity for exploring the relationship between the folk-group and the lore of the group. Because the character of the group will, naturally, condition the character of the lore, an understanding of the social context is essential to a proper understanding of that lore. This folkloristic truism applies as much to Scottish balladry as to Breton beliefs or Bantu riddling.[1]

The *sine qua non* of traditional ballad societies was their nonliteracy. As Lord says:[2]

> In societies where writing is unknown, or where it is limited to a professional scribe whose duty is that of writing letters and keeping accounts, or where it is the possession of a small minority, such as clerics or a wealthy ruling class (though often this latter group prefers to have its writing done by a servant), the art of narration flourishes, provided that the culture is in other respects of a sort to foster the singing of tales. If the way of life of a people furnishes subjects for story and affords occasion for the telling, this art will be fostered.

Other factors besides nonliteracy that fostered the singing of tales in a culture can be identified from the striking similarities in social pattern that occur among European folk-groups where traditional ballads flourished. The Spanish, Yugoslavian, and Danish ballad societies that produced much of the best in the Romance, Balkan, and Nordic balladries had a great deal in common. J. E. Housman outlines the common factors when he describes the archetypal ballad society: 'It seems probable, then, that traditional balladry . . . thrives best in a homogeneous feudal and agricultural society, and preferably in a border region subject to political or social tension'.[3] An examination of how these factors operated in the Northeast should, then, reveal how the way of life in this particular ballad culture furnished both 'subjects for story' and, the first concern, 'occasion for the telling'.

Entwistle describes the chronology of the European ballad societies as, in a wide sense, 'medieval', that is, they begin 'after the great migrations and crusades have subsided, and medieval man has settled down to cultivate his own acre' and they end with 'the practice of reading'.[4] In the Northeast of Scotland medieval man had little chance to settle down and cultivate his own acre before the middle of the fourteenth century. From the twelfth century onwards, the regional society had been in a state of flux as the Anglo-Saxon and Anglo-Norman incomers gradually supplanted the Celtic inhabitants. And in the first part of the fourteenth, mainly because Bruce's powerful enemies, the Comyns, held much of the Northeast, the land suffered considerably during the Scottish Wars of Independence. After the turning-point of the first war, the Battle of Barra, Bruce laid waste to the countryside in the savage 'herschip' (harrying) of Buchan that people remembered for fifty years, and later, when secure on the throne, he redistributed the lands among his own adherents. Only after all the turmoil had subsided, and a common language had been established, could the regional ballad tradition have taken firm root. But the patterns of society which emerged at this time were to remain, basically unchanged, for the next four centuries.

The social patterns that obtained in the rural Northeast from the mid-fourteenth to the mid-eighteenth centuries undoubtedly provided an atmosphere conducive to the singing of traditional tales. It was an agricultural society but, more important, it was a particular kind of agricultural society. The methods of land management and cultivation and the concomitant settlement type all point to a form of social organization that was communal in spirit and co-operative in its activities. This particular kind of agricultural society provided conditions in labour and living where an oral culture would naturally thrive.

The main settlement type in the Northeast was the fermtoun, a small farming township consisting, on the average, of eight houses, whose inhabitants held their lands and dwellings directly from the laird, the proprietor of the estate, by lease or tack. In the prototypical toun the eight houses were occupied by eight co-tenants holding equal amounts of land, for this is the arrangement upon which the system of land division is predicated. Based not on acreage but on the amount of tillable land, this system had for its central unit the ploughgate (or ploughgang or simply 'ane pleuch'), that area of land which could be cultivated by one plough-team, and which in practice was roughly equivalent to 104 acres. It was sub-divided into eight oxgates (or oxgangs), each oxgate being originally the amount of land owned by a joint-tenant who contributed one ox to the toun plough-team.[5] The mathematically exact division of one toun's lands into eight oxgates worked by eight tenants is, however, rarely found in the extant rentrolls and leases because the system had to adapt itself to such varying circumstances as differences in the quality of the land and size of the oxen-team and population changes. Growth in population gave rise to a sub-tenant class, composed of cottars, who worked small holdings, and grassmen, who rented enough grassland to maintain one cow. Although the sub-tenant had the use of the toun plough for his own plot, he was quite dependent on the main tenant he rented from and worked for, because, when a tack was renounced, all the lesser tenants had to vacate the property along with the principal. The toun, however, still remained a corporate unit, for in most cases the tacks were made out to a group of tenants, either co-tenants corporately responsible for all the rent, or single tenants each responsible for his or her share of the joint-rent.[6]

The standard English practice of having a three-field system with regular rotation of winter crop, spring crop and fallow land was almost unknown in Scotland, which used the more primitive system of infield and outfield cultivation.[7] The infield or intoun which, as the name implies, lay adjacent to the township, constituted the best, because regularly manured, fields, while beyond lay the irregularly manured and tilled falds and faughs of the outfield. As the only dyke or fence was the impermanent head-dyke that separated the arable from the pasture, regularly laid out fields as we know them did not exist; the 'fields' were enclaves of tillable land, of various shapes and sizes, scattered among land too boggy or stony to cultivate.

19

These fields were divided into the rigs or strips which gave their name to the runrig method of group cultivation. By this method the rigs were shared amongst the joint-tenants so as to ensure that each holding had an equivalent amount of good and bad land. Sometimes a stipulation about the allotment of runrig appears in the tack between heritor and tenant:[8] 'And all the above parties do heirby oblidge themselves to agree to the division of the mixed land in the said toun of Todlachy in the same maner that the tenents of the said toun are bound by there tack.' That the runrig system demands active co-operation among the tenants for its smooth working is clearly evident from its complex process of distribution:[8]

> The s[d] M[r.] Archibald Grant shall sett in tack to the s[d] William Couper three haughs of the intown of Black-hillocks lyeing closs to the Water of Done presentlie possest by John Davidson, William Couper, Robert Wilson and Elspat Couper, as also two rigs of the uper intown of Hillocks and four faugh buts lyeing on the north side of the Burn of Pittfichie, the s[d] two rigs presentlie possest by Robert Grant, and s[d] four buts by Malcolm Callom and sick like the s[d] William Couper is to have ten outfeild folds and the faughs belonging to them, viz.: the Stonefold, the Bleufold, the Broomfold, Plyfold, Broadfold, and ane oy[r] fold lyeing south of y[t], the fold lyeing north of the Hen Croft, the faughs lyeing west and south west the s[d] Hen Croft presentlie possest by the s[d] Robert Grant, and ane other fold lyeing north west from the yeard of Pitfichie possest by the s[d] Robert Grant, as also the Bear fold possest by William Gellon and the Sour fold possest by William Robertson, the house, barn and keall yeard belonging to the s[d] John Davidson, the half of the corn yeard possest by the s[d] Malcolm Callom.

If tenants violated the co-operative principles of the runrig system, the system itself could provide means for their enforcement, as the minutes of the Monymusk Baron Court show; for when there was a complaint[8]

> that the ridg in the Barally in use to be laboured by James Thomson & John Coupland in Delab is considerably

less than the ridg in use to be laboured by John Wood
& Elspet Craig in Delab and that some part of the s^d
ridg wch is lesser was left unmanured, the bailie fined
each of the s^d James Thomson and John Coupland in the
summe of fourtie shilling Scots money and ordeaned them
in all tyme comming to labour w^t the s^d John Wood and
Elspet Craig equally and for that effect to chang ridges
yearly.

Before runrig there had existed an even more communal agricultural system, that of 'township possession', whereby the
cultivators not only worked the land together but also divided
amongst themselves the produce.[9]

The systems of group cultivation and group farm organization
had a pronounced effect on the kind of life led by the folk. The
papers of the eighteenth-century Aberdeenshire agriculturalist,
Sir Archibald Grant of Monymusk, show that the everyday life
of the northeastern farmer was to a marked degree communal
and co-operative. Grant's 'Plan for Neither Coullie' supplies one
illustration of this:[10]

Cowley in two, 3 or 4—al in partnership in maner
following: one only to live at Neither Cowley, & to cast
lotts for their habitations & yards, & all the rest common.

To plow all work, sow & pasture in comon, also to reap
in comon; . . . If any furnish more than one serv^t, either
constant or harvest, to be allowed as usuall in generall
acc^t, & each to have one or two cows belonging to comon
stock, the milk but not calfs for each use.

20 oxen & 10 horses & 9 persons includeing y^{m}selves
to make 4 ploughs will manage it well, each party to
take equall number of serv^{ts} in maintinance or allowed
for it if unequall; & wool divided by weight when all
cliped, & sorted; advantage from sale of sheep, graseing
cattle, or milk cows, other than those for their own use,
to be common.

Conditions of tack are . . . to sell no corn with fodder,
nor sell any corn, meal or bear but with comon consent;
nor graise, bye or sell cattle otherways; to graise for
Heritor in comon stock, 100 weders & 50 ews . . . &

B

> when any of y^m faile or dye or give up, those who remain
> to hold the whole or choise their associates. . . .
>   Their houses & stations to be determind by lott, & all
> cattle & horses to be by birlymen made as equall as
> possible; & straw & chaff to be used for mantinance of
> sheep & feeding cattle for comon benefite; tools furnished
> & mantaind at comon charge.

Symptomatic of the egalitarian spirit that animated the rural
communities is the casting of lots, whether, as here, for the
houses, or, as had been customary, for the allotment of rigs.
The medieval burghs followed the same practice with communal
trade purchases and land holdings.[11] The frequency of the
phrase 'They keist the cavils them amang' in the local ballads
reflects the egalitarian and co-operative principles that permeated
the lives of the ordinary folk.

The tacks, it has been observed, were usually issued to a group
of tenants. The stipulations of these tacks show how the community operated as a unit. For example, the tenant promised to
perform certain 'services': 'to send a man one day each year to
the heritor's service . . . to give a draught of his horses each
year for lime, one for scleat & one for timber, with other harrages
& carriages alike w^t neighbour & others of so much labouring.'
The tenant also contracted 'to do dutie to Kirk, Miln & Officer
ust & wont', which required that he pay so much meal to the
minister, the miller, and the ground officer.[12] Those within the
community who lived by the soil provided the basic victuals for
those who did not.

Even the rents fixed by the tacks were paid collectively. In
the Forbes Rent Roll for 1552 the toun of Logy has four tenants
who farmed two ploughgates, and paid as part of their rent, two
lambs and two wethers: Sande Mechell, farming 'ane pleut',
paid 'ane lam' and 'ane custome weddir'; Wille Mechell, with
four oxingang, paid 'half ane lam' and 'half custome weddir';
James Elmislie and Jonat Warrack, each with two oxingang, both
paid 'ane quartar Lam' and a 'quartar weddir'. Each of the eight
tenants of the toun of Cultircullane possessed four oxingang and
each paid as part of the joint rent a 'half qtar. custome cow'.
Not only the joint-tenants of one toun but also neighbouring
touns banded together in the payment of rent, as two memoranda

of the same rentroll illustrate: 'Memorand, y^t Stragarnik, Kirktoune, and Lary pais ane custome cow to my Lord, ilkane yair zere abowtt' and 'Memorandu, yat ye half miln off catty, ye croft of bandorre, and ye half of Inchbair pais zeirlie xiij s. iiij equalie amang ym., qlk. makkis furth ye xl s. for ye custome cow.'[13] The payment of services, duties and rents owing to the heritor all demonstrate how the rural community functioned as a corporate entity.

During the four seasons, the toun's folk would engage in a diverse range of activities, almost all of which, major and minor, were performed in common.[14] The yearly round began with the ploughing, harrowing, and sowing which, because of the climatic vagaries of an Aberdeenshire springtime, were carried through with great speed. Summer was mainly given over to cutting, dressing, and carting the fuels, peat and turf, from the mosses and moors, but at this time the tenants would also erect the head-dyke, repair steadings, build a new byre, or indulge in activities as miscellaneous as cutting thistles, removing stones from the fields, 'helping to bleed cattle', or breaking 'fir sticks for fire'. The harvest, which in the Northeast gives its name to the season—hairst—was the crown of the year. Despite the severity of the labour, all the workers seem to have revelled in the cheer of 'the shearing'. Anticipating the idea that brought Musak to the factories, one Mearns farmer used to engage a piper for the duration of the harvest to lighten the work of the 'hyeuks'.[15] After the harvest itself came the secondary tasks, the carting, the making of ropes, and the 'eddering of rucks' (which translates into rather pale English as 'the making of haystacks'). Much of late autumn, and indeed some of spring, the toun's folk spent cutting, mixing, and distributing 'muck fail', a dressing compounded of soil and manure whose effectiveness was out of all proportion to the time spent in its preparation. So ineffective was it that one local gentleman who lived before the Heritable Jurisdictions Act was moved to declare that 'noblemen and muck fail would assuredly prove the ruin of Aberdeenshire'.[16] Winter was the slackest stretch of the year when the farmers busied themselves with odd building jobs and some ploughing but had ample time for leisure. Besides these more seasonal occupations, threshing in the pre-breakfast hours was a year-round activity, and the herding of cattle and sheep took up many of the months.

Each toun had a common pasture, where every tenant had a 'souming', and toun herds, sometimes boys but quite often the physically maimed or mentally deficient males of the community, looked after the animals. In many districts it was customary to send the livestock in summer to the hill pastures, the shielings, where they were minded by these toun herds.

The agricultural system of group farm organization and group cultivation produced a particular kind of rural settlement, the fermtoun.[17] This settlement type, which dominated the local settlement pattern, intensified the co-operative spirit of community engendered by the conditions of northeastern labour. Almost unknown were villages of the English kind: units of from two to three hundred people grouped in orderly fashion round a village green and church, and under the surveillance of the local squire and parson.

The nucleated farming townships were not arranged according to any formal plan; the eight or so houses of the average toun huddled together at the centre of the infield in quite haphazard fashion, while on the edges of the toun lands might stand one or two crofts inhabited by cottars or shepherds. The amount of land belonging to a toun or cultivated by one tenant, and the population of a toun, all varied in accordance with the location and quality of the land. The barren hills of Mar had, as a rule, smaller touns and individual plots than the comparatively flat lands of Buchan and Formartine.[18] Other factors also worked to grade the size of the touns. Some were the basic unit, containing just the farm workers; some were augmented by a 'wolhous' or 'ailhous' or 'smedy' or one of the various 'milns'; and others, like most Kirktouns, were enlarged by the presence of up to a dozen rural tradesmen. An example of the larger toun-hamlet is the Buchan toun of Whythill, which in 1696 contained 71 adults—38 men and 33 women; the farmers comprised seven tenants, ten sub-tenants, six servants, one grassman, and one 'his sone'; the tradesmen comprised three chapmen, three tailors, two weavers and an apprentice, two tinklers, two shoemakers, and one couper.[19] The second group gives some idea of the trades followed by the folk who occupied the touns along with the cultivators. Weavers, cordiners, masons, wrights, and smiths, who in some instances had their 'sucken' (legal territory) just like the millers, operated from within the toun, while others used the toun as a base for operations that carried them further afield.[20] One of the latter was the main trader in the rural communities, the chapman, who in those days was generally a man of some substance. The tailor also would serve a wide area, utilizing the material spun by the women of the attended household and woven by the local weaver. Equally peripatetic were the various cairds such as the horners, who manufactured spoons, and the tinklers, who made and mended pots and pans. These travelling tradesmen had an importance for rural society beyond their trades for they were the channels of communication by which the touns exchanged news, and, in all probability, lore.

The touns formed distinctive and, to a certain extent, self-contained social units. The working conditions emphasized the separate identity of each toun, and the distance, for most, from the heritor's house engendered an independent capability among the responsible joint-tenants. Because they lived very much as a communal group, the toun-folk lived by the principles of 'Good Neighbourhood'. Good Neighbourhood, or *vicinitas*, necessitated (as the name implies) living amicably with one's fellow toun-folk, and prosecuting one's full share of the corporate labour. The 1511 rental for the Bishopric of Aberdeen shows not only that tenants could lose their rights of tenancy if they did not follow these principles, but also that they were responsible for their sub-tenants maintaining the same precepts.[21] The guardians of Good Neighbourhood were the barleymen. These men, normally two in number and chosen by both heritors and tenants, umpired in matters of rural disputation when those involved could not agree amongst themselves. Differences of opinion over tacks, improvements to steadings, the allotment of rigs, the respective rights of an incoming and an outgoing tenant, all fell within the province of the barleymen.[22]

A tradition of communal existence was not peculiar to the rural touns as it was an equally marked characteristic of the burghs for much of the four centuries under consideration. The burgh was designated a 'communitas' in the charters, and in every aspect of burgh life it was a community, and a closely-knit community at that. It was a self-governing and financially autonomous organization, whose arable land, grazing, peat grounds, and in the case of Aberdeen, fishings, were shared by

25

the burgesses. Trading ventures were pursued in common; buying and selling were done in an open market. When a new burgess was admitted to the company of his fellows, he swore an oath to be 'leel and feel' to the community of the burgh, and to observe *vicinitas*. Travelling merchants, by the principle of withernan, could be held liable for the debts of a fellow burgher. The Council Register for 1574 reveals that the burgh craftsmen in Aberdeen were bidden to and from work by the 'Almany Quhissil' accompanied by a 'tabourine'. This sense of corporateness existed on a national as well as on a local scale, the main burghs being accustomed to joint discussion and action in concert.[23]

The bulk of the population, however, inhabited the rural touns, these almost self-contained organisms within which the folk were accustomed to live by the precept and practice of communal co-operation. Though the mobile elements of rural society, the travelling craftsmen and traders and regional congregating at kirk, market, and fair, prevented the toun from lapsing into introverted isolation, during by far the greater part of the year it had to rely on its own resources for work and recreation. And the communal habits of the work would naturally have carried over to the recreation. To emphasize the communal aspects of the life, however, is in no way to posit a kind of collective Utopia; as is only to be expected, the Baron Court Books and the Kirk Session Records show human nature in all its idiosyncratic contrariness.[24] But such a community as the toun, unlettered, comparatively isolated and self-reliant, living and working co-operatively, would provide an eminently suitable environment for a sturdy oral tradition. An oral culture would thrive in the communal environment, because the processes of oral transmission depend upon corporate activity, and a flourishing tradition can be maintained and developed only by group participation. The Northeast toun, dependent upon itself for labour and recreation, and communal in both work and leisure habits, would undoubtedly furnish the ballads with abundant 'occasion for the telling'.

Although the toun or clachan was once thought to be a peculiarly Celtic type of rural settlement, it existed, in its essential form, not only in Britain but also in Brittany, northwestern Germany and the neighbouring Dutch and Danish regions, and districts in Scandinavia. In these areas this type of rural settlement,

> connected with a restricted, but permanently tilled and
> heavily manured infield, preferably in open strips,
> surrounded by outfields with a fieldgrass or field-heather
> cultivation and extensive common heathlands under
> severe Atlantic climate and soil-conditions, appeared as
> the dominant feature, forming a striking parallel to the
> Nw [northwest] German *Drubbel* with the *Langstreifenflur*
> on the Esch. Although the social structure may differ in
> respect of property-status, size of holdings, etc., there
> remain still many features which connect these settle-
> ments of small rural groups with an expressed team
> spirit. There are several comparable features of joint-
> property or co-operation ('run-rig'—pooling etc.)
> throughout these regions.[25]

The areas where the toun was the dominant settlement type approximate to Entwistle's suggested matrix for the Nordic ballads:[26] 'The common centre for these Nordic ballads, if there were one centre, would thus seem to have been the northern parts of Germany, and the first area of diffusion to have been the rim of land round the North Sea from Jutland to East Anglia.' From the regional viewpoint, we can now add to the Northeast's ethnic and trading connections with northwestern Europe the link of a common settlement type. But there is a wider signifi-cance. These areas all possess evidence of old and strong oral cultures, so it is likely that a correlation between the toun type of communal rural settlement and a thriving ballad culture may exist for more European regions than the Northeast of Scotland.

Chapter 4

The Border Region

For much of its history Scotland has contained two nations, the Celtic Highlanders and the Anglo-Saxon Lowlanders, enjoying different social organizations, different customs, different languages, and a mutual distrust. The Northeast was a border region for these two races. Geographically, it belongs to both Highlands and Lowlands for, though it is a continuation of the eastern coastal plain, it also lies to the north of the Highland Boundary Fault, and is set apart from the rest of the Lowlands by the Mounth. Once a Celtic territory, the Northeast became predominantly Anglo-Saxon by medieval times, though its western districts remained populated by Gaelic-speaking Highlanders. The consequent interaction between the two races had cultural, social, and political effects, and of these the political are the most immediately evident. As in other European border regions, the threatening proximity of an alien race animated the ballad society with continual political and military tensions.

For some centuries the history of the region was characterized by the conflict between retreating Gaels and incoming Anglo-Saxons. When, in the eleventh century, the Saxon influence first began to grow in Scotland, the Northeast became the battleground for the war between Macbeth and Malcolm, whose struggle bears little relation to the Shakespearian portrayal, for, while dynastic in origin, it had pronounced racial and regional overtones. Macbeth, descended from the old line of Scottish kings and son of the Mormaer of Moray, was a figure uncompromisingly Celtic; Malcolm, on the other hand, had spent many years of his life at the English court, had married for his second wife a Saxon princess, and was altogether very pro-Saxon. It was the victories of Malcolm at Lumphanan and Essie, and his ensuing supremacy, that decided the Northeast was never to be a centre of Celtic particularism like Macbeth's family territory, the 'Kingdom of Moray' to the west. Only in the thirteenth century was this Celtic province incorporated into the kingdom of Scotland, though, as it remained a wild and lawless region, it was to prove a source of continual disquiet to the Scottish kings for some time. The threat presented by this dangerously unstable province led the kings to regard the Northeast as the outermost bastion of their consolidated kingdom, and consequently brought about a swift feudalization of the region. By the fourteenth century Anglo-Norman feudalism had superseded the old Celtic monastic, administrative, and landholding systems, though not without being modified in the process.[1]

Even after the Northeast had been established as a predominantly Lowland Saxon region, it served as a battleground for conflicting Lowland and Highland forces. In 1411 the battle of Harlaw was fought in Aberdeenshire and in its way it was an encounter of no little importance. An older generation of Scottish historians used to see it as a battle for the domination of Scotland, the battle which determined once and for all whether Lowland Scotland was to be predominantly Celtic or predominantly Anglo-Saxon, but this opinion has been modified by modern historians. They are inclined to see it in more medieval terms as the result of a feudal squabble over land, specifically, the Earldom of Ross. The major claimant for this earldom was Donald, Lord of the Isles, who, fearing the rapacity of the then Regent of Scotland, the Duke of Albany, collected a large army of Highlanders and set out to occupy the earldom's lands in the Northeast. The people who had most to lose from this incursion were the burgesses of Aberdeen who, fearing the rapacity of Donald and his caterans, helped organize a large body of Lowlanders under the leadership of Alexander Stewart, Earl of Mar, to protect the Northeast. The provenance of the troops, and the edict, customary after a battle of national importance, that the heir of any man killed at Harlaw was to receive his ward, relief and marriage free from the king, would seem to suggest that the struggle, if not for the 'domination' of Scotland, was viewed by contemporary Lowlanders as a more-than-local defence of Lowland Saxon prosperity against the onslaught of Highland barbarism. This battle gave rise to the region's earliest historical ballad, 'The Battle of Harlaw' (163).[2]

After Harlaw, the Celts made their presence felt in the north-east mainly through a long series of creachs and spulzies, of cattle-lifting raids and forays. They also took part in the Civil Wars, but raiding was their regular kind of hostile activity, and this was a direct result of the conditions and environment of Gaelic society. The social unit of Gaeldom was the clan, a patriarchal organization whose firmest ties were the bonds of kinship. The clansmen accorded their familial chiefs a fervent loyalty which, however, co-existed quixotically with a firm sense of personal independence. These qualities are amusingly exemplified in the anecdote about a drunken quarrel between the Laird of Grant and his kinsman, Dalrachany:[3]

> Dalrachany got up, and told him he would suffer
> that blow from him as his chief, but that he would not
> suffer the second blow of any subject, and the laird
> redoubling the blow, Dalrachany engaged with him and
> took him by the collar, and . . . he threshed him most
> heartily.

Social and economic factors combined to make of the Gaels a warlike people. The status of the chieftain depended largely on the number of men he could call to the field, so, despite the inability of his lands to support them, he insisted on maintaining a large following which, of course, had to be allowed to display its martial prowess; and in like fashion, the status of the minor chieftains depended on their committing daring acts of aggression. The mountain lands occupied by the Gaels were poor agricultural country, and even the emphasis on grazing and hunting did little to strengthen a weak and unstable economy. Naturally, they eyed hungrily the fertile lands of the Lowlands, which, they maintained, belonged by right to them: 'They have also a Tradition amongst them that the Lowlands were in Ancient Times, the Inheritance of their Ancestors, and therefore believe they have a right to commit Depradations, whenever it is in their power to put them in execution.'[4] By robbing the corn and cattle of those who had stolen their patrimony, the chieftains both remedied the clan's economic deficiences and maintained their own social status.

To Highlanders who could move easily through the Cairngorm passes, the upper lowlands of Aberdeenshire and Banffshire were natural targets for despoliation. Their reiving techniques were quite straightforward:[5]

> They go out in Parties from Ten to Thirty Men, Traverse large Tracts of Mountains till they arrive at the Lowlands where they design to Commit Depradations which they chuse to do in places distant from the Clans where they Inhabit; They drive the Stolen Cattle in the Night time, and in the Day remain on the Tops of the Mountains or in the Woods (with which the Highlands abound) and take the first occasion to sell them at the Fairs or Markets that are annually held in many parts of the Country.

The standard method of dealing with the caterans involved a practice that has given modern English the word 'blackmail'. Lairds whose lands bordered the mountains paid to the Highlanders as protection money 'the Black Meal'. By this method, the laird ensured his lands freedom from reivings as long as he kept up his contributions; if it happened that some cattle were lifted, the chieftain had to make good the loss. Most of the vulnerable heritors contributed to this old-style protection racket because, otherwise, their holdings were certain to be harried. Two extant documents show that this system operated in the Northeast as late as 1744. One is a letter, a kind of trade circular, sent by Cluny MacPherson round the lairds who, as the euphemism put it, 'contributed to the watch undertaken by him', while the other, kept in the Farquharson records, is its sequel, an 'Obligation by Ewan Macpherson of Clunie . . . whereby the Laird of Clunie agrees to maintain a sufficient watch for preserving the Cattle of the said heritors and their tenants, or recovering them, if stolen, Beginning on 22nd May, 1744.'[6]

Not all the heritors paid the blackmail; some relied on their own abilities to recover their cattle. If a laird tracked down the caterans with his own posse, he, if more powerful in numbers, would seize the animals, and if less powerful, would buy his own cattle back. The ordinary heritor rarely prosecuted the thieves both because of the expense of the legal process and the fear of reprisals by the clan. If a wealthier landowner apprehended the caterans, he contracted an arrangement with the chieftain—'to keep, as they call it, good Neighbourhood'—whereby the laird promised not to prosecute and the chieftain offered a double indemnity, raised by the united efforts of the clan and paid in cattle lifted from the other side of Scotland. The offering of 'Tascal-Money' could also recover cattle. The aggrieved laird would send to the area under suspicion men who offered bribes to any who would reveal the whereabouts of the cattle and the caterans. So offensive was this method to the Highlanders that the entire Clan Cameron took a mutual oath against the accepting of Tascal-Money.[7]

As the Commissions against the caterans granted by kings and Privy Councils produced little tangible success, some heritors, such as the Lord Forbes of the late seventeenth century, took individual action against the reivers. The likely results of such action are shown in the 'Account of loss My Lord Forbes lands sustained by the Robberies and depradations of the Highlanders, Anno [16]89 and [16]90'. Six fermtouns in the upper Lowlands— Logie, Edinbanchrie, Marchmarre, Westhills, Windseye, Cushney—were utterly ravaged, the total damage sustained being valued at £3,858. Ten years later, however, the local lairds jointly set up in opposition to the caterans, for in 1700 the heritors in the Presbyteries of Kincardine and Alford, where much of the Forbes lands lay, made 'Bonds . . . to concert measures for the peace of the country'.[8] Although the number of 'broken men' liable to disturb the peace of the country increased after the failure of the Fifteen rebellion, the government's raising of companies of 'Black Watch' did drain off some of the warlike spirits, and finally, after the Forty-Five, when roads were built and military garrisons established in the Highlands, the practice of cattle-lifting came to an end.

Because the Northeast was a border region, its upper lowlands suffered considerably from the raids of the caterans, but extensive as the ravaging was, it did not match in extent the continual depredations on the lowlands of Moray. A letter from Cameron of Locheil to the Laird of Grant in which he apologizes to a fellow freebooter for a misdirected raid, illustrates, as well as the familial bonds of the clans, the Highlanders' attitude to Moray:[9]

> Respd. and Lowing Cousin.—My heartly commendations being mentioned to you. I have received your letter concerning this misfortunate accident that never fell out

the like between our houses the like before in no man's
days; but praised be God, I am innocent of the same, and
my friends, both in respect that they went not in your
bounds, *but to Murray lands, where all men taken their
prey* nor knew not that Moynes was ane Graunt, but
thought he was ane Murray man, and if they knew him
they would not stor his land more than the rest of your
bounds in Strathspey. . . '

The fertile Laigh of Moray suffered to such a degree because
the Highlands of Moray and adjacent Badenoch were covered
with lawless clans, most notably the MacIntoshes, MacPhersons,
and Grants. These clans were also the ones which most often
despoiled Aberdeenshire and Banffshire, although the prospect
of a rich creach in these shires quite frequently drew caterans
from as far afield as Lochaber.[10]

Not all the reivers, however, came from beyond the region,
for the Northeast itself harboured 'broken men' and 'clannit
men'. Attached to the 1587 Acts of Parliament is a 'Roll of þe
names of þe landislordis and baillies of landes duelland on þe
bordouris and in þe hielandis quhair brokin men hes duelt and
presentlie duellis' which includes the major landowners of the
region, the Earls of Huntly, Erroll, and Mar, and the Master of
Forbes.[11] Although there were many clannit men, there was only
one outright clan—the Farquharsons, who inhabited much of
the Northeast's border zone. They occupied a rather ambivalent
position, being sometimes regarded as the most westerly of the
Lowlanders and at other times as the most easterly of the
Highlanders; in 1641 the Privy Council granted John Farquharson of Invercauld a Commission to defend the Sheriffdoms of
Angus, Mearns, Aberdeen and Banff, but thirty years later
Alexander Farquharson had to contract with the Privy Council a
'Bond to the Peace' for himself and his clan.[12] The Farquharsons
seem to have belonged to Major's second category of 'Wild Scots'
(Highlanders)—those who possessed 'a wealth of cattle, sheep
and horses, and these, with a thought for the possible loss of
their possessions yield more willing obedience to the courts of
law and the king.'[13] Yet it is the Farquharsons who are the
cattle-lifters in 'The Baron of Brackley' (203).

The tensions between the Highlands and the Northeast Lowlands provided material for a number of ballad-stories. Local ballads in which Highlanders figure prominently include 'The Battle of Harlaw' (163), 'Willie Mackintosh' (183), 'James Grant' (197), 'The Baron of Brackley' (203), 'Bonny Baby Livingston' (222), 'Eppie Morrie' (223), 'Lizzie Lindsay' (226), 'Charlie Macpherson' (234), and 'Dugall Quin' (294). Their stories tell of a baron killed during a cattle-lifting, a Highland freebooter who burns a Lowland castle, a Highland freebooter vainly hunted by his enemies, and the abductions of Lowland lasses by Highland gallants. These ballad-stories, however, record more than events. 'The Battle of Harlaw' records not just the physical result of the tensions, the battle, but also the psychological—the emotional attitudes of the northeastern folk to the Highlanders over a number of centuries. The texts of this ballad-story illustrate how the tensions produced in the local folk an ambivalent reaction to the Highlanders: on the one hand they were feared because of their depredations, and on the other were chuckled at as comic fellows from the hills. This conception of the Gael as at once a wild cateran and an unconscious comedian ripe for burlesque is paralleled in Scottish literature, as, for example, in the poem from the Bannatyne MS., 'How the First Hielandman was Made by God of ane Horse Turd', with its incisive quatrain:[14]

> God turned owre the horse turd with his pykit staff,
> And up start a Hielandman black as ony draff.
> Quod God to the Hielandman, 'Where wilt thou now?'
> 'I will doun in the Lawland, Lord, and there steal a cow.'

This attitude altered to a more neutral one when, after 1750, the tensions slackened, and some texts of 'Harlaw' show that the original story of the ballad likewise was being altered to accommodate the change in attitude.[15] This particular ballad-story suggests how ballads may interest historians, for it captures not just the events of the Highland-Lowland tensions, but also the psychological effects of these tensions; it describes not only what men did but also how they felt. The tensions of the Highland border gave rise to ballad-stories like 'Harlaw' based on actual events; but Highland society, as we shall see in the next chapter, exerted an even more powerful, though more indirect, influence on the formation of ballad-stories.

Chapter 5

The Clannit Society

Proximity to the Gaels resulted in more than border hostilities. Other kinds of interaction between the two races affected significantly the ethos, organization, and generally violent atmosphere of northeastern society. The Northeast, of course, had already been influenced by the thousand years of Celtic occupation. While the most obvious legacy is the large number—almost ninety per cent—of local place-names derived from the Gaelic, other inheritances included the systems of land management and rural settlement described earlier. The evidence of the Celtic *Book of Deer* indicates that land division by ploughgate and davoch (four ploughgates), group cultivation (once by teams of men wielding spades), and the organization of society by communal rural township were features of early Celtic society; the close correspondences between Lowland fermtoun and Highland clachan also point to their having a common origin in the early Celtic township.[1] Culturally, as has been observed, the Celts dowered their successors with a plentiful body of folk-melody, and much lore. But later influences also helped shape the regional society. When, between the twelfth and fourteenth centuries, the Northeast was transformed from a Celtic region into a Lowland region, the processes of change did not operate only in one direction. Just as the Celtic landowners voluntarily adopted many of the ways and administrative methods of the Anglo-Norman incomers, so the Anglo-Normans incorporated Celtic features into their feudalism.

The resulting social organization of the Northeast was a compound of feudal and clan systems that can best be described as 'clannit'. The primary bond of the clan system was that of kinship, whereas the feudal plan was basically a system of landholding arrangements; and these two systems merged in the

Northeast where the landholding arrangements were fortified by the ties of blood-relationship.[2] Such families as the Gordons were organized on neither a strictly feudal basis nor a strictly clan basis, but a mixture of both; they were clannit houses. These clannit houses laid great stress on the ties of kindred and consequently on the family name, though in the fifteenth century the name could be gained through adoption as well as blood. One Lord of Gordon of that time wished to increase his power and so declared that to every man who became his vassal he would present a boll of oatmeal; since the agreement's crucial stipulation insisted that the new vassals took the family name, those who accepted were thereafter known as the 'Bow o' Meal' Gordons.[3] Later, this clannit house had no need of such ploys, for it grew in power and influence until Gordons were found planted in almost every corner of the Northeast. The head of the house—the 'Cock o' the North'—drew allegiance from the scattered Gordon lairds because he was not only head of the house but also their feudal superior. As the Gordon Rent Roll of 1600 shows, he used the medieval practice of subinfeudation, by which the lord who held land direct from the king would have minor lords hold land from him in the same way, to bind together, in letter as well as in spirit, the various septs and branches of the family.[4]

The employment by the northeastern lairds of a form of tenancy popular in the Gaelic Highlands indicates that the relationship between laird and tenant often resembled that of chief and clansman more closely than that of superior and vassal. By this type of tenancy, known as 'steelbow tenure', the laird helped to set up an incoming tenant in seed and stock and was repaid at the tenant's outgoing. The sixteenth-century Forbes Rent Roll notes that the toun-tenants of Buthny 'his of my Lordis, to ye lawboring of ye ground xxxij bollis aitts, viij bollis bere, and viij oxin, prysit to xiij £ xv s.', and that in another toun 'ye tennentts of Carnaverane ressavit fra my Lord viij £ to by oxin, and sall pay ye sam agane at yair furthpassing'.[5] The lairds, then, contrived to inject some of the emotionally binding relationships of the clan into the feudal structure.

They fused the familial organization with the feudal primarily in order to have a large body of dependants who would follow the laird, willingly and without duress, in any warlike activity against reiving clans, feuding neighbours, or foreign invaders. The lists of the heritors in the Aberdeenshire and Banffshire highlands who, in 1699, gave bonds for the peaceable behaviour of their men record the existence of many men not registered in the Poll Book of 1696.[6] These men were 'sorners', personal retainers of the laird who did little or no agricultural work but who were always ready for local raid or national campaign. As Leslie said of the lairds: 'Gret families thay feid and that perpetuallie, pairtlie to defend thame selfes frome thair nychtbouris, with quhome oft thay haue deidlie feud, partlie to defend the Realme.'[7] The lairds were able to afford the upkeep of these 'gret families' because of the system that existed until well into the eighteenth century of paying rents in kind. Almost the only way in which the large heritors could profitably utilize the immense amounts of meal, fowl, and livestock paid to them as rent was to maintain these sorners. These conditions resulted in the laird and his sorners having a relationship not unlike that of the clan chieftain and his comitatus. The features of the Celtic clan system that were incorporated into the Northeast's social organization during the feudalization did not atrophy but rather increased in importance as the region became more solidly Lowland, because in times of general turbulence they proved useful to lairds frequently called upon to defend the Realme from invaders or themselves from 'nychtbouris', whether clans or other lairds.

Under the clannit system the head of a Lowland house was able to capitalize on his dual position as family chief and feudal superior. When in need of fighting men, he could call out not only those of the family name but also those who were not kindred but feudal vassals. When clansmen held land from a Lowland laird —as the MacPhersons and MacIntoshes held their Badenoch lands from the house of Gordon[8]—anomalous situations were bound to occur. In 1562, for example, Huntly called out his MacIntosh tenants who, on their way to join his forces, were accosted and commandeered for the Queen's party by their clan chief; they then helped their chief defeat their superior at the Battle of Corrichie.[9] The claims of the crown were likely to come third on the scale of priority to those of both chieftain and superior. In 1691 Lieutenant Mackay of the 'Garrision of Badenoch' wrote to the Duchess of Gordon that Cluny MacPherson would permit the king to raise a company of troops from his clansmen, 'only his kinsmen out of respect and reference to your grace, and the family of Huntly, to whom they are vassalls, refuse obedience without your grace's order.'[10] Clannit houses and clans were also linked in another way. From the fifteenth to the seventeenth century it was customary for Lowland lairds to band together in Bonds of Alliance, Manrent, or Friendship, but some of these bonds were also made out between Lowland houses and Highland clans. A Bond of Manrent and Maintainance, a kind of bond that 'would seem to have taken its origin in a desire to create a kind of feudal relation, like that of Lord and Vassal, between parties who were not linked together like them by the tenure of land' was granted by Huntly to the Maclean in 1536 and to the Captain of Clan Cameron in 1543.[11] As the country was at one time entangled by a network of alliances, these covenants undoubtedly helped to escalate any local feud. But individual interactions between clans and houses were not so significant in maintaining unsettled conditions as the general interaction between the clan and feudal organizations that had produced the clannit system.

The clannit system had two important effects on the life of the Northeast: it fostered a sense of homogeneity among lairds and tenants and it encouraged bellicosity between the lairds. In doing so, it reinforced what seem to have been national characteristics. There are indications that Scottish society as a whole tended towards homogeneity more than most contemporary societies. Serfdom died out early in Scotland, largely because the frequency of war and feud influenced fundamentally the relationship between superior and vassal. As Coulton succinctly puts it: 'To call upon men on Monday to help you in repelling an invader . . . and on Tuesday to treat them like cattle again, is not possible in the long run.'[12] The Scottish nobles treated their own tenants in a much more friendly fashion than most of their European counterparts: 'thay ar frie of al custumes, wt quhilkes ar opprest the subiectes of utheris princes.'[13] From an early date efforts were made to safeguard the livelihood and rights of the ordinary tenant-farmer; an Act of the Parliament of July 1366 laid down that:[14]

No prelate, earl or baron or anyone of any rank, cleric

or lay, shall ride, to the destruction of the land, with a
greater retinue in persons or horses than becomes his
rank, and that no-one shall lead with him spearmen or
archers riding through the land unless there is a reasonable
cause about which they shall be held to make an oath to
the king's ministers holding an inquiry on this matter,
on pain of imprisonment.

The absence of such uprisings as Wat Tyler's Revolt, the Jac-
querie rebellions, or the German Peasants' War, attests the
comparative harmony of the Scottish tenant-farmer's relationship with his local laird.

Two sixteenth-century writers, both of whom probably hailed
from the Northeast, indicate that the people enjoyed 'a gret
freedome and libertie'. Perhaps because of the Wars of Independence, the Scots were early believers in ideas of political liberty;
by 1521 Major could enunciate as a fundamental political
principle that 'The king holds his right as king of a free people
nor can he grant that right to anyone against the will of that
people.'[15] Fifty years later Bishop Leslie commented on the
Scottish body politic:[16]

Of this may ony man esilie collecte in our people yit to
be a certane form of Repub. Eftir that forme, in latine
Democratia, yt is a forme of commoune weil quhair the
people haue the hail authoritie wtout ony vthir state,
notwithstanding with vs, eftir that maner nocht aluterlie
sa, bot wt sik temperance, that cheif vpon thair king and
counsel maist graue of the nobilitie, the Repub. does
depend.

The democratic elements within the 'commoune weil' manifest
themselves in the relation of tenant to laird; the tenants 'keep a
horse and weapons of war, and are ready to take part in his
quarrel, be it just or unjust, with any powerful lord, *if they only
have a liking for him*, if need be, to fight to the death' (italics
added).[17] This national tendency towards a democratic homogeneity was intensified in the Northeast by the egalitarian life
of fermtoun and burgh and by the clannit social system. There
were in the region none of the massive barriers between aristocracy and peasantry common elsewhere; distinctively, the North-

east was characterized by a clannit homogeneity whereby lairds and tenants were linked through family bonds, loyalties, and mutual respect.

The other national characteristic fostered by the clannit system was the bellicosity of the lairds and their followers. Between local feuds and national campaigns, the Scots experienced more of war than their English or European counterparts. Hector Boece, the first Principal of Aberdeen's King's College, laments their intemperance and wishes 'the Albianis had sic grace that thay micht leif with concord amang thaimself',[18] while John Major shows how their pride and hastiness of temper, which gave rise to the simile 'fier comme un Ecossais', gave rise also to feud and vendetta:[19]

> If two nobles of equal rank happen to be very near
> neighbours, quarrels and even shedding of blood are a
> common thing between them; and their very retainers
> cannot meet without strife . . . From the beginning of
> time families at strife with one another make bequest of
> hatred to their children.

In the Northeast the lairds could indulge their belligerent tendencies quite freely because the bonds between laird and tenant engendered by the local social system ensured them a ready supply of willing fighting men. In fostering the sense of homogeneity and the lairds' bellicose tendencies the clannit system contributed greatly to the general turbulence of the northeast.

The clannit system had developed because of unsettled conditions but, once established, it helped perpetuate the unsettlement. For much of the period under discussion the Northeast was rife with violence. The border affrays created hostile tensions enough, but even more disruptive were the tensions generated by the incessant feuding among the Northeast lairds. Under the luckless Stewarts, many of whom died early, Scotland generally suffered from a pronounced weakness in the central government, and this allowed the unruly lairds to prosecute their feuds more or less with impunity. Weak central government also encouraged the growth of the great houses. In the Northeast the Gordons wielded enormous power, but rarely for peaceful purposes. With huge amounts of rent in kind available to maintain the sorners, they were embroiled, through the Bonds of Alliance and Manrent and the neighbourhood disputes of the family's ubiquitous branches, in a continual series of raids, reprisals, and vendettas.

As the feuds significantly affected northeastern life, and its balladry, they merit some attention. Feuding, of course, was not a prerogative of the Gordóns, but widespread among the lairds. The Synod of Aberdeen in its complaint to James I in 1606 over the region's 'miserabill confusione' gave these as the causes: 'In commonweill, FIRST, Monye deadlie feudis arysin amangst Forbesis and Irwingis, Leslyes and Leythis, quhilk are licklie be thair pairties to draw on the haill countrey to bloodie factionis. SECONDLIE, That everie man that plesis wearis gunis, pistolis, rydis with jacks, spearis, knopsknais, without controlment.'[20] The feud between the Leiths and the Leslies, which also took in the Abercrombies and the Gordons of Newton, is perhaps a representative one of these days, involving as it did bloodshed, murder, robbery, adultery, rapine, outlawry and spells in the Tolbooth. The account of this feud in the Register of the Privy Council of Scotland provides an insight into how the turmoil affected the ordinary tenant-farmer. Adam Abercrombie complained to the Privy Council that when John Leith of Harthill and his men searched for one of his tenants, Henry Clerk, and failed to find him[21]

> they took a broust of new beir dranke out a parte thairof and spilt the rest upon the floore, brake up his kists and beeff fatts, cutted his seckes with swords and durkes, spulzied and tooke his haill salt beiff, muttoun and other victuall being within the hous, with his bed cloathes and what ellis they could find in the hous.

When Leith did lay hands on Henry Clerk, he imprisoned him in irons for five days:

> and before he lett the poor man goe he tooke him deepelie sworne that he sould never strike pleuche nor harrow in the lands of Aldrayne . . . Lykeas the said John Leith of Harthill be himselfe and his commissioners threatned the whole tennents of Aldrayne nather to strike pleuche nor harrow upon the saids lands, otherwayes he vowed to God to hang thame everie man over thair awne balkes.

41

> Upon occasion whereof the haill labourers and occupyers
> of the lands of Aldrayne left the ground, so as thare wes
> not a reiking hous within aucht plewes of the saids lands,
> aucht crofts and a mile of ground, except onelie Johne
> Ker, who maried ane Leith to his wife.

Clerk's answer to Abercrombie's request to complain officially,
that 'he nather would nor durst compleane, and that it would
cost him his life if it were knowne he had a purpose to compleane',
illustrates further just how hazardous was the lot of a tenant-
farmer whose laird was weaker than an oppressive neighbour.

The Forbes–Leslie feud that was interlinked with the Leslie–
Leith feud was initiated by a son of 'Red Sir Andrew' Leslie of
Balquhain, a famous local laird who sired seventy children,
seven of them in one night. Inspired by paternal example, the
son abducted the betrothed of Sir John de Forbes and precipitated
a feud that lasted two hundred years and found its bitterest
expression in the cruelty of the sixteenth-century freebooter,
John Strachan of Lynturk.[22] It is an index of the very real havoc
these men wreaked that neither Strachan nor the seventeenth-
century brigands such as John Dugar and Gilderoy turn up in
traditional song as beneficent freespenders like Robin Hood or
Jesse James.[23] The general lawlessness of the region is mirrored
in the existence not only of these freebooters, but also of terrorist
gangs like the 'Societie of the Boyis' and the 'Knychtis of the
Morter'. A letter to the Earl of Huntly from the Privy Council
describes the first group:[24]

> having associat unto thameselffis ane nomber of deboscheit
> and laules lymmaris . . . they haif most unlauchfullie and
> seditiouslie bound thameselffis in ane fellowschipp with
> aithis, vowis, and protestationis of mutuall defence
> and persute, and that every one of thair quarrellis salbe
> coummoun to all, and that the purpois and interprise of
> ony one of thame salbe prosequuted, bakkit, and followit
> oute be the haill Societie aganis all and quhatsomeuir,
> without respect of personis. Lyke as thir same lymmaris
> keepis thameselffis togidder, committing open and avowed
> reiffis, heirschippis, and utheris enormities in all pairtis
> quhair they may be maisters and commandaris.

Huntly's measures against the gang could not have been very effective, for two years later appeared the Knychtis of the Morter, composed mainly of Forbeses. As it was 'a foull reprotche and scandell to this oure natioun that suche a handfull and infamous byk of laules lymmaris salbe so lang sufferit to haif residence and resting in ony pairt of oure said kingdome', Irvine of Drum, no friend of the Forbeses, was given a commission against this 'maist unlauchfull, rebellious, and detestable societie and felloeschip', who 'go athort the cuntrey armed with hacquebutis and pistoletis, attending the occasioun to commit robreis, slaughteris and oppressionis quhair thay bore quarrell'. It is in such an atmosphere that a Garioch laird could enter in the fly-leaf of the family bible:[25]

> This day oor Jock stickit Glaister o' Glack's auldest son,
> Glory be to God the Father, God the Son, and God the
> Holy Ghost.

The local Lowland feuds were often exacerbated by the lairds' employment of Highlanders. After the events dramatized in 'The Fire of Frendraught' (196), which grew out of a Gordon–Crichton–Leslie feud, the Gordons mercilessly harassed Crichton of Frendraught with hordes of 'lawless and broken Highlandmen', 'so that his lands have been caste waste, as tenants will not run the hazard of dwelling thereupon, being so often spoiled of their goods and their lives threatened'. The Highlanders ruthlessly spulzied the tenants

> whois haill goods they have lifted, layed thair lands waist,
> hanged one of the poore tennents upon the gallowes of
> Strabogis, burnt the said Laird of Fendraucht his
> barnyaird, and compellis suche of the tennents as remaines
> upon the ground to pay thame blackemaill, and with ane
> high hand of rebellion they have resolved to make
> thameselffes maisters of the said Laird of Fendraucht
> his estait and to possesse thameselffes therein and to
> keepe the same by strenth of armes in contempt and
> defyance of his Majesteis royall auctoritie.

It is small wonder that when Crichton refused to pay taxes in 1635 because his lands were devastated, the Lords of the Privy Council 'compassionatting the distrist estate of the Laird of

Fendraucht in respect of the manie incursionis, heirships and depredationis committed upon his tenents' recommended to the Lords of the Exchequer that exactions should be temporarily halted. But such a feud as this did not involve only the Crichtons, the Gordons, and lawless Gaels finding Lowland compensation for a year of Highland scarcity. The Privy Council ordered the sheriffs of Aberdeen, Banff, Elgin, Forres, Nairn and Inverness 'to conveene and raise in armes the haill noblemen, gentlemen and others fensible persons within thair severall jurisdictions in proper person' and, if the broken men were to 'abandoun the incountrie' and flee to the adjacent Highlands, the lords of the nearest lands were to 'raise the countrie people, pas, follow and persew the saids brokin men with fire and sword'. What began as a localized feud rippled out to include Highlanders, sheriffs and lairds of both Northeast and neighbouring shires, and the tenants of the western Lowlands who, burnt out of their homes one week, were likely to be hunting down raiders the next.[26]

Involvement with national affairs as well as with the Highlands also intensified and spread the local enmities. When the central government made one of its periodic attempts to subdue or punish the Highlands, it often delegated its authority, through the vice-regal 'Lieutenandry of the North' or a specific commission, to a local noble, who in the Northeast was Normally the Earl of Huntly but sometimes his great enemy, the Earl of Moray. National politics lay behind James VI's granting Huntly a commission in 1592 to apprehend the Earl of Moray; Huntly, displaying great zeal in a duty where national coincided so conveniently with personal interest, killed the earl instead of capturing him. While this murder provoked one ballad (181), its aftermath in the Northeast helped create two more. After the murder, the MacIntosh vassals of the dead earl, together with the Farquharsons and other members of Clan Chattan, devastated the Gordon lands in Strathdee, Glenmuick and Abergeldie, killing, amongst other Gordon lairds, the Baron of Brachlie. Huntly was returning from his retaliatory raid on the Clan Chattan lands when he discovered that Willie MacIntosh and 800 men of Clan Chattan were at that time laying waste his own lands in Strathbogie; these he defeated at the Stapliegate in the Cabrach.[27] 'Willie Mackintosh' (183) and 'The Baron of Brackley' (203) are based on these events.

Though the Northeast was comparatively remote from the centres of political government, the power of its nobles and its strategic position often embroiled it in the country's affairs, particularly when national issues could be used to settle local scores or further local ends. The long and stormy feud between the Gordons and the Forbeses provides one example of this. Ever since the collapse of the old Earldom of Mar led to their becoming the two most powerful families in the region, they normally ranged themselves with opposing sides on national issues—the post-Reformation fighting in the sixteenth century, the Civil Wars of the seventeenth, down to the Forty-Five, when the leading Hanoverian in the region was Duncan Forbes and the Jacobite lieutenant in the Northeast was Lord Lewis Gordon. Out of the Gordon–Forbes hostility came what is probably the most widely known of the northeastern feud ballads, 'Edom o Gordon' (178). The ballad recounts the burning of Corgarff Castle and the Gordons' slaughter of the Forbes defenders, and its stanzas illustrate the ambience of feud: the heroic defiance, the brutal murder of the young, the implacable loyalty of retainer to laird:

> Ye paid me well my meatt, lady,
>   Ye paid me well my hire,
> But nou I am Edom of Gordon's man,
>   To ye mane lat the fire.   (I: 13)

and the bereavement of a survivor, the wifeless laird who mourns as would a tenant-farmer for whom oats and barley were, in fact, life itself:

> O I hae corn, an' I hae bere,
>   An barley in a bing,
> But I wad gie it a' this nicht
>   To hear my lady sing.   (*Last Leaves*, C:6)

The Gordons and the Forbeses were distinguished by different characters and patterns of behaviour; Dr Douglas Simpson sums up the difference neatly: 'In the main, the Forbeses are practical, earnest and realistic, with a shrewd capacity to judge the winning side. And in the main, the Gordons were the romantic gallants, the heroes of the lost causes. They are the "Gay Gordons".'[28] In the light of this it is significant that while the Forbeses appear notably in 'The Battle of Harlaw' and 'Edom o Gordon', and fleetingly in 'Bonny John Seton' (198), the Gordons appear in all the other northeastern ballads of feud and war. The semi-historical ballads also show how far the Gordons caught the ballad-makers' imagination, for a Gordon figures prominently in 'The Earl of Aboyne' (235), 'The Duke of Gordon's Daughter' (237), and 'The Rantin Laddie' (240).

The Northeast, then, was a border region, itself basically Lowland but much affected both politically and socially by neighbouring Highland society. The influence of the Celtic social system reinforced the national democratic tendencies and helped produce that clannit homogeneity which marked regional society. This clannit homogeneity in turn aggravated the generally turbulent conditions, as did the reiving raids of the Highlanders; and out of the turbulence came 'subjects for story'.

The ballad society of the Northeast was an agricultural society, whose most marked characteristic was its communality; in this respect it resembles ballad areas in northwestern Europe. It was not a feudal society in the strict sense, but rather a clannit and homogeneous society where tenant-farmers and small chieftains existed together amicably, like the knights and yeomen of Denmark.[29] The Northeast was remote but escaped cultural introversion because the potentially static regional society was animated by certain dynamic relationships that encouraged the spread of traditional material: the isolated touns of the rural districts were linked through the peripatetic tradesmen and local foregatherings, and the region as a whole, though barriered from the rest of the Lowlands by the Mounth, enjoyed a vitalizing contact through trade with the continent. The area was a border region, where the meeting of the Gaelic and Lowland Scottish races and cultures provided both social crossfertilization and political tension. To judge by the analogies of Yugoslavia, where the cultures of Protestant Teutons, Mohammedan Turks, Roman Catholic Latins, and Orthodox Slavs all intersected, and Spain, where the cultures of Mohammedan Moors and Castilian Christians intermixed, it seems probable that the frontier hostilities of the two races were at least equalled in importance for balladry by the energizing interpenetration of their cultures. Interaction with not only Gaelic culture but also continental cultures invigorated and enriched the regional ballad culture, whose tunes are related to the Celtic and whose texts are related to the Scandinavian. In this northeastern society, the feuds and reivings created both ballad atmosphere and ballad-stories, and the communal environment of the fermtoun furnished plentiful 'occasion for the telling'. On the basis of northeastern society and its analogies with the major European ballad areas, it is now possible to amend Housman's description of the archetypal society of ballad folk to read thus: traditional balladry flourished in a nonliterate, homogeneous, agricultural society, dominated by semi-independent chieftains, that is situated in a remote, hilly, or border region where cultures meet and feuds and wars abound; this kind of society provided both subjects for ballad-story and occasions for ballad performance, and lasted till the advent of widespread literacy.

Part II

The Oral Tradition:
the Ballads

Chapter 6

Balladry and Oral Poetry

Ballads are normally studied by folklorists in North America and by literary scholars in Britain, a situation which reflects balladry's dual status. The ballads are folklore because folklore consists of 'the material handed on by tradition, either by word of mouth or by custom and practice'.[1] Again, they are poems, though poems of a distinctive kind because of their origin in the tradition of nonliterate societies. By origin, then, balladry is a genre of oral poetry. Recently the essential nature of oral poetry has been illuminated by Albert Lord, and his account of the oral method of composition is producing widespread repercussions in the study of both literature and folklore. His work provides the master-key to an understanding of material orally composed and transmitted by nonliterate people. As with most pioneering works, however, a penalty must be paid for the very radicalism of its insights: by showing how different the oral method of composition is from the literate, Lord has rendered much of our current terminology obsolete or ineffectual. Ambiguities now abound in the terms available for a discussion of oral material, because the denotative and connotative meaning of these terms are rooted in a literate context. Standard terms of literary criticism, such as 'author' and 'original text', and of folkloristic criticism, such as 'transmission', have vastly different meanings in oral and literate contexts.

The difficulties, however, do not lie only in standard critical terminology. The connotations of a word like 'illiterate' indicate our ingrained assumptions about the creative intelligence of people who cannot read and write. 'Illiterate' people, we are liable to assume, are, *ipso facto*, backward and incapable of sustained literary activity. How, if this were true, could we explain away the ability of the Kara Kirghiz poet, Sagymbai

Orozbakov, to compose a poem 40,000 lines long when he is 'illiterate'?[2] And he is just one, though a particularly strong-lunged one, of many oral singers of quality and stamina. Lord's explanation of how nonliterate singers like Orozbakov and Avdo Mededovic can compose artistically sophisticated poems forces us to revise radically many of our literate preconceptions about literature, particularly our view of the relationship between composition and transmission. To consider transmission as a separate operation makes sense in a literate context, but is fatally constricting in an oral context, because there transmission is just part, though an integral part, of an all-inclusive process: ' "oral transmission", "oral composition", "oral creation", and "oral performance" are all one and the same thing'. Likewise with our conception of 'author': 'Our oral poet is composer. Our singer of tales is a composer of tales. Singer, performer, composer, and poet are one under different aspects *but at the same time*. Singing, performing, composing are facets of the same act.'[3] The process of oral 'transmission' is essentially a process of re-composition, because the oral poet re-creates each story at each performance, during each performance. A mature traditional singer can hear a story of perhaps some thousands of lines, once, and can thereafter re-tell the story at even greater length. The literate mind boggles. The oral poet can do this, can compose rapidly in performance, because he has learned the phrases and rhythms of a poetic language, the language of tradition, which he can think in almost as easily as we can think in the phrases and rhythms of our prosaic language.

The traditional singer does not learn individual songs as fixed texts, but learns instead both a method of composition and a number of stories. By this method he re-composes each individual story every time he performs. While, however, he re-creates the story's narrative essence, he actually creates the individual lines and shapes the individual structure at the moment of performance: he composes the text as he re-composes the story. Each rendering of the story is, then, an 'original text'. The nonliterate singer is able to compose poems in the traditional way because he has mastered the tradition's phrases and rhythmic patterns, which may be looked on—though the metaphor does not do full justice to the dynamism of the creative process—as many-layered moulds into which the story-idea is poured.

Oral poetic texts can be recognized as such because they contain the traditional phrases and patternings intrinsic to the oral method of composition. The most overt sign of the oral style is the 'formula', which may be defined as 'a group of words which is regularly employed under the same metrical conditions to express a given essential idea'. Formulas may appear as individual phrases such as 'the wine-dark sea' and 'the berry-brown steed', or as clusters of lines. Oral poems are also characterized by what Milman Parry has called the 'adding style'. In poems built up line by line this shows most clearly in the parataxis of grammar, but in poems built up stanza by stanza it shows most clearly in a parataxis of narrative image, a stylistic trait that in the ballads has been compared to cinematic montage and the technique of the strip-cartoon. The phrase 'adding style' implies a narrative looseness which does not in fact exist, because binding rhythms unify the poems, and produce highly patterned artefacts. In addition to their sometimes intricate aural patterns of assonance and alliteration, oral poems frequently possess quite complex architectonic patterns. These latter patterns manifest themselves, structurally and conceptually, in all kinds of balances and parallelisms, contrasts and antitheses, chiastic and framing devices, and in various kinds of triadic groupings. A conceptual pattern called by Lord the 'tension of essences', whereby certain narrative elements automatically cohere, would suggest that there are other hidden patterning forces, as yet undissected, working within oral tradition. Just as the aural patterns reflect the nonliterate person's highly developed sense of sound, so these architectonic patterns reflect how his mode of apprehension is spatial as well as simply linear and sequential.[4]

By demonstrating how a traditional poetry is composed, Lord has clarified our understanding of oral poetry's characteristics of style. Many years ago the Danish folklorist, Axel Olrik, investigated a group of genres (including folksong, folktale, myth, saga and legend) which he collectively designated the *Sage*, and, by examining the characteristics of style, attempted to deduce from them 'rules for the composition' of the *Sage* genres which he then called the epic laws of *Volksdichtung*.[5] In the light of Lord's findings, we can now see that what Olrik understood as *Sage* and *Volksdichtung* we would understand as material that belongs to both oral literature and folklore, material orally

c

composed-and-transmitted, and that what Olrik termed 'laws' are primarily descriptions of textual characteristics resulting from the oral method of composition-and-transmission.

These 'laws' extend our knowledge of the hallmarks of oral style, but they also, when ordered, provide us with further insight into the artistic and psychological processes of oral composition. Olrik notes in general that the *Sage* has its own internal Logic (*die Logik der Sage*), that it has much Patterning (*die Schematisierung*) and Repetition (*die Widerholung*), and that the *Sage* work has Unity of Plot (*die Einheit der Handlung*). The Unity of Plot derives to a large extent from particular kinds of Patterning and Repetition. These specific patterns demonstrate how what I shall call unitary, binary, and trinary forces are at work in tradition shaping the individual songs and narratives. The unitary force shows in the *Sage* work's concentration on the Single Plot Strand, the Leading Character, and one or more Striking Scenes (*die Einsträngigkeit, die Hauptperson, die Hauptsituationen plastischer Art*). The binary force shows in the *Sage*'s many balances and parallelisms, which Olrik formulates as a series of laws: the Law of Contrast (*das Gesetz des Gegensatzes*), the Law of Twins (*das Gesetz der Zwillinge*), the Law of Two to a Scene (*das Gesetz der szenischen Zweiheit*), the Law of Opening and Closing (*das Gesetz des Einganges und des Abschlusses*) and the Law of Initial Position (*'Toppgewicht'*) and Final Position (*'Achtergewicht'*). And the trinary force shows in the *Sage*'s frequent arrangement of material in threes, a characteristic that is probably the most evident of *Volksdichtung*'s structural patternings and one that Olrik recognizes in his Law of Three (*das Gesetz der Dreizahl*). The unitary force differs in kind from the binary and trinary forces, and the difference between them illuminates one aspect of the oral creative process. In the artistic mind of the oral singer or narrator complementary impulses are at work, one reductive, the other expansive: the reductive impulse compels the oral maker to jettison ruthlessly all extraneous matter in order to concentrate on the story's essence—the Single Plot Strand, the Leading Character, and the Striking Scene; on the other hand, the binary and trinary rhythms enable the oral maker both to expand dramatically the bare essentials of the story and at the same time to bind together these expanding elements in patterned unity. The co-existence of these two shaping influences, the reductive and the expansive, reveals how, in a nonliterate artist's consciousness, an unsophisticated linear mode of apprehension functions conjointly with a more complex spatial mode of apprehension.

Olrik's 'laws' are held in some quarters to be superorganic, that is, to exist above and beyond the individual artist, and to govern him rigidly in his artistic creation.[6] There is a grain of truth in each part of this conception: in the first part because the rhythmic forces which lie behind these 'laws' operate in the individual's works and also throughout the tradition, and in the second part because these rhythmic forces do constitute powerful shaping influences on the individual compositions. But to divorce these 'laws' from the conscious will of the oral artist, and to see them as rigidly constricting his creative freedom, is to undervalue seriously the positive creativity of the traditional maker. The 'laws' which Olrik enumerates are not superorganic at all; they simply codify some of the ingrained characteristics of oral style that grow organically out of the nonliterate maker's traditional method of composition.

In this instance, as in many others, we are able to see the precise significance and function of oral stylistic traits only by knowing how the method of oral composition operates. This just emphasizes how important it is to see oral composition not as a debased or primitive form of written literary composition but as a sometimes sophisticated autonomous method of literary creation. It comes as a peculiar kind of shock to realize, with all the implications, that most of mankind have been nonliterate and that their literature, where it existed, has been oral. The very incongruity of the phrase 'oral literature' underlines how fundamentally we associate literature with writing, how easily we assume that written literary composition is the only form of literary composition. Having discarded that assumption, we are then liable to find difficulty in fully understanding the oral method itself, because our own frames of reference and habits of perception are literate. Consequently, when investigating the oral method we need to be chary of our basic assumptions about literature, particularly as they are built into our critical and descriptive terminology, for if we insist on examining the oral process through the lenses of literacy our reward will be, not keener sight, but blurred vision.

These difficulties show very clearly in attempts to conceive of the oral method as a process of 'memorization' or 'improvisation' when the normal literate acceptations of these terms have little relevance to an oral context. The process of traditional oral transmission is not, as the inflexibly literate would have it, merely a process of memorization by rote. To the literate mind, the process of transmission posits firstly, a fixed text, and secondly, a chain of attempts to memorize the verbal content of that text. It is conceived of as a largely visual process: the words are seen, then committed by repeated readings to memory, where they are perhaps retained by an act of visual imagination. The nonliterate person does not possess this kind of visual imagination; words for him cannot be translated into pictorial symbols, they exist as sound-groups; his faculty for imaginative retention is largely auditory. For basically the same reason, the lack of a capacity for literate visualization, he has no conception of a fixed text; the belief that a story and the words in which it is told must be the same or else the story is altered would be to him incomprehensible. He has none of the sophisticated literate mind's word-fixation; he makes no attempt to render the actual words of the story as he heard it, but he does make a strenuous effort to render the story itself exactly as he heard it. For him, the story's the thing.[7]

In the nineteenth century a Tsarist official, V. V. Radlov, observed the Kara Kirghiz oral singers in action and gave his impression of their method:[8]

> Every minstrel who has any skill at all always improvises
> his songs according to the inspiration of the moment, so
> that he is not in a position to recite a song twice in
> exactly the same form; but one must not suppose that
> this process of improvisation involves composing a new
> poem every time. The procedure of the improvising
> minstrel is exactly like that of the pianist. As the latter
> puts together into a harmonious form different runs
> which are known to him, transitions and motifs according
> to the inspiration of the moment, and thus makes up the
> new from the old which is familiar to him, so also does
> the minstrel of epic poems. Through an extensive practice
> in production, he has whole series of 'elements of

production', if I may so express it, in readiness, which he
puts together in suitable manner according to the course
of the narrative. . . . The art of the singer consists only
in arranging all these static component parts of pictures
with one another as circumstances require, and in
connecting them with lines invented for the occasion.

Now the minstrel can utilise in his singing all the
formative elements specified above in very different ways.
He knows how to represent one and the same picture in
a few short strokes. He can depict it more fully, or he
can go into a very detailed description with epic fullness.
The greater the number of different formative elements
at the disposal of the minstrel, the more diversified will
be his performance, and the longer will he be able to
sing without tiring his listeners by the monotony of his
descriptions. The amount of the formative elements and
the skill in putting them together is the measure of the
skill of the minstrel. A skilled minstrel can recite any
theme he wants, any story that is desired, extempore,
provided that the course of events is clear to him. When
I asked one of the most accomplished minstrels whom I
had learnt to know if he could sing this or that song, he
answered me: 'I can sing any song whatever; for God
has implanted this gift of song in my heart. He gives
me the word on my tongue, without my having to seek
it. I have learnt none of my songs. All springs from my
inner self'. . . . The improvising minstrel sings . . . just
as the words flow from the tongue of a speaker without
his producing intentionally and consciously the articulations
necessary to produce them, as soon as the course of his
thoughts requires this or that word. The accomplished
minstrel can sing a day, or a week, or a month, just as
he can speak, and narrate all the time.

This account seizes on the essentially re-creative nature of the
oral process, but at the same time shows how easily the literate
mind can slip into false assumptions about the oral mind and its
artistic workings. Radlov's use of the term 'improvisation'
illustrates clearly how most of the available descriptive terms
come trailing clouds of literate connotations. Improvisation con-

notes for Radlov, as for most of us, 'inspiration of the moment', and thereby fails to convey the inherently ordered and disciplined character of the oral process. Again, Radlov's comment that 'The art of the singer consists only in arranging all these static component parts of pictures' exemplifies another fallacy, a more sophisticated version of the earlier memorization fallacy, that is attractive to the literate mind: the notion that the process is a dully mechanical one, whereby the singer memorizes by rote narrative and verbal units and then, dipping into his rag-bag, strings them together 'with lines invented for the occasion'. This view does not do justice to the dynamic aspects of the creative process. One must, then, in conceiving of the oral technique, steer between the Scylla of mechanical memorization and the Charybdis of improvisation by inspiration. Rather, the process is a kind of dynamic memorization, analogous to the way in which we use language, or a kind of disciplined improvisation.

Oral composition is, then, an essentially re-creative process. The oral composer re-creates each story at each performance by moulding the story in the shaping dies, verbal and architectonic, of his tradition. These principles are basic and hold good for all oral traditions, but the particular manifestations of these principles vary from tradition to tradition, from one regional and linguistic group to another. In Europe, there is a crucial division between the oral traditions of the West, where songs are rhymed and largely strophic, and the oral traditions of the East, where songs are rhymeless and largely unstrophic; and, of course, local peculiarities diversify still further variation between national and regional traditions.[9] The principles apply equally to Yugoslav and Scottish traditions, but the practical processes that embody these principles differ, because the end product of the Yugoslav tradition is the epic song whose thousands of unrhymed decasyllables are built up line by line, whereas the end product of the Scottish tradition is the tight ballad-drama whose main unit is the rhyming stanza. The basic difference in the forms ensures that the verbal, structural, and musical patterns through which the oral composer creates his structured story in song will have textual manifestations particular to the individual traditions. It also ensures a difference in the practical process of composition. The architectonic unit that Lord calls the 'theme' performs an important conceptual and structural function in the composition of the long Yugoslavian poems, but has no similar existence in the shorter Scottish ballads, where the architectonic forces are more nakedly structural. The first tentative effort to apply Lord's findings to British balladry fell short of its goal primarily because of its implicit assumption that not just the strategy, the general principles, but also the tactics, the particular acts of composition and particular textual results, would be the same for both Yugoslav and Anglo-Scottish traditions.[10]

The textual characteristics of Anglo-Scottish balladry have, of course, been analysed and enumerated by many scholars, though it is only in the wake of Lord that they can be seen in their proper perspective, in relation to a special method of composition. Some scholars have also provided insights into the method itself. G. L. Kittredge remarks of the ballad poet that 'he improvises orally', a statement he expands in a footnote:[11]

> Improvisation in verse is a lost art among us, and we
> instinctively regard it as a very special mark of exceptional
> genius. But this is a serious misapprehension. It survives
> in full vigor among the folk in most countries, and is
> well known to be far less difficult, in itself, than the art
> of speaking extempore in well-turned prose sentences.

Will Walker, Child's main Aberdeen helper, makes the same point: 'we must remember that improvisation and impromptu adaptation were far more common among rural maidens and mothers in Scotland, during the centuries that are past, than they are now'.[12] These insights were, however, lost in the critical mêlée between 'Individualists' and 'Communalists'. The 'Ballad War', wasteful and unproductive as it was in many ways, at least focused attention on the process of ballad composition, though the pervasive bipolarized view of the process as *either* individual *or* communal composition precluded a really fruitful revelation.[13] It was the scholar who put paid to this controversy, G. H. Gerould, who came closest to realizing the full implications of the old truism that ballads have flourished best in nonliterate communities. 'Folk without writing', says Gerould, 'know the art of composition in language, and preserve the memory of what they have composed'; the ballads are 'the flower of an art formalised and developed among people whose training has been oral instead of visual.'[14]

Other scholars have probed near or into the method of composition through considering the significance of ballad style or form. W. P. Ker notices the operation of a distinct process, if not a method of composition, when he says ' "The Ballad" is *form*' because of its 'power of taking up new subjects, and treating them according to the laws of the Ballad'.[15] Entwistle, for whom again 'The Ballad is form', declares that 'Anyone could compose a ballad who knew how to express events in a ballad manner' which means, *inter alia*, that 'the course of the tale must have the prescribed order and formulas'.[16] The most enlightening insight, however, into the relationship between ballad style and the oral process has been supplied by the early nineteenth-century Scottish collector, William Motherwell. In the Introduction to his *Minstrelsy*, Motherwell comments on the ballads' distinguishing features: 'their general structure and . . . those commonplaces and curious burdens'; these features 'serve as landmarks, and helps to the memory of the reciter', and constitute 'the bounding line which exists between what is the Oral and what is the Written poetry of a people'.[17]

Both Motherwell and Entwistle emphasize the importance of the structure, or order, and the formulas, or commonplaces, in ballad poetry. In general, contemporary studies of oral poetry concentrate most on formulas, although Whitman's work on Homer deals in large measure with the highly patterned structurings of the *Iliad*. Contemporary studies of folklore, on the other hand, are more likely to concentrate on structural analysis. In myth, Claude Lévi-Strauss has shown how the structure of a myth should be organized in diachronic sequences for synchronic reading in order to elucidate the myth's meaning.[18] In folktale, the English translation of Vladimir Propp's *Morphology of the Folktale* has provoked a number of structural studies, most notably Alan Dundes's *The Morphology of North American Indian Folktales*. In this book Dundes draws on structural linguistics for his basic schema, just as Robert Georges utilizes the concepts and terminology of generative–transformational grammar in his 'Structure in Folktales'.[19] Not surprisingly, Lord, Lévi-Strauss, Dundes, and Georges all find language the most useful analogy with which to illustrate the creative processes of oral tradition. Here is how Lord relates the methods of language and oral poetry:[20]

> The method of language is like that of oral poetry, substitution in the framework of the grammar. Without the metrical restrictions of the verse, language substitutes one subject for another in the nominative case, keeping the same verb, or keeping the same noun, it substitutes one verb for another. In studying the patterns and systems of oral narrative verse we are in reality observing the 'grammar' of the poetry, a grammar superimposed, as it were, on the grammar of the language concerned. Or, to alter the image, we find a special grammar within the grammar of the language, necessitated by the versification. . . . The speaker of this language, once he has mastered it, does not move any more mechanically within it than we do in ordinary speech.
>
> When we speak a language, our native language, we do not repeat words and phrases that we have memorised consciously, but the words and sentences emerge from habitual usage. This is true of the singer of tales working in his specialised grammar.

In the Scottish Northeast, and presumably elsewhere, ballads were once composed in traditional fashion by local singers of tales who had mastered the patterns and systems of their poetic language. The strongest evidence of this lies in the texts of the ballads of Mrs Anna Brown.

Chapter 7

The Oral Ballads of Mrs Brown

The ballads of Anna Gordon, better known as Mrs Brown of Falkland, constitute the oldest extant corpus (repertoire of one singer) in Anglo-Scottish balladry. They were mostly learned before 1759, at a time when the Northeast was still largely nonliterate, and the old conditions of life had not yet been disrupted by social upheaval. For Child, these ballads provided a touchstone of quality: 'No Scottish ballads are superior in kind to those recited in the last century by Mrs Brown of Falkland.'[1] That they are among the oldest and best of ballad texts provides warrant enough for a study of the corpus, but their age and quality are of secondary, though related, importance to their major distinction: they exemplify the traditional mode of oral composition by which ballads were once created and transmitted. Anna Gordon's ballads, wrote her father, 'proceded upon a system of manners, and in a stile of composition, both words and music, very peculiar, and of which we could recollect nothing similar'.[2]

Anna Gordon's background hardly tallies with our likely preconceptions about a 'folk' environment. She was born at Old Aberdeen in 1747, one year after Culloden, and spent the first half of her life at 'Humanity Manse' beside King's College, where her father, Thomas Gordon, held the Chair of Humanity. Gordon occupied this post till a year before his death, when he was appointed, at the age of eighty-three, Professor of Greek; much, it seems, could be expected of scholars in those days. Gordon's interests were not confined to things academic, however, as he participated prominently in one of the earliest clubs devoted to agricultural improvement.[3] Anna Gordon's mother was Lillias Forbes, one of the three daughters of Baillie William Forbes, first of Rubislaw and later of Disblair. When Forbes bought Disblair in 1696 he sold Rubislaw, by a quirk of co-incidence, to Sir George Skene of Fintray, whose descendant was James Skene of Rubislaw, the close friend of Scott and the man who obtained the other large group of old northeastern ballads, the 'Old Lady's Collection'.[4] Anna Gordon was nearing middle age when in 1788 she married the Reverend Andrew Brown, a former chaplain to the 21st Foot who had been presented to the Church of Falkland in Fife five years before. After nineteen years there, he became minister at Tranent, where he died in 1805, in his sixty-first year. Five years later, on 11 July 1810, his wife, Anna Brown, died in Old Aberdeen and was buried at Old Machar.

Anna Gordon learned her ballads from her mother's side of the family, and the indications are that she inherited her musical ability from the Forbeses as well. William Macmath examined the account of William Forbes of Disblair's personal estate, and in a letter to Child made this observation:[5]

> I think there is one remarkable thing about the deceased
> gentleman's personal estate, distinguishing it from that
> of the ordinary northern laird of that time. I mean the
> prominence assumed by his 'Musicall Instruments' and
> 'Musicall Books.' His music books are mentioned separately
> from the rest of his library and at a Public Auction
> brought almost as much as all the rest . . . Music was
> probably the hobby of Mr Forbes.

Forbes's daughter Anne, one of the 'Ladies of Disblair', was Anna Gordon's main ballad source, as Thomas Gordon explains to Alexander Fraser Tytler:[6]

> An aunt of my children, Mrs Farquherson, now dead,
> was married to the proprietor of a small estate near the
> source of the Dee, in the division of Aberdeenshire called
> Braemar, a sequestered, romantic pastoral country . . .
> This good woman, I say, spent her days, from the time
> of her marriage, among flocks and herds at Allan-a-quoich,
> her husband's seat, which, even in the country of Braemar,
> is considered as remarkable for the above circumstances.
> She had a tenacious memory, which retained all the
> songs she had heard the nurses and old women sing in

that neighbourhood. In the latter part of her life she
lived in Aberdeen, and being maternally fond of my
children when young, she had them much about her,
and was much with us. Her songs and tales of chivalry
and love were a high entertainment to their young
imaginations. My youngest daughter Mrs Brown, at
Falkland, is blessed with a memory as good as her aunt
and has almost the whole store of her songs lodged in
it. . . . Mrs Farquherson, I am sure, invented nor added
nothing herself.

Writing in middle age to Fraser Tytler, Mrs Brown remarks on
her association of the songs with her memories of childhood:[7]

You judge rightly in supposing that I should take
pleasure in recalling those scenes of infancy & childhood
which the recollection of these old songs brings back to
my mind, it is indeed what Ossian call[s] the joy of
grief the memory of joys past pleasant, but mournful to
the soul—but enough of this prattle. . . .

She did not learn all her ballads from her aunt, however; she
learned some from her mother, and some from a maid-servant
who had been a retainer in the Forbes family for many years.[8]
As far as they can be traced, then, Anna Gordon's ballads are
stories of a woman's tradition; her three immediate sources
were women, and the most important of the three, Anne
Farquharson, derived hers from the nurses and old women of
Allanaquoich.

We are faced with a paradox: the woman who preserved the
finest representatives of the old oral tradition, the tradition of
the nonliterate rural folk, was herself an educated woman,
daughter of a Professor and wife of a minister. This paradox is,
however, apparent rather than real, because it is possible, at a
certain point in the tradition, for a person to be both literate
and an oral composer. It is only when a person ceases to be
re-creative along traditional lines and accepts the literate concept
of the fixed text that he or she can no longer be classed as oral.
This normally occurs 'not when writing is introduced, but when
published song texts are spread among singers', when the singer
with his new literate respect for the printed word comes to

think of the printed text of the song as the right and only way
of the song: 'The change has been from stability of essential
story, which is the goal of oral tradition, to stability of text, of
the exact words of the story.'[9] That Mrs Brown did not accept
the concept of the fixed text, but did in fact re-create her ballad-
stories, has been amply demonstrated by Bertrand Bronson. For
Mrs Brown 'there was nothing sacred about the mere words of
her ballads. . . . As clearly appears from her contemporaneous
texts of the same ballads, she viewed her proper function as an
active participation, not a passive, inert reception.' By comparing
her different versions of the same ballad-stories, he shows that
she carried in her memory 'Not a *text*, but a *ballad*: a fluid
entity soluble in the mind, to be concretely realized at will in
words and music'. For example, Mrs Brown produced two
versions of 'The Lass of Roch Royal' (76D, 76E) whose differences
make it clear 'that what Mrs Brown was trying for in the version
of 1800 was, not to recover her own text of 1783, but to recover,
or re-create, the ballad itself, the essential, ideal "Lass of Roch
Royal" '. On the basis of Mrs Brown's 'co-operative and re-
creative' attitude to her texts, Bronson says that 'We come into
contact here with a vital active stage of oral tradition. It is
creative, or at least re-creative, and is at a vast remove from
the state of mental sleepwalking in which the older ballads have
latterly been perpetuated.' In short, 'a living and vital tradition,
such as is typified by Mrs Brown' indicates that 'The golden
age of balladry, whenever it occurred, was an age when there
was a maximum of creative and re-creative energy coursing
through the ballads and a minimum of merely passive re-
recording'.[10] Mrs Brown re-created her ballads, and re-created
them in the traditional manner, for, as we shall see later, her
ballad-texts carry the hallmarks of the oral style.

The circumstances in which Mrs Brown learned and remembered her ballads help us to understand the paradox, to
realize just how a literate woman could produce these traditional
texts. First, she learned the ballads, which is to say, the ballad-
stories and the method of composition, when very young. In a
letter to Alexander Fraser Tytler accompanying nine ballads she
sent him, she says:[11]

they are written down entirely from recollection, for I

> never saw one of them in print or manuscript; but I
> learned them all when a child, by hearing them sung by
> the lady you mentioned (Mrs. Farquharson), by my own
> mother, and an old maid-servant that had been long in
> the family. I dare say I may have fragments of others,
> but I could not so easily recollect them, except the ballads
> they belonged to were mentioned.

The ballads were learned by the age of ten, according to a letter
from Robert Anderson to Bishop Percy, and by the age of
twelve according to Child.[12] Mrs Brown was not unduly pre-
cocious; other Scottish singers born in the eighteenth century
also learned their ballads at an early age. In a comment dated
4 August 1826 on a version of 'Gil Morrice', Motherwell notes:
'This copy is from the recitation of Margaret Paterson alias
Widow Michael a very old woman residing at Dovecote ha'
Barhead. She is a native of Banffshire and learned the ballad
there in her infancy. . . . It is 70 years since she committed it to
her memory.'[13] Mrs Harris, daughter of the minister of Blair-
gowrie in Perthshire, learned her ballads from 'an old nurse
Jannie Scott, whose store of ballad lore was inexhaustible, who
chaunted them to the child who picked up a mere tithe of the
songs before she was 10 years of age'.[14] As the education of
women was in the Northeast for long considered unimportant,
and sometimes totally superfluous, it is possible, though, given
her father's profession, not entirely probable, that Anna Gordon
learned her ballad-stories and method of composition before she
learned to read and write.

Once she had learned the ballads Mrs Brown kept them in
her head, without writing them down. In a letter to Fraser
Tytler she writes:[15]

> I have lately by rumaging in a by-corner of my memory
> found some Aberdeenshire ballads which totally escaped
> me before they are of a different class from those I sent
> you not near so ancient but may be about a century ago.
> . . . I never saw any of them either in print or Manuscript
> but have kept them entirely from hearing them sung
> when a child.

Mrs Brown's stressing in both these letters that none of the ballads were seen either in print or manuscript indicates that she kept her traditional ballads quite separate in her mind from printed songs. While it seems probable that Widow Michael, Mrs Harris and another singer, Mary Barr, were like Mrs Brown in keeping ballads in mind without any aid from print or writing, it is quite clear that Mary Barr, Mrs Harris and yet another, Mrs Gibb, were like Mrs Brown in distinguishing firmly between traditional and printed songs. Of Mary Barr, Kinloch writes: 'She says she never committed anything to memory that she found in print; all the ballads and songs she can repeat were orally communicated to her, upwards of fifty years ago, since which time she has not attempted to burthen her memory with learning any others.'[16] In a letter sent to Child, Amelia Harris writes: 'My mother often remarked that she had only a tithe of old Jannie Scott's ballads—some of them were too coarse for singing—she did not sing them to us, if she kept them in mind. And what we saw in the hawkers' baskets we did not trouble to commit to memory.'[17] In a letter to John Francis Campbell James Gibb writes:[18]

> I can however furnish you with copies of one or two others of the following kinds; 1. What I take to be popular imitations of the old ballads, dating about the end of last century or the beginning of this. These were noted down at the same time also from the dictation of my mother. She learned them when a girl from broadsheets &c and the distinction between them and the fragments which I now send you was evidently clear & complete in her mind.

From this it is clear that many Scottish folksingers of the eighteenth and nineteenth centuries drew a firm line between the old and the new, the oral and the printed balladry; they did in fact distinguish—in the phrase that is anathema to some ballad scholars—a ballad aristocracy. It is also possible to infer from this evidence that the old oral mode was retained by more singers than one might at first suspect; but only detailed studies of their individual corpora can confirm or deny such a supposition.

Mrs Brown, then, learned her ballad-stories and the old re-creative technique of composition at an early age, retained the ballad-stories in her mind by a purely auditory process without any recourse to writing, and kept them mentally distinct and separate from written material. It is as if she possessed a bicameral mind, the one part literate and the other oral, the one part capable of writing letters, and the other capable of composing ballads orally. Mrs Brown, however, is no solitary phenomenon. Russian bards of this century such as Marfa Kryukova, Peter Ryabinin-Andreev, and Ergash Dzhumanbulbul have all been literate, and yet have also been prolific oral composers of *byliny*. [19] These, like Mrs Brown, belong to a particular stage in their tradition's development; they come at the very end of the oral period, just before the advent of widespread literacy fragments irretrievably the old oral culture.

Mrs Brown's ability to compose letters by one method and ballads by another must also be seen in terms of the cultural environment of her time. Her capacity for mentally separating the two processes is a particular manifestation of a general dichotomy so pronounced in eighteenth-century Scotland as to be dubbed a 'national schizophrenia'. [20] The roots of this schizophrenia are to be found in the combined effects of the Reformation, the Union of the Crowns, and the Union of the Parliaments, which was, in a much more literal sense than the Chancellor realized, indeed 'the end of an auld sang'. These events debilitated the national Scottish culture and, more specifically, precipitated the decline into a vernacular of the Scots language, a medium which was formed by and reflected the particular psychology and temperament of the Scottish people. By the eighteenth century, Scots who wanted to get on in the world had to learn 'to speak properly', as the revealing phrase has it, that is, to speak English. Literate Scots became accustomed to carrying two languages in their heads: English for writing, Scots for speaking, English for 'proper' occasions, Scots for 'real' life. The upshot was a peculiarly Scottish dissociation of sensibility whereby, as Edwin Muir put it, Scotsmen *felt* in Scots and *thought* in English. [21] This psychic cleavage helps explain why Scotland retained such a rich stock of folk literature up to the present century. Because their language was the language of feeling and their ethos exemplified the native outlook on life, the Scottish ballads provided—as works in English could not—aesthetic correlatives organically suited to the Scottish spirit and emotional constitution, and thereby fulfilled an important need in the national psychology; they helped maintain a sense of native identity against the pervasive threat of alien anglicization.

In eighteenth-century Scotland the effects of literacy are intrinsically bound up with the effects of the anglicization of Scottish life; literacy meant not just learning to read and write but learning to read and write *in another language*. For Scotsmen, the fragmentation of consciousness that attends the arrival of literacy became polarized in the two languages: English became primarily visual and cerebral, and Scots became primarily aural and emotional.[22] The split between 'real' language and 'proper' language shows clearly in Scottish written literature, and most obviously in the qualitative contrast between the English and Scots poems of Burns, or in our time of MacDiarmid, and between the English narrative and Scots dialogue of Scott's novels. English was, and is, likely to freeze or at least severely impede the creative flow of a native Scots speaker. Given a climate where literate Scots were accustomed to speak and feel in Scots and write and think in English, it is clear that Mrs Brown's dichotomizing of literate letter-writing in English and oral ballad composing in Scots is simply an extension of the basic dichotomy. She composed ballads in Scots because Scots was for her the language of *real* speech and *real* feeling, and the total process of oral composition in Scots afforded her the deep emotional satisfaction that writing in English could not give. Once again, consideration of the processes of literary creation leads us back to the psychological functions and emotional roots of language.

When Mrs Brown died, there existed three Brown Ballad MSS.: the Jamieson Brown MS., the Tytler Brown MS., and the Fraser Tytler Brown MS. The first two, both written down in 1783, owe their existence to a request from William Tytler, the Scottish historian and antiquarian, as Mrs Brown explains in a letter to his son, Alexander Fraser Tytler:[23]

> This MS. of which Mr. Jamieson is now in possession was originally made out with the intention of being sent to your father but upon his additional request of having the tunes of the Ballads noted down my father ordered Bob Scott, then a very young boy & a mere novice in musick to try to do it & he & I set to work but found the business so crabbed that in order to abridge our labours

> a little we selected what we thought the best of the
> Ballads whose tunes being added in the best manner
> we could were sent to your father—the longer MS.
> which I thought had been destroyed It seems Bob Scott
> laid up & has since given to Mr. Jamieson.

This 'longer MS.' of twenty ballads, which was later expanded by songs that Jamieson obtained directly from Mrs Brown, had been given in 1799 by Robert Scott, then Professor of Moral Philosophy at King's College, to his colleague, Gilbert Gerrard, Professor of Theology, who sent it to Jamieson. After Jamieson's death the MS. found its way into the possession of Robert Pitcairn, of Adam Sim of Culter, and latterly of David Laing; it is now among the Laing MSS. at the University of Edinburgh.

In a letter to Alexander Fraser Tytler Thomas Gordon describes the genesis of the second MS., the Tytler MS., and in doing so reveals how the ballads were recorded:[24]

> In conversation I mentioned [Mrs Brown's songs] to
> your father, at whose request my grandson, Mr. Scott,
> wrote down a parcel of them as his aunt sung them.
> Being then a mere novice in musick, he added in his
> copy such musical notes as he supposed, notwithstanding
> their incorrectness, might give your father some imperfect
> notion of the air, or rather lilts, to which they were sung.
> Both the words and the strains were perfectly new to
> me, as they were to your father. . . .

This MS. has a rather chequered history, being for long presumed lost beyond recall. From their seat in Inverness-shire, Aldourie Castle, the Tytlers had frequently lent the MS. to such interested antiquarians as Monk Lewis, who rewrote some of the stories for his *Tales of Wonder*,[25] and Scott, who had the MS. in his possession twice, in 1795, and again in 1800, immediately prior to the publication of the *Minstrelsy*. When Child set out to examine all the ballad manuscripts, the Tytler MS. was the sole known one his intensive researches failed to turn up, and he therefore presumed it had gone astray on one of its many borrowings. In 1793 and 1794, however, the MS. had been borrowed by Joseph Ritson, who was then preparing his *Scottish Songs* for publication. Ritson copied it in its entirety, though he printed none of the contents and even declared to Fraser Tytler in his letter of thanks that in his view the pieces, as poetry, had very little distinction, although he conceded 'them to be genuine [and] in certain respects curious'.[26] Ritson's copy of the MS., however, turned up prior to the First World War in the Shakespearian Library of Marsden J. Perry of Providence. It was later bought by Dr Rosenbach of Philadelphia who presented it in 1920 to Harvard University, where it is now kept in the Houghton Library.[27] And recently the original MS. has been discovered at Aldourie Castle.[28]

Also at Aldourie Castle is the Fraser Tytler MS., which was procured on Scott's behalf by Alexander Fraser Tytler in 1800. Replying to Fraser Tytler's request for more ballads, Mrs Brown hopes[29]

> to be able to send six or seven at least good long ones
> with the musick noted down for each has its own
> appropriate tune & some of them I think are pretty
> enough though all in the plaintive style as indeed all the
> old scotch Melodies are that I ever heard.

This is the smallest of the three MSS., containing nine as opposed to the twenty and fifteen ballads of the others. As Child had transcripts made of the Jamieson MS. and the Fraser Tytler MS., copies of all three Brown MSS. are now to be found at Harvard University Library.

Before this century the recording of an oral poem posed a large difficulty: the singer composed too rapidly for any scribe to write down the text with either accuracy or completeness. While recording apparatus has solved the problem for this century, transcribers in earlier times were forced to alter the normal conditions of oral performance, sometimes for better, sometimes for worse, in order to catch the text in writing. The different circumstances of recording affect the act of composing enough to warrant our classifying the texts produced by the different conditions. There is the modern *text of the actual performance*, recorded by machine; there is the *oral dictated text*, written down, as Homer's probably were, by a scribe from a singer proceeding at sub-normal speed; and there is the *oral autograph text*, usually, though not always, inferior to the second variety, written down by an oral poet who is himself

71

literate.[30] Evidently it was Mrs Brown's practice to have someone take down the ballads from her singing, because all the texts whose method of recording is mentioned are oral dictated texts. Thomas Gordon has already described the method by which the Tytler MS. was recorded, and Jamieson does likewise in a prefatory note to his MS.: it is 'A faithful transcript of Popular Ballads, written from the recitation of his Aunt Mrs. Brown of Falkland . . . by Mr. R. Scott'. In addition to these, Jamieson personally recorded four texts in 1800 from Mrs Brown's recitation—'Willie and Earl Richard's Daughter', 'Sir Hugh', 'The Mother's Malison', 'Bonny Baby Livingston' (222Ab)—and received another three in letters—'Lamkin', 'The Baron of Brackley', and 'Bonny Baby Livingston' (222Aa). In sending the last text to replace 222Ab, Mrs Brown notes that 'I found I had the whole story in my memory, and thought it better to write it out entire'. That she 'wrote it out entire' for Jamieson does not presuppose her writing it down in the first place, as the procedure over 'The Baron of Brackley' indicates; though, again, she wrote out the text of this ballad for Jamieson, her husband had first transcribed it from her singing.[31] The Fraser Tytler MS. was also written down from the recitation of Mrs Brown, probably by her husband.[32] Her prevailing practice in the transcription of the texts underlines how strongly aural the process of ballad recitation was for her, and how thoroughly she dissociated the act of composition from the act of writing.

Both the Tytler MS. and the Fraser Tytler MS. were used by Scott in compiling his 'Border' *Minstrelsy*, not, however, without his incurring Mrs Brown's displeasure. In a letter written to Jamieson in 1802, she declares how 'vexed' she was at Scott's publishing her name without her permission, and asks Jamieson not to do the same.[33] This must have been a source of considerable disquiet to Mrs Brown as her nephew, Robert Scott, repeats the request to Jamieson just prior to the publication of his *Popular Ballads and Songs*, which drew heavily on Mrs Brown's corpus.[34] Her displeasure illustrates further how the national dichotomy widened in the eighteenth century. The old homogeneity of Scottish society that allowed Anne Farquharson to learn her traditional ballads from rural nurses and old women at Allanaquoich, and the old homogeneity of taste that allowed both aunt and niece to delight in these ballads, had been superseded in

1802 by a new social concern for propriety, gentility, and station. Parenthetically, it is worth remembering that Thomas Bowdler hailed from Edinburgh and published his edition of Shakespeare, not in Victoria's reign, but in 1818. In Scotland these new social attitudes were likely to be predicated upon the inherent virtue of all things anglicized. Anna Gordon found it natural and satisfying to know her ballads, but Mrs Brown of Falkland, a lady of the manse, could not admit publicly to a knowledge of these rude though curious Scottish songs.

Mrs Brown's life spans a crucial sixty years. When she was born in 1747 the Northeast had, in essentials, changed little in the previous four hundred years, but when she died in 1810 it had undergone an agrarian, an industrial, and a social revolution. She learned her ballads just after mid-century, before general literacy destroyed the oral mode and before the revolutions transformed the country, but by the turn of the century antiquarians had already begun their search for relics and lore of the old untransformed Scotland. Born one generation earlier, she would probably have remained unrecorded: born one generation later, she would not have been able to compose her ballads by the old oral method.

Chapter 8

The Substance of the Ballads

Mrs Brown's corpus contains thirty-three ballad-stories, and, because of her re-creations of these stories, a much higher number of ballad-texts. Twenty of her versions are designated A-texts by Child and another four, being the only versions extant, may be looked on as honorary A-texts. Altogether, thirteen of her thirty-three stories have never been recorded in Britain outwith the Northeast.

Before, however, we go on to examine how Mrs Brown's ballad-stories were orally composed, we shall first consider what these stories are about. The ballads may be conventionally classified by general subject-matter in three groups: Magical and Marvellous Ballads, Romantic and Tragic Ballads, and Historical and Semi-historical Ballads. Into the first group fall 'Gil Brenton' (5A), 'Willie's Lady' (6), 'The Twa Sisters' (10B), 'King Henry' (32), 'Kemp Owyne' (34B), 'Allison Gross' (35), 'Thomas Rymer' (37A), 'Clerk Colvill' (42A), 'Young Bekie' (53C), 'Bonny Bee Hom' (92A), and 'Sir Hugh' (155A). The second group comprises 'The Cruel Brother' (11A), 'Young Bicham' (53A), 'Fair Annie' (62E), 'Child Waters' (63B), 'Lady Maisry' (65A), 'The Lass of Roch Royal' (76D,E), 'The Bonny Birdy' (82), 'Fause Foodrage' (89A), 'Jellon Grame' (90A), 'Fair Mary of Wallington' ('The Bonny Earl of Livingston') (91C), 'Lamkin' (93A), 'The Gay Goshawk' (96A), 'Brown Robin' (97A), 'Brown Adam' (98A), 'Johnie Scot' (99A), 'Willie o Douglas Dale' (101A), 'Willie and Earl Richard's Daughter' (102A), 'Rose the Red and White Lily' (103A), 'The Mother's Malison' (216B), 'Lady Elspat' (247), and 'The Kitchie-Boy' (252C). And the third group consists of 'The Baron of Brackley' (203C) and 'Bonny Baby Livingston' (222A). As the placing of the two variants of 'Young Beichan' (53A and C) would indicate, these groups overlap to a fair extent. Most of these are in quatrains, but five (5, 6, 10, 11, and 203) are couplet ballads.

These ballad-stories, however, did not constitute her entire stock. In a letter to Fraser Tytler (which once again demonstrates that her command of written syntax was much shakier than her command of ballad syntax) she writes:[1]

> I have lately by rumaging in a by-corner of my memory
> found some Aberdeenshire ballads which totally escaped
> me before they are of a different class from those I sent
> you not near so ancient but may be about a century ago.
> I cannot boast much of their poetical merits but the
> family incidents upon which they are founded the local
> allusions which they contain may perhaps render them
> curious & not uninteresting to many people they are as
> follows—
> >   1st the Baron of Braichly
> >   2nd the Lass of Philorth
> >   3rd the Tryal of the Laird of Gycht
> >   4th the Death of the Countess of Aboyne
> >   5 the Carrying off of the Heiress of Kenady

These titles represent versions of 'The Baron of Brackley' (203), 'Lord Saltoun and Auchanachie' (239), 'Geordie' (209), 'The Earl of Aboyne' (235), and 'Charlie MacPherson' (234); the first of these has survived because she later sent it to Jamieson, but her versions of the others have never been recovered. In the letter to Jamieson that contains 'The Baron of Brackley', she writes:[2]

> Glenkindie, or rather Glenskeeny [?] I have heard &
> there is a Ballad in Percie's collection that is very much
> the same he is there called Glass gerrion but is the same
> story in all . . . I doubt not that in the course of conver-
> sation I might recollect something that might be new to
> you, tho' I do not recollect anything at present.

Given her knowledge of this ballad-story, it is distinctly possible that she may have contributed to the composite 'Glenkindie' printed by Jamieson (Child's 67B), which was procured mainly from Mrs Brown's nephew, Professor Robert Scott. Be that as it may, this one singer knew in all thirty-eight ballad-stories, one-eighth of all stories in the Anglo-Scottish ballad tradition.

The strongly romantic and marvellous cast of her ballad stock reflects the regional tradition's richness in the romantic and even more particularly, the magical categories. The corpus, however, does not reflect the region's wealth of indigenous historical and semi-historical ballads. This imbalance presumably resulted from her sources of all being women, and therefore constitutionally more inclined to the marvellous than the martial. Even the historical ballads she knew owed their remembrance to their romantic qualities, for in each a female character occupies a central, and normally empathetic, role. Mrs Brown's stock, therefore, very definitely constitutes a woman's corpus, and may perhaps represent a woman's tradition within the regional tradition. This raises the intriguing but, given the available evidence, largely unanswerable question as to how large a part women played in the regional tradition as a whole. Certainly women outnumber men as recorded sources in the transitional period between general orality and general literacy, but this fact tells us little about the pre-1750 tradition. During the heydey of ballad recording in the region, rural women received a much skimpier education—if they received one at all—than the men, and consequently were likely to retain longer into the literate period the habits of the old oral culture. We cannot, however, argue about the place of women in the tradition's oral period on the basis of evidence from the transitional or modern, literate, periods.

The thirty-three ballad-stories are set in a certain world, the ballad world, and the nature of this stylized limbo helps illuminate some of the functions of the old ballads. The ballads are distanced; they have settings which distance them from the everyday work of the plough and the byre. Their ambience is aristocratic and their characters noble; the queens and ladies, kings, knights and squires enact their roles in castles, halls and bowers shadowily peopled by the maries and porters and pageboys of the noble household.

The traditional ballad maker enjoyed depicting the well-born or wealthy heroes—'Large o' limb an lith'—and heroines—the 'weel-faurd mays'—and the luxurious magnificence of the aristocratic life. His opening shots show the heroes sitting in Silver Wood or standing in a stable door behind which are no muddy plough-oxen, but milk-white steeds, and the heroines sitting in a bower, looking out the shot-window, or playing at the ba'; but never are they shown ploughing, threshing, feeding hens or milking cows, for these characters enjoy the aristocratic luxury of daily leisure. The maker relished describing the nobles' fare, the 'baken meat and the claret wine' and 'the good white bread', delicacies unknown to farming folk living exclusively off oatmeal. He delighted in picturing the high-born's splendour of dress and appurtenance. The heroine of 'Young Bicham' turns up to claim her bridegroom and astounds the porter:

> For on every finger she has a ring,
>   An on the mid-finger she has three,
> An there's as meikle goud aboon her brow
>   As woud buy an earldome o lan to me.   (53A: 17)

The heroine in 'Gil Brenton' arrives for her wedding sorrowing, but with an impressive retinue:

> There was twal an twal wi beer and wine,
> An twal and twal wi muskadine:
>
> An twall an twall wi bouted flowr,
> An twall an twall wi paramour:
>
> An twall an twall wi baken bread,
> An twall an twall wi the goud sae red.   (5A: 3–5)

Looked at from one viewpoint, these descriptions satisfied a naïve taste for finery; they were, for the women, an early equivalent to a magazine account of a Balenciaga collection. They are not, however, mere fantastical embroideries, but integrated parts of the stories' unfolding, highlighting in each case the basic tensions in the narrative. What appears to us as uncomfortably hyperbolic would not jar on an audience for whom the whole aristocratic style of life, perhaps glimpsed by some, imagined by most, was hyperbole.

The distanced settings of court, castle, and greenwood have rarely any precise, geographically identifiable, location, for they belong to a stylized landscape—a starker version of the Spenserian landscape—that represents both the imagined aristocratic world, and the wide world of adventure outwith the ploughman's experience. The hero who 'maun sail the sea' is not travelling with a practical purpose to a particular place; he is venturing into the unknown world 'out there', a world plangent with possibilities as the fermtoun was not. Those settings that are located by name contribute to the distancing because the names are accepted correlatives for romantic far-away places: the young Scottish knight goes to 'the English court' or 'the court of France' to gain fame and adventure; the bonny foot-boy lands on 'the coast of Spain'; Young Bicham journeys from the mysterious metropolis of London to the land of the heathen Moors: all lunar to the northeasterner. These places, however, are never particularized; they are all part of the ballad landscape, standard emblems of story-lands where rents have never to be paid.

The Otherworld, as well as the aristocratic world, distances the tales from drab mundanity. The mermaid-siren, the Belly Blin, the Queen of Elfland, the seely Court, the spellings, unspellings, magic rings, speaking corpses, and talking harps, all helped satisfy the folk's appetite for glamourie, romance and the marvellous, an appetite whetted by their unvarying struggle to plough and reap, raise and feed.

The distancing of substance calls for correspondence in style. Ballad language in general is stylized, but certain words within that language carry a specifically aristocratic flavour. 'Paramour', for example, does not at first sight look like a regular ballad word, and yet it crops up in 'Gil Brenton', 'Willie o Douglas Dale', and 'Willie and Earl Richard's Daughter', far from specific in denotation, but always with the same vaguely romantic connotation; in 'Gil Brenton':

> An twall an twall wi bouted flowr
> An twall an twall wi paramour (5A: 4)

in 'Willie o Douglas Dale':

> O in a little after that
>   He keepit Dame Oliphant's bowr,
> An the love that passd between this twa,
>   It was like paramour. (101A: 8)

in 'Willie and Earl Richard's Daughter':

> Earl Richard had but ae daughter,
>   Fair as a lily-flower,

And they made up their love-contract
Like proper paramour.   (102A: 2)

And, again in 'Willie o Douglas Dale', appear the lines,

Whan night was gane, an day come in,
An lions gaed to their dens   (101A: 14^{1,2})

which bear no relation to the realities of the British countryside,
but which set the necessary eerily romantic atmosphere. In diction
and image, then, we can observe a process of linguistic distancing
analogous to the narrative distancing.

Side by side with the distancing is another, complementary
process, that of localizing, whereby the distanced world is seen in
terms of the folk's own life.[3] The position of the knight or squire
at court is like that of a labourer at a farm: they all 'serve for
meat and fee'. The heroine of 'Gil Brenton' lives an aristocratic
existence,

We had nae mair for our seven years wark
But to shape an sue the king's son a sark.   (5A: 44)

but her attitude to the end of the week is that of a servant lass,
glad of a respite from hard work:

O it fell on a Saturday's afternoon,
When a' our langsome wark was dane . . . .   (5A: 45)

For his seven years' service to the Queen of Elfland, Thomas
receives, as any laird's retainer might, a coat and shoes, though
in his case they are 'of even cloth' and 'of velvet cloth'. In 'The
Mother's Malison' the well-born hero sets off on his coal-black
steed to visit the well-born heroine in her bower; when he arrives
there he discovers that the bower, like any decent farmhouse at
night, has 'its doors steeked, and windows barred'; he then asks
for 'some out-chamber' where he might pass the night. 'Chamber'
may appear to accord completely with an aristocratic setting, but
in the Northeast, the word 'chaumer' was the normal word for
a room in any of the outhouses in the farm steadings where
provender was stocked and farm servants billeted. That this is
the sense in which the word is used is clear from the answer
given the hero:

> For I've nae chambers out nor in,
>   Nae ane but barely three.
>
> The tane o them is fu o corn,
>   The tither is fu o hay;
> The tither is fu o merry young men;
>   They winna remove till day.   (216B: 13³–14)

The aristocratic residence is here visualized in terms of a rural farmhouse, and something similar occurs in 'Lamkin'. In this story the castle-dwellers—referred to in the ordinary phrase of the farm as 'the men o' the house' and 'the women o' the house' —absent themselves from the 'castle' in order to perform the normal toundwellers' tasks: the men are 'at the barn-well thrashing' and the women are 'at the far well washing'.

The ballad maker, then, apprehends this imagined aristocratic life through the folk's rural life, and gives this aristocratic world a concrete actuality by utilizing the details of the folk's own world. He encourages the willing suspension by incorporating references to the social events and pastimes of the rural community, the kirkings, the christening feasts, the 'herrying' of birds' nests, the playing 'at the ba' or with 'the puttin-stane', and by mentioning places and objects well-known to the toun-folk: the mill-dam and market place, the 'reef-tree of the house', the 'shaver for his beard', the 'comber till his hair', and the 'gaggs and sheers' of a difficult childbirth. He also describes realistically a setting which, though not his own, yet was geographically near: in the semi-historical ballad 'Bonny Baby Livingston', the heroine is abducted when she, like any farmer's wife, 'goes forth to view the hay', and is taken to a highland clachan where the boys are dressed in 'philabeg and bonnet blue', the lasses are milking cows and ewes, and the men are armed with claymores.

The maker sometimes emphasizes how different the imagined aristocratic world is by back reference to his own. He stresses that things of vital importance in the workaday world are of little moment in the other; money, for example, matters little in the aristocratic world. The heroine gives Young Bekie 'five hunder poun ... to spen, an nae to spair'; Clerk Colven pays 'crowns fifteen' for such a trifle as his lady's belt; and heroes are so insouciant over finance that they can afford to spurn tochers or send disappointed brides away with doubled tochers. Again, if the things of the ordinary world threaten to smudge the aristocratic patina of the other, the maker transforms the ordinary into the extraordinary: the domestic 'bason' and kemb' of 'Allison Gross' are of silver; the hammer of Brown Adam, the smith who 'blows his bellows well', is 'o the beaten gold'.

The nature of these complementary processes, distancing and localizing, establishes beyond doubt that for some time previous to the eighteenth century the bulk of the performers and audience of the regional tradition were the rural folk, the tenants, grassmen, weavers, smiths and cordiners of the fermtouns; but they were probably not the only participants. Anyone who was nonliterate could take part in the tradition, and in centuries previous to the eighteenth many, if not most, of the minor lairds would have belonged to the nonliterate category. The region's social homogeneity would reinforce the likelihood of their joining in the local customs of the regional culture. Even in the eighteenth century we have an actual instance, in Anne Farquharson, of the wife of a minor laird participating in the local tradition of the nurses and old women at Allanaquoich.

The ballads that were sung mainly in the fermtouns are, then, set in imagined worlds remote from the workaday worlds of the tounfolk. The folk did not sing about the folk. Certainly, they sang of the human passions and emotions that are the common property of king and cottar, but the actors in the ballads are nobles and the background aristocratic. Because of northeastern society's homogeneity, there existed few or none of the class rivalries and hatreds later fomented by the industrial revolutions, and consequently the folk had no antipathy to singing songs whose heroes were noble. In fact, quite the reverse was the case, for the lives of the great in court and castle represented for the folk the glamorous world of romance and adventure outwith their ken. Today, people devour a newspaper's society pages, and display a voracious interest in the ersatz aristocracy of Hollywood; then, the ballads provided for the folk, *inter alia*, a vicarious enjoyment of life's luxuries and glories, and a world of imaginative escape from the hard realities of daily toil. Once, however, the folk's life changed, the ballad world changed and these ballad functions changed.

It is hardly possible to see the ballads functioning as a kind of tribal encyclopaedia, like the Homeric epics, but they probably did, like the Greek poems, reinforce the regional society's *ethea*, the laws of moral and behavioural custom concerning a man and his family, his friends and his enemies.[4] Rarely, however, do we come across the overt directive, as in this oddly out of place stanza in 'King Henry':

> Lat never a man a wooing wend
>> That lacketh thingis three;
> A routh o gold, an open heart,
>> Ay fu o charity.   (32: 1)

Only with the advent of general literacy do the moral tags and interjections begin to spread through the ballad-texts. The old ballads are descriptive rather than prescriptive; they influenced their audience through human example, of steadfast lover or restrictive parent, rather than moral precept. For, like all oral literature, the ballads are concerned with action, with doings, performed by people who are exemplars of—in this case—the heroic virtues necessary in a border society. The ballad emphasis is on people in action, people *doing*, not, as with much written poetry, on people *being*. Just as 'Homeric Greek is innocent of any connection with the verb to be', the ballad language abjures the flat statement of being for the active description of doing. Take Mrs Brown's version of a well-known kind of stanza:

> An she gid by the first table,
>> An leugh amo them a';
> But ere she reached the second table,
>> She let the tears down fa.   (62E: 11)

It is not a matter of her being happy, and then being sad; she laughs, and then she weeps. The following stanza underlines her sorrow and does so again through a specific, concrete action:

> She's taen a napkin lang an white,
>> An hung't upon a pin;
> It was to dry her watry eyes,
>> As she went out and in.   (62E: 12)

Like Homeric Greek, the ballad language is 'a language of act and event'.[5] This preference for doing rather than being and for the concrete rather than the abstract is of course what generates much of the ballad's particular power, and what distinguishes oral from most literate poetry.

The ballads are stories of doings and doers, and it is the ballad actors who, firstly, provide us with the best perspective on the narrative substance and, secondly, introduce us to the patterns of oral structuring. Every ballad in this corpus has as its narrative base a relationship between two people; normally a third person then threatens to disrupt this relationship. The story hangs on the threat, and the central pair's reactions to the threat. The basic story-telling pattern of situation + complication–development–resolution manifests itself in the ballad in a fairly straightforward way: the situation establishes the relationship of the two main characters, and the complication the third character's threat to that relationship; the development deals with the efforts to promote or combat the threat, and the resolution concerns the happy cementing or tragic dissolution of the relationship. Already we can perceive one of the main tendencies in oral structuring, the tendency to group by threes. The norm in these ballads is for the stories to have three emotionally interacting characters. The phrase 'emotionally interacting' is important, for the major, emotionally involved characters must be distinguished from the mere narrative agents, the porters, page-boys and the like.

Though the character mould is set for three, it is flexible enough to accommodate two, four or six characters. Three ballads contain just two characters, and of these, two ('King Henry', 'Thomas Rymer') embody very old motifs, and the third ('Bonny Bee Hom') is the shortest of all Mrs Brown's texts, being more a detached, inflated motif than a complete and rounded story. In most of the ballads, the three characters who make up the situation + complication also take part in the development, but in some the Third Character of the situation is partially or totally supplanted by another Third Character in the development. In 'Brown Robin' and 'Johnie Scot' the emotional opposition of the heroine's father to the central relationship (her love-affair) is narratively personified by, respectively, the porter and the Italian champion. In 'The Kitchie Boy', while the threesome of the situation comprises hero, heroine and the father whose implicit opposition sends the hero abroad, the development is concerned with the Spanish lady's efforts to break the main relationship. In 'Lamkin', where the basic situation concerns

Lamkin's attempt to avenge himself on lord and lady, the development contains another Third Character with a grudge against the central pair in the nourice, whose presence balances the lord's absence. And in 'Lady Elspat', the Third Character who threatens the relationship is counteracted by another who resolves all happily. As a general rule, when a fourth character comes to the forefront, one of the original three fades into the background. This fact may help to explain the presence of the otherwise inexplicable episode in 'Willie o Douglas Dale' where, tacked on to the main story, is a superfluous scene with the nourice. As the third party of the situation, the heroine's father, does not participate in the developing action the oral maker may have responded to the pull of the traditional character pattern by introducing another actor to the cast. Two ballads have six characters. 'Fause Foodrage' has two sets of three characters: the breaking of the central relationship (of King and Queen) by Fause Foodrage, which constitutes the first section of the ballad, is avenged in the later sections by their son who has been reared by Wise William and his wife. The longest of Mrs Brown's ballads, 'Rose the Red and White Lily', contains a double triangle, with two heroes, two heroines, and two Third Characters, one who is evil and complicates the action, and one who is good and resolves the action. Whether the ballads have, as most do, three characters who remain constant in situation and development, or have a surrogate Third Character, or have two sets of three characters, the basic character pattern is consistent: it is triangular.

In all the stories the central relationship is between male and female; and in all bar 'Sir Hugh' it is some kind of amatory relationship, either forced or voluntary. Once we establish that there is always a central pair and that this central pair consists nearly always of 'hero' and 'heroine' (the terms are convenient rather than connotatively accurate), then we can see that the Third Character holds the key to understanding the similarities and variations of the basic narrative patterns. Looked at in this way, the stories may be divided into three groups: stories of family opposition, stories of the other love, and stories of murder and revenge. More than half the stories have as the Third Character a close member of the family—his mother, her mother, father, or brother—and in fifteen cases these characters stand in direct opposition to the match of hero and heroine. Variations on the basic pattern occur in 'Child Waters' and 'Fair Mary of Wallington'. In the first, where the hero puts the heroine through a severe series of trials, his mother is well-disposed towards the girl; in the other, her mother pushes the heroine into a marriage she does not want because she knows she will die in childbirth. The second group, stories of the other love, contain Third Characters who compete with one of the central pair for the love of the other. A variation on the basic pattern in 'Allison Gross' has the hero being rescued from an unwanted relationship with Allison the witch by another woman, the Fairy Queen. One ballad, 'The Kitchie-Boy', falls into both groups because, having both the opposed father and the other woman, it interlinks the two story patterns. Four ballads make up the third group, stories of murder and revenge: in 'Jellon Grame', the heroine is murdered by the 'hero', but is avenged by their son; in 'Fause Foodrage', the heroine is imprisoned and the hero murdered by the villain, but they are avenged by their son who has been brought up by a surrogate mother and father; in 'Lamkin', the heroine is murdered by the villain and his accomplice but is finally avenged by the hero; in 'Sir Hugh', the hero is murdered by the 'heroine', but retribution comes when his mother's search reveals the speaking corpse. There are, then, just three story-patterns, of high, middling and low frequency, in this singer's corpus. Interestingly, the staple of the popular novelist, the triangle that is 'eternal', is not the most common story-theme in Mrs Brown's repertoire.

Many of the stories have in addition to the central triangle minor characters, figures who are not directly involved in the crucial interaction. Some, normally sisters and brothers, fulfil a function like that of a confidant in a play: they are there to point up and highlight the emotional situation. In 'Fair Mary of Wallington', for example, it is the sister's reaction to the heroine's death that reveals the full measure of the mother's guilt. Other minor characters are narrative agents, whose function is to propel the story swiftly, without necessitating any involved account of cause and effect that would detract from the emotional core of the story. Into this category fall numerous page-boys and bonny boys, the miller and harper of 'The Twa Sisters', the birds of 'The Gay Goshawk' and 'The Bonny Birdy', and the

D

Belly Blin of 'Willie's Lady' and 'Young Bekie'.[6] The minor figures are not gratuitous interlopers, for they serve a double purpose: they lend the story emotional emphasis and narrative fluency while not impeding or clouding the central interaction of the major characters.

Seen in terms of the characters, the narrative substance yields only a few story-patterns. The interaction of hero and heroine with Third Character produces just the three story-themes: those of familial thwarting, the other love, and of murder and revenge. There are three kinds of basic narrative moulds, each flexible enough to encourage variation from the standard casting. The ballad world then, helps illuminate the nature of the ballad audience and the ballad's functions within that audience, and the ballad characters help illuminate the narrative substance. Our knowledge of the patterning of character and story will, in the next chapter, shed light on the structuring of the ballads, which in turn will enable us to return to a further consideration of character and action.

Chapter 9

The Structure of the Ballads 1

The stories we have been discussing were re-created by Mrs Brown at each singing. Knowing something of how oral poetry operates in general, we shall now examine the structures of these texts to see how the oral technique of re-creative composition functioned in the Northeast's ballad tradition. Ballad structure has not been a popular topic for study; it generally attracts a few perfunctory comments about 'abrupt transitions' and 'incremental repetition' and is then dismissed. The structures of the old ballads, however, deserve much closer attention than they have received because they demonstrate the genre's original orality and show how the oral sensibility operated in an acoustical literary medium. And, as Whitman's study of the complex architectonics of the *Iliad* has shown, traditional structures may hold the key to an aesthetic understanding of oral art.

Oral structures are liable to escape our literate attention because they are the products of a different kind of sensibility working in what are to us alien conditions. When organizing a written poem or piece of prose, we have the aid of the page: we can revise, we can move forward or backward over the written pages in order to give our piece coherence. Except in such anomalies of a literate culture as scholastic examinations, we do not have to produce instantaneous organized coherence, which is what the oral composer has to produce. He can, and does, of course, rehearse songs for the performance, but whether in rehearsal or in performance he has none of our visual props: he must control his material entirely in the mind. He must be able to marshal his material compactly but not rigidly and to develop his story-line flexibly but not loosely. To effect this, he works through certain structural-mnemonic rhythms or patternings.

As we have earlier observed, the oral maker normally tells a tale which has a fairly obvious skeletal essence. For easier mental storage of a story he deals with tales which can be reduced to simple essentials. Yet the finished stories he tells are often of considerable complexity. How then do we reconcile these two facts? Though he may carry in the mind a stripped-down version of the story, the maker also has at his creative disposal patterned rhythms which enable him to expand and elaborate the story while yet maintaining control over it. These are the binary, trinary, and annular patternings; the maker organizes his material by pervasively grouping its units through balancing, tripling, and framing arrangements.

To understand the overall architectonic structure of the old ballads, we must first realize that there is more than one 'structure'. There are, in fact, three major synchronic structurings: the stanzaic structure, which involves the arrangement in scenes of a unified group of stanzas; the character structure, which involves the deployment of the actors; and the narrative structure, which involves the arrangement of the units of action. At times the three structures correspond exactly; at others, particularly in the longer ballads, they co-exist in a kind of structural counterpoint. In the longer stories they act as checks upon each other, preventing the complexity of any one part of the ballad from getting out of hand. The binary, trinary and annular patternings permeate all three structures and the overall architectonic organization of the ballad. First we shall consider the operation of these patternings in the stanzaic structure.

The habit of thinking in balances, antitheses, appositions and parallelisms is intrinsic to the oral mind. It manifests itself both conceptually, in the arrangement of the narrative 'ideas', and verbally, in the arrangement of the line and stanza word groups. This principle operates to build up a single stanza:

> Lord John stood in his stable-door,
>> Said he was bound to ride;
> Burd Ellen stood in her bowr-door,
>> Said she'd rin by his side.   (63B: 3)

It also operates to build up a pair of stanzas, as we can see from the stanza that follows and balances the above:

> He's pitten on his cork-heeld shoone,
>> An fast awa rade he;

> She's clade hersel in page array,
> An after him ran she. (63B: 4)

This pair of stanzas is linked by a common appositional pattern,
in which a plan or intention is first declared, then carried out or
executed. These stanzas, then, balance internally and with each
other, but this is not all, for as a pair they balance the preceding
pair of stanzas:

> 'I warn ye all, ye gay ladies,
> That wear scarlet an brown,
> That ye dinna leave your father's house,
> To follow young men frae town.'

> 'O here am I, a lady gay,
> That wears scarlet an brown,
> Yet I will leave my father's house,
> An follow Lord John frae the town.' (63B: 1, 2)

Within this pair the conceptual antithesis of first the warning
then the flouting is reinforced by the verbal parallelism, while
together this pair of stanzas in speech balance the succeeding
pair in direct narrative. The conceptual balances are most obvious
when reinforced by the verbal, or by the alternation of speech
and narrative, but are really ubiquitous in such frequent appositional patterns as plan and act, command and execution,
question and answer,

> Till they came till a wan water,
> An folks do ca it Clyde;
> Then he's lookit oer his left shoulder
> Says, Lady, can ye wide?

> 'O I learnt it i my father house,
> An I learnt it for my weal,
> Wenneer I came to a wan water,
> To swim like ony eel.' (63B: 5, 6)

and expressed emotion and apposed event:

> 'Lye still, lye still, my ain dear babe,
> Ye work your mither wae;
> Your father rides on high horse-back,
> Cares little for us twae.'

> O about the midst o Clyden water
>   There was a yeard-fast stane;
> He lightly turnd his horse about,
>   An took her on him behin.   (63B: 10, 11)

One of oral literature's most pervasive tendencies is to group its material in threes. Like the binary force, the trinary operates on all levels of a ballad; within, for instance, a half-stanza,

> Ye lee, ye lee, ye gentle knight,
>   Sa loud's I hear you lee;   (82: 4)

or a complete stanza,

> 'Is this the Duke o Albany,
>   Or James, the Scottish King?
> Or are ye some great foreign lord,
>   That's come a visiting?'   (99A: 25)

or a triad of stanzas,

> But the firstin stap the lady stappit,
>   The water came til her knee:
> 'Ohon, alas!' said the lady,
>   'This water's oer deep for me.'
>
> The nextin stap the lady stappit,
>   The water came till her middle;
> An sighin says that gay lady,
>   I've wat my gouden girdle
>
> The nextin stap the lady stappit,
>   The water cam till her pap;
> An the bairn that was in her twa sides
>   For caul begane to quake.   (63B: 7–9)

or in a triad of balancing stanzas,

> 'O see you nae yon castle, Ellen,
>   That shines sae fair to see?
> There is a lady in it, Ellen
>   Will sunder you an me.'
>
> 'There is a lady in that castle
>   Will sunder you and I:'

90

'Betide me well, betide me wae,
   I sal go there an try.'

'O my dogs sal eat the good white bread,
   An ye sal eat the bran;
Then will ye sigh, an say, alas!
   That ever I was a man!'

'O I sal eat the good white bread,
   An your dogs sal eat the bran;
An I hope to live an bless the day,
   That ever ye was a man.'

'O my horse sal eat the good white meal,
   An ye sal eat the corn;
Then will ye curse the heavy hour
   That ever your love was born.'

'O I sal eat the good white meal,
   An your horse sal eat the corn;
An I ay sall bless the happy hour
   That ever my love was born.'   (63B: 13–18)

As they stand, these may be described as simple triads, but the trinary rhythm may blend with the rhythms common to stanza construction—rhythms predicated on a four-unit structure—to produce extended triads. Individual stanzas are normally built on the balance of lines one and two against lines three and four, with the climax of the stanza coming in either line three or line four. In the most common kind of extended triad the triadic core is followed by a coda, and the complete pattern resembles that of a stanza with a third-line climax. The preceding triad, for example, is followed by:

O four an twenty gay ladies
   Welcomd Lord John to the ha,
But a fairer lady than them a'
   Led his horse to the stable sta.

An four an twenty gay ladies
   Welcomd Lord John to the green,
But a fairer lady than them a'
   At the manger stood alane.   (63B: 19, 20)

As an individual stanza might do, though on reduced scale, this extended triad contains conceptual and stylistic balances: the three pairs of stanzas deal with his intended treatment of her when they reach the castle, while the final pair show the actual treatment at the castle; the three pairs are in dialogue of rising dramatic power, while the final pair are in quiet narrative and round off the scene by reducing the tension. Less frequently, the trinary rhythm may blend with the other rhythm of stanza construction, where the climax comes in the fourth line, to produce a different kind of extended triad.

'Kemp Owyne' is one ballad structured completely with scenes of balances and triads. The first scene has both balancing and extended triad rhythms:

1   'Come here, come here, you freely feed,
           An lay your head low on my knee;
      The hardest weird I will you read
           That eer war read to a lady.'

2   'O meikle dollour sall you dree
           An ay the sat seas oer ye['s] swim;
      An far mair dollour sall ye dree
           On Eastmuir craigs, or ye them clim.'

3   'I wot ye's be a weary wight,
           An relieved sall ye never be
      Till Kempion, the kingis son,
           Come to the craig and thrice kiss thee.'

4   O meickle dollour did she dree,
           An ay the sat seas oer she swam;
      An far mair dollour did she dree
           On Eastmuir craigs, or them she clam;
      An ay she cried for Kempion,
           Gin he would come till her han.

The second scene has two pairs of balancing stanzas:

5   Now word has gane to Kempion
           That sich a beast was in his lan,
      An ay be sure she would gae mad
           Gin she gat nae help frae his han.

6   'Now by my sooth,' says Kempion,
      'This fiery beast I['ll] gang to see;'
    'An by my sooth,' says Segramour,
      'My ae brother, I'll gang you wi.'

7   O biggit ha they a bonny boat,
      An they hae set her to the sea,
    An Kempion an Segramour
      The fiery beast ha gane to see:
    A mile afore they reachd the shore,
      I wot she gard the red fire flee.

8   'O Segramour, keep my boat afloat,
      An lat her no the lan so near;
    For the wicked beast she'll sure gae mad,
      An set fire to the land an mair.'

The dramatic crux of the ballad, her unspelling, is a triad of balancing stanzas:

9   'O out o my stye I winna rise—
      An it is na for the fear o thee—
    Till Kempion, the kingis son,
      Come to the craig an thrice kiss me.'

10   He's louted him oer the Eastmuir craig,
      An he has gien her kisses ane;
    Awa she gid, an again she came,
      The fieryest beast that ever was seen.

11   'O out o my stye I winna rise—
      An it is na for fear o thee—
    Till Kempion, the kingis son,
      Come to the craig an thrice kiss me.'

12   He louted him oer the Eastmuir craig,
      An he has gien her kisses twa;
    Awa she gid, an again she came,
      The fieryest beast that ever you saw.

13   'O out o my stye I winna rise—
      An it is na for fear o ye—
    Till Kempion, the kingis son,
      Come to the craig an thrice kiss me.'

14 He's louted him oer the Eastmuir craig,
    An he has gien her kisses three;
   Awa she gid, an again she came,
    The fairest lady that ever coud be.

The coda reverts to the two balancing pairs of stanzas:

15 'An by my sooth,' say[s] Kempion,
    'My ain true love—for this is she—
   O was it wolf into the wood,
    Or was it fish intill the sea,
   Or was it man, or wile woman,
    My true love, that misshapit thee?'

16 'It was na wolf into the wood,
    Nor was it fish into the sea,
   But it was my stepmother,
    An wae an weary mot she be.'

17 'O a heavier weird light her upon
   Than ever fell on wile woman;
   Her hair's grow rough, an her teeth's grow lang,
   An on her four feet sal she gang.'

18 'Nane sall tack pitty her upon,
   But in Wormie's Wood she sall ay won,
   An relieved sall she never be,
   Till St Mungo come oer the sea.'

Like the first stanza and the first scene, the ballad itself is built on the rhythm of the extended triad: two introductory scenes, the climactic third, and the coda. To look at it another way: three pairs of balancing pairs flank a climactic triad of balancing pairs. With balances within balances and triads within triads, the total ballad has the look of a Chinese box. As we are, for the moment, concerned only with the stanzaic structure, we shall pass by the other structures except to note the appositional pattern that occurs in the balance between scene one and the coda. Where the ballad begins with the mother delivering the weird on the heroine, it ends with the hero delivering the weird on the mother. The pattern is a kind of split balance or framing device.

Framing—the annular device or ring composition, as it is

known to the Homerists—is one of the hallmarks of oral poetry, because it is a habit of construction that grows organically out of the restrictive conditions of oral creation.[1] We who are literate can store our material on the page and structure it at leisure; the oral maker must store his material in the mind and structure it in performance so that even while he deals with any one part of a poem, he can keep a grip on the interrelations of all parts of the poem. He must have a firm sense at any one moment of where he has been, where he is, and where he is going. The frames enable him to have just this.

Like the balancing and triadic rhythms, framing operates on both the minor level of scene construction and the major level of ballad construction, and may be simply conceptual or, more pronouncedly, conceptual and verbal. In its simplest forms a frame consists of a balancing pair of stanzas which flank a single stanza or a balance or a triad. The complete unit, a framed balance or triad, is what normally constitutes a ballad scene. ('Kemp Owyne' represents a more elementary form of construction because, although the ballad as a whole has the framing of scenes one and four, internally the scenes are built up through binary and trinary patterns only.) The primary function of the frame is to shape manageable units, the scenes of the ballad-story. In 'Child Waters', for example, stanzas 5 to 11 constitute one scene: 5 and 6 are a balancing pair, 7 to 9 a triad, and 10 and 11 another balancing pair. The structuring of the scene does not end there, however, for 5 and 11 and 6 and 10 are also balancing frames. In stanza 6 the heroine defiantly declares her ability to cope with the river unaided, and in stanza 10 she resignedly admits the need for help. Stanza 5 introduces the river episode,

> Till they came till a wan water,
> An folks do ca it Clyde;
> Then he's lookit oer his left shoulder,
> Says, Lady, can ye wide?

and stanza 11 rounds it off:

> O about the midst o Clyden water
> There was a yeard-fast stane;
> He lightly turnd his horse about,
> An took her on him behin.

The triad describes dramatically the act itself, while the frames provide the cause and effect of the act. The cause, the hero's initial brute insensitivity, contrasts with the effect, his later tacit concern, and this reversal, carried by the frames, both shapes the scene and sets it in its general narrative context by fore-shadowing the major reversal in attitude at the ballad's crux. Basically, however, the frame's function is to hold the material together in a kind of narrative vice; the frames are—to yoke the heterogeneous—like a pair of aural bookends. The oral maker progresses by a 'divide and control' policy; he breaks down his

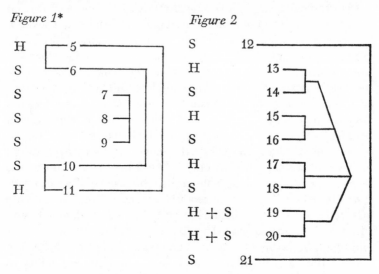

Figure 1*

Figure 2

narrative into constituent scenes, then uses the frames to impose a tight unity within each scene. The form repeats itself on a major level, for he also uses the constituent scenes of some ballads as framing scenes to unify the ballad itself.

To depict adequately the ballad's oral structuring in visual form is difficult, and to some extent distorting, but diagrams do throw into relief characteristics of that structuring not imme-diately apparent to the literate mind. Two scenes from 'Child Waters' are shown in a diagrammatic form (Figures 1 and 2) which attempts to convey the stanzas' interrelations. Figures 1 and 2 make clear how the framing stanzas bind the scenes

* For these abbreviations see p. xii.

together. Like those of the first scene, stanzas 12 and 21 firmly enclose a triadic rhythm, introducing and rounding off a particular unit of the narrative:

12   'O tell me this now, good Lord John,
       An a word ye dinna lee,
    How far it is to your lodgin,
       Whare we this night maun be?'

21   Whan bells were rung, an mass was sung,
       An a' men boun to meat,
    Burd Ellen at a bye-table
       Amo the foot-men was set.

The first stanza raises the topic of the castle, while the latter establishes them at the castle and outlines what her place is to be. A framing stanza, however, may do more than simply round off one scene. Stanza 21 also leads into the next section of the ballad, which begins: 'O eat an drink, my bonny boy'. On occasion, a stanza is the latter half of one framing pair and first half of another. As well as marking off individual scenes, the framing stanzas may, then, also link one scene to the next.

Moreover, the maker uses a frame not only to link but also to integrate scenes. In 'Lamkin', the scene between Lamkin and the nourice is welded to the scene between the nourice and the lady by a framing device; the triad between the first pair—'O whare's (a) the men (women, bairns) o this house'— is succeeded by these four stanzas,

'O whare's the lady o this house,
   that ca's me Lamkin?'
'She's up in her bower sewing,
   but we soon can bring her down.'

Then Lamkin's tane a sharp knife,
   that hang down by his gaire,
And he has gien the bonny babe
   a deep wound and a sair.

Then Lamkin he rocked,
   and the fause nourice sang,
Till frae ilkae bore o the cradle
   the red blood out sprang.

> Then out it spak the lady,
>> as she stood on the stair:
> 'What ails my bairn, nourice,
>> that he's greeting sae sair?   (93A: 11–14)

which lead into another triad ('O still my bairn, nourice')
between lady and nourice. Stanza 11 is linked to the previous
triad by the central concept ('where is 1, 2, 3, 4') and the verbal
patterns, and stanza 14 to the succeeding triad by the central
concept (the 'greeting' of the baby), but in their joint emphasis
on the lady they balance each other: the one speaks of bringing
her downstairs from her bower, the other has her standing on
the stairs. Again we can see how the internal unit dwells on the
act itself (the murder of the baby) while the frames carry the
cause (the desire to attract the lady downstairs) and the effect
(the attraction as far as the stairs).

The oral maker also uses the frame to express contemporaneous
action, as in 'Lady Maisry', where stanza 17 introduces the idea
of the punitive fire,

> 'O whare is a' my merry young men,
>> Whom I gi meat and fee,
> To pu the thistle and the thorn,
>> To burn this wile whore wi?'

and the balancing stanza 18 introduces the idea of rescue:

> 'O whare will I get a bonny boy,
>> To help me in my need,
> To rin wi hast to Lord William,
>> And bid him come wi speed?'

Stanzas 19 to 25 deal with the boy's successful rousing of the
hero, and then stanza 26 returns to the heroine at the stake, just
as the hero is approaching:

> Or he was near a mile awa,
>> She heard his wild horse sneeze:
> 'Mend up the fire, my false brother,
>> It's na come to my knees.'

By framing the idea of the rescue with the idea of the fire, the
maker achieves considerable suspense. Instead, however, of cross-

cutting between fort and Fifth Cavalry, he shows the peril of the fort, then stays with the Cavalry until just before the rescuers' arrival.

Again, the oral maker uses the frame to dispense narrative information dramatically. Consider as an example the first scene of 'Lady Maisry'; the initial stanza contains the two narrative ideas, (a) the lords are wooing Maisry, and (b) she is refusing them:

> The young lords o the north country
>   Have all a wooing gone,
> To win the love of Lady Maisry,
>   But o them she woud hae none.

The next two stanzas merely repeat, with verbal variation, idea (a),

> O they hae courted Lady Maisry,
>   Wi a' kin kind of things;
> An they hae sought her Lady Maisry
>   Wi brotches an wi' rings.

> An they ha sought her Lady Maisry
>   Frae father and frae mother;
> And they ha sought her Lady Maisry
>   Frae sister an frae brother.

and stanza 4 brings back idea (b) to join idea (a):

> An they ha followd her Lady Maisry
>   Thro chamber an thro ha;
> But a' that they coud say to her,
>   Her answer still was Na.

With a fine feeling for dramatic effect, however, the maker has held back the crucial idea (c) for stanza 5:

> 'O had your tongues, young men,' she says,
>   'An think nae mair o me;
> For I've gien my love to an English lord,
>   An think nae mair o me.'

The narrative ideas, then, are deployed in this order: ab aa aa ab bc. While it might appear from this that stanzas 1 and 4 are the balancing frames and stanza 5 a coda (a pattern discernible in stanzas 1 to 5 of 'Bonny Baby Livingston'), the verbal patternings of 2, 3 and 4 make it clear that they are a triad, and stanzas 1 and 5 the framings. The three essential narrative ideas are contained in stanzas 1 and 5; the other three stanzas are not strictly necessary to the story. This gives us an insight into the narrative method of the maker and the part played in that method by the frame. These stanzas may be viewed as fixed points on the narrative line, from which the maker swings out in semi-circular expansions; by being fixed, the framing stanzas prevent the maker from losing his sense of the story's direction because they keep taking him back to the straight narrative path. In the framed five-stanza unit, the expansion of the three, easily remembered, essential narrative ideas into a satisfyingly dramatic scene exemplifies in minuscule how the maker can plump his thin narrative outline into a full-blown ballad.

At its most pronounced, framing becomes chiastic structuring. Chiasmus, the arrangement of a work's units in inverse order (abccba), is used frequently by the oral mind where the literate mind, with its different habits, would use a straightforward linear arrangement. Figure 3 illustrates how a scene may be chiastically ordered. Chiasmus is intrinsic to oral creation because of the basic, structural-mnemonic function of annular organization. Frames, however, serve a variety of functions: they enable the maker to break down his narrative into constituent units and impose a tight control on these units; to link and integrate these units; to express contemporaneous action; and, finally, they enable him to keep to his narrative line while the binary and trinary rhythms allow him to expand dramatically. Annular structuring, especially in its chiastic form, shows how the oral mind operates spatially. The maker manages to control material that is stored in the mind and not on the page through these frames which are organized not by linear but by spatial relationship. Framing, then, helps explain how the maker responds to the restrictions of nonliteracy by utilizing a narrative method that is at once practical and aesthetically satisfying. But this method, it should be emphasized, indicates firmly that the oral mind and sensibility, and hence the oral aesthetic, differ in kind from their literate equivalents.

Although the examples of the binary, trinary, and annular

patterns so far given have been relatively straightforward, these patterns are sometimes combined to produce rather more complex units. In 'Fause Foodrage', for example, the common pattern of a triad of balancing stanzas is varied to include a final unit of balancing stanzas, so that stanzas 6 to 13 run: 6/7 8/9 10–11/

Figure 3

Structures:	Stanzaic	Character	Tonal*	Narrative
a	4	H + S	n + sp	Meeting of H + S
b	5	H	sp	H introduces himself to S
c	6			S expresses her attraction
	7	S	sp	to H
d	8	H + S	n	Act of love
c	9			S laments her pregnancy
	10	S	sp	to H
b	11	H	sp	H proposes elopement to S
a	12	H + S	n + sp	Elopement of H + S

* where n = narration and sp = speech[2]   (101A)

Figure 4

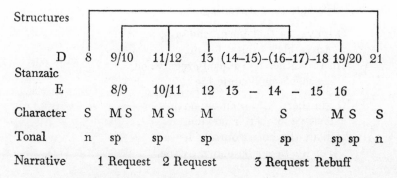

Structures								
D	8	9/10	11/12	13	(14–15)–(16–17)–18	19/20	21	
Stanzaic								
E		8/9	10/11	12	13 – 14 – 15	16		
Character	S	M S	M S	M	S	M S	S	
Tonal	n	sp	sp	sp	sp	sp sp	n	
Narrative		1 Request	2 Request		3 Request Rebuff			

12–13. In 'The Lass of Roch Royal' (76E), the final unit of a triad subsumes another, framed, triad: stanzas 8 to 16 run 8/9 10/11 12 13–14–15 16. Mrs Brown's other text of this ballad-story (76D), recorded seventeen years earlier, demonstrates further how changes can be rung on the basic pattern, and also how a singer may vary the structuring of the same conceptual unit of a story in different re-creations. Figure 4 shows the same scene in the two versions. The basic pattern is the triad of requests which in E takes the form of a balance, a balance, and a framed triad. In D the first two units of the minor triad are expanded into balances and, as counterweight, the frame becomes an extended frame through the addition of another balancing stanza; and, because the triads of D are quite complicated, the maker feels the need to keep tight control on the scene by enclosing it within the framing of 8 and 21.

In these examples, the third unit of the common triad is expanded; on other occasions, however, it is the fourth unit of an extended triad that is expanded. In stanzas 16 to 25 of 'The Kitchie-Boy', for example, three balances are climactically followed by a simple frame, so that the sequence runs 16/17 18/19 20/21 22/23–24/25. 'Willie o Douglas Dale' has a minor variation on this pattern in stanzas 15 to 25 where the sequence runs 15/16 17/18 19/20 21 22/23 24/25. In this instance, the three balances are followed by an extended frame, which carries the climax of the scene and the ballad:

> He's bent his bow, and shot the deer,
>   An thro the green wood gane,
> An ere that he came back again
>   His lady took travailing.
>
> 'O up ye tak that horn,' she says,
>   'An ye blaw a blast for me;
> Gin my father be in good green wood,
>   Sae seen's he'll come me ti.'
>
> 'O gin there be a man on earth
>   That ye loo better nor me,
> Ye blaw the horn yoursel,' he says,
>   'For it's never be blawn by me.'

O he's bent his bow, an shot the deer,
  An thro the green wood has he gane,
An lang or he came back again
  His lady bare him a son.

O up has he tane his bonny young son,
  An washn him wi the milk,
An up has he tane his gay lady,
  An rowd her i the silk.   (101A: 21–5)

These examples in which the end of the triadic unit is heavily
weighted all illustrate what Olrik calls the principal characteristic
of folk narrative—'*Achtergewicht* ("the Weight of the Stern")
combined with the Law of Three'.[3] A different kind of combination of patterns is observable in stanzas 22–7 of 'Child Waters'
where one triad frames another. Here three stanzas of hero–
mother dialogue are embedded in three stanzas of hero–heroine
dialogue:

'O eat an drink, my bonny boy,
  The white bread an the beer:'
'The never a bit can I eat or drink,
  My heart's sae full of fear.'

'O eat an drink, my bonny boy,
  The white bread an the wine:'
'O I canna eat nor drink, master,
  My heart's sae full of pine.'

     But out it spake Lord John's mother,
       An a wise woman was she:
     'Whare met ye wi that bonny boy,
       That looks sae sad on thee?

     'Sometimes his cheek is rosy red,
       An sometimes deadly wan;
     He's liker a woman big wi bairn,
       Than a young lord's serving man.'

     'O it makes me laugh, my mother dear,
       Sic words to hear frae thee;
     He is a squire's ae dearest son,
       That for love has followd me.'

> 'Rise up, rise up, my bonny boy,
>   Gi my horse corn an hay:'
> 'O that I will, my master dear,
>   As quickly as I may.'

The narrative necessities that produced such a construction will be discussed later, but from this episode it is quite clear that Olrik's 'Law of Two to a Scene' does have exceptions. When faced with a particular difficulty, the maker has sufficient inventive skill to create a scene with three characters, using an ingenious variation on his standard rhythms. On occasion, the maker will have two rhythms co-existing in the same unit, as in the previously quoted stanzas 1–4 of 'Child Waters'. These can be seen as a pair of balances (1/2–3/4), but they can also be seen as a framed balance (1 2/3 4). In stanza 1 is the uncharacterized warning not to follow young men frae the toun; in 2 and 3 she expresses her intention of following Lord John; in stanza 4 she ignores the warning by following Lord John frae the toun. This exemplifies in small compass what occurs in many of the longer ballad-texts, where often a number of patternings are intertwined.

The examples of how the binary, trinary, and annular rhythms operate on the level of stanza and scene provide an important insight into the oral process. The maker organizes his material in scenes formed by certain basic structural patterns. The basic structural units of these patterns, the simple balance, triad, and frame, allow the maker considerable scope, since they can be expanded and combined to produce new and more complicated structural units as the narrative demands. The process is not unlike that by which new verbal formulas are evolved from the old; in fact, one could call the balance, the triad, and the frame formulaic structural units. All of Mrs Brown's ballads are built up of these formulaic structural units, deployed in both simple and complex variations of the binary, trinary, and annular patternings.

Chapter 10

The Structure of the Ballads II

Like the stanzaic structure, the ballad's character structure is formed by these binary, trinary, and annular patternings. The trinary pattern shows itself in the three-character norm, where it acts, not as an expansive force as in the stanzaic structuring, but rather as a reductive or controlling influence. The standard three-character pattern not only aids the mental storage of the story but also makes it easy for the maker to fit his regular number of characters into regular patterns of deployment. In the character structure, however, the trinary pattern is less prominent than the binary and annular patterns.

Figure 5	*Figure 6*
S	H + b
S	S + b
S + M ─┐	H + S
H + M ─┘	
H	
H	

The binary pattern is apparent, generally, in the frequency of the two-character scene, and, more specifically, in the way the maker uses one character in two separate scenes to balance and thereby link these two scenes. The mother in 'The Lass of Roch Royal', for example, integrates the two halves of the story, one dominated by the heroine, the other by the hero; Figure 5 shows the character structure.

The maker likes to link scenes through a common character.

This is particularly evident at the beginnings of some ballads where the first two scenes, introducing hero and heroine respectively, are integrated through a minor character. In 'Jellon Grame', for example, the two main characters are not brought into confrontation immediately; the first scene introduces the hero dictating a message to a page-boy, and the second the heroine receiving the message from the page-boy, while the climactic confrontation comes in the third scene; Figure 6 shows the structure of this section. The maker's ingrained recognition of the need to build to a climax without slackening his grasp on the

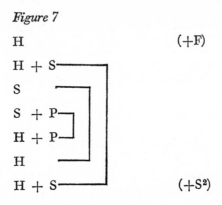

Figure 7

H   (+F)

H + S

S

S + P

H + P

H

H + S   (+S²)

material shows again in his use of a character like the porter in 'Young Bicham'. He purposefully refrains from throwing the hero and heroine together after her journey across the sea; each has first a scene with the porter. For all that has been written about jagged transitions in the ballad, the oral maker exhibits a firm sense of how to pace a story. The 'Young Bicham' structure is given in Figure 7. A number of points emerge from the Figure. As frequently happens, one character is carried over from each scene to the next, to provide a narrative fluency. Clearly, the two scenes with the porter are the ballad's fulcrum, but while the porter looms large, the Third Characters that belong to the motifs that make up the story—the heroine's release of the hero from her father's prison, and the hero's impending marriage to another woman—recede into the background and form a vestigial frame. The diagram indicates how the tendency to balance the characters' appearances is not confined to adjacent scenes but is in fact found throughout the story; the balancing becomes framing.

Framing is one of the most effective devices at the maker's command, and the framing of characters one of his favourite patternings. The framing may be of the verbal kind, as in 'Kemp Owyne', which begins with the mother delivering the heroine's weird, and ends with the hero delivering the mother's weird, though the mother does not appear on stage at the end; or it may be of the active kind, with the Third Character playing a part in the final interaction. The oral maker feels the need to tie up the

Figure 8

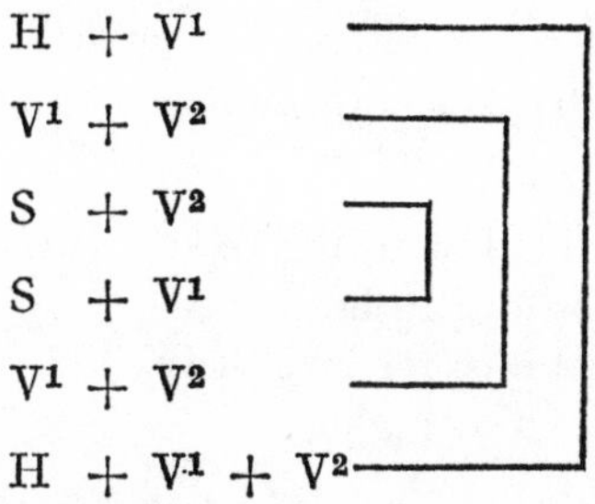

$$H + V^1$$
$$V^1 + V^2$$
$$S + V^2$$
$$S + V^1$$
$$V^1 + V^2$$
$$H + V^1 + V^2$$

ends, for in most stories there is at least a verbal reference to the complicating Third Character. A character may frame an entire ballad, like the mother in 'Kemp Owyne', or Lord Wearie in 'Lamkin', where the character structure is as shown in Figure 8. Utilizing the frame in this fashion is one way of controlling a story whose characters exceed the norm of three.

There is a group of five ballads, all with a total of three scenes, in which one character frames the action of the third scene. In 'Brown Adam', the initial two scenes containing only the hero (stanzas 1 to 4, 5 to 8) are followed by a climactic scene whose core is a triadic confrontation between heroine and villain, which is framed by the hero:

> Whan he came till his lady's bowr-door
>   He stood a little foreby,
> And there he heard a fu fa'se knight
>   Temptin his gay lady.
>
> O he's taen out a gay gold ring,
>   Had cost him mony a poun:

'O grant me love for love, lady,
  An this sal be your own.'

'I loo Brown Adam well,' she says,
  'I wot sae does he me;
An I woud na gi Brown Adam's love
  For nae fa'se knight I see.'

Out has he ta'en a purse of gold,
  Was a' fu to the string:
'Grant me but love for love, lady,
  An a' this sal be thine.'

'I loo Brown Adam well,' she says,
  'An I ken sae does he me;
An I woudna be your light leman
  For mair nor ye coud gie.'

Then out has he drawn his lang, lang bran,
  And he's flashd it in her een;
'Now grant me love for love, lady,
  Or thro you this sal gang!'

'O,' sighing said that gay lady,
  'Brown Adam tarrys lang!'
Then up it starts Brown Adam,
  Says, 'I'm just at your han.'

He's gard him leave his bow, his bow,
  He's gard him leave his bran;
He's gard him leave a better pledge,
  Four fingers o his right han.   (98A: 9–16)

In like fashion, the hero of 'The Bonny Birdy' frames the colloquy
of his faithless wife and the villain; stanzas mourning the death
of the Baron of Brackley frame the dalliance of his faithless wife
and Inverey; the Lord Justice frames the last scene of 'Lady
Elspat'; and, in more shadowy fashion, the dead boy and his
miracle frame the last scene of 'Sir Hugh'.

In many ballads one of the three characters does not appear
until the final scene or scenes, and in these instances the character is often integrated by a kind of framing process. This is the
case with the disappointed bride of 'Young Bekie', and the

nourice of 'Willie o Douglas Dale'. In 'Child Waters', it is the integration of the mother in the character structure that enables us to see with some clarity how the last Act of this ballad is unified. The stanzaic structure of this Act is rather complex, with three triads, the first of which frames the second, preceding three balances, as shown in Figure 9. Figure 10 shows in essence

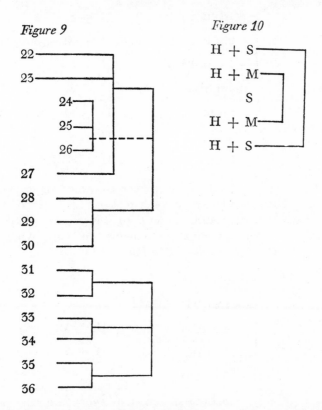

Figure 9

Figure 10

the character structure of stanzas 22–36. The two scenes between hero and mother enclose the crucial event of the Act (stanzas 28 to 30), the heroine's delivery of a son 'even amo the great horse feet'. Only in the light of the character structure do we see clearly how the entire Act with its three triads and three balances is fundamentally integrated. The maker is dealing simultaneously with more than one set of structural patternings. Often they correspond, but often, as here, they produce a kind of structural counterpoint. The interplay of the structurings modifies the geometric simplicity of any one of the individual structures. The two structures of the last Act of 'Child Waters', when put together, appear as in Figure 11.

Figure 11

┌─ 1st triad : 1 + 2	H + S
│ 2nd triad	H + M
└─ 1st triad : 3	H + S
3rd triad	S
balance	H + M
balance	H + S
balance	H + S

The Bb version of 'Child Waters', recorded seventeen years after the Ba version, illustrates how the maker may be both stable and variable in re-creating a story. In the last Act of the Bb version, the character structure remains the same, while the stanzaic structure alters, as seen in Figure 12.

Figure 12

┌─ 1st triad : 1 + 2	H + S
│ 2nd triad	H + M
└─ 1st triad : 3	H + S
3rd triad	S
balance	H + M
triad	H + S
triad	H + S

The basic organization does not change, but the later version, by replacing a pair of balances with the two strongly apposing triads, has a much more dramatic conclusion. In ballads such as this, it is the integrated framing of the Third Character that

110

provides the key to an understanding of a complicated architectonic.

The full extent to which characters are balanced and framed throughout a ballad becomes apparent when the character structures of complete ballads are outlined. Figs 13 and 14 show

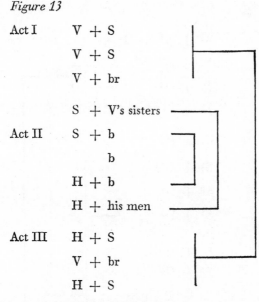

Figure 13

those of two long ballads, 'Bonny Baby Livingston' and 'Rose the Red and White Lily', the first having the normal three-character base, and the second the unusual grouping of six characters, with double hero and heroine. As the three scenes of Act I, when taken together, balance the three scenes of Act III, and Act II balances on the fulcrum of the boy with the message, it can be readily recognized from Figure 13 that the entire character structure is a balanced unity. Figure 14 shows the structure of the six-character ballad. Because of the six characters, the patternings here are quite complicated. As one expects, individual scenes within Acts are linked by the normal patterns, but in addition the ballad as a whole is framed by those balancing scenes within Acts I and III in which the heroes and heroines confront the evil Third Character, the mother, and the good Third Character, the king.

Finally, the binary and annular patterns manifest themselves in the introduction of narrative agents or minor characters whose appearance is, to the literate mind, often superfluous. The maker responds to the pull of the appositional pattern (what in this context Olrik would call the Law of Two to a Scene) by intro-

Figure 14

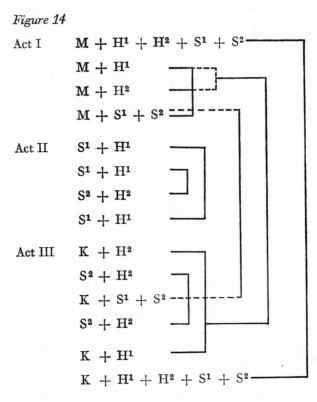

Act I $M + H^1 + H^2 + S^1 + S^2$

  $M + H^1$

  $M + H^2$

  $M + S^1 + S^2$

Act II $S^1 + H^1$

  $S^1 + H^1$

  $S^2 + H^2$

  $S^1 + H^1$

Act III $K + H^2$

  $S^2 + H^2$

  $K + S^1 + S^2$

  $S^2 + H^2$

  $K + H^1$

  $K + H^1 + H^2 + S^1 + S^2$

ducing a counterbalance to a major character in an otherwise unpopulated scene. The brothers of 'Kemp Owyne' and 'Bonny Baby Livingston' are cases in point. The sister of 'Fair Mary of Wallington' illustrates how economically the maker uses these characters called forth by the balancing impulse. At the beginning, it is from her conversation with the heroine that we learn the sisters are all doomed to die in childbirth, and after the heroine's death, when the sister now stands in the situation the heroine was in, it is from her conversation with the mother that we learn of the mother's culpability. The sister, then, is first used as a confidante, and latterly takes over the heroine's role. It is only after the heroine's death, however, when the sister takes over this role, that the maker brings the mother on stage: he makes certain that, even though the story has four rather than the normal three characters, he never has to deal with more than three at any one time. The tendency to control the minor characters by pairing is observable again in 'Lady Maisry', where a good 'bonny boy' balances an evil 'kitchie boy', and in the framing scenes of Act II of 'Bonny Baby Livingston', where the scene between heroine and villain's sisters is balanced by one between the hero and his men.

The selfsame rhythms that motivate the arrangement of the stanzas and the characters determine also the ballad's narrative structure. In part, of course, a story's shape is decided by the logic of the narrative, but the narrative units in the old ballads are ordered by the now familiar method of oral organization. Amenability to development through the traditional patterns was probably a major criterion for a story's acceptance into a ballad tradition.

On the level of stanzas and scene, the trinary arrangement of the narrative ideas corresponds to the stanzaic triads; at the core of the last scene in 'Sir Hugh', for example, is this extended triad:

> She's doen her to the Jew's castell,
>   Where a' were fast asleep:
> 'Gin ye be there, my sweet Sir Hugh,
>   I pray you to me speak.'
>
> She's doen her to the Jew's garden,
>   Thought he had been gathering fruit:
> 'Gin ye be there, my sweet Sir Hugh
>   I pray you to me speak.'
>
> She neard Our Lady's deep draw-well,
>   Was fifty fathom deep:
> 'Whareer ye be, my sweet Sir Hugh,
>   I pray you to me speak.'
>
> 'Gae hame, gae hame, my mither dear,
>   Prepare my winding sheet,
> And at the back o merry Lincoln
>   The morn I will you meet.'   (155A: 12–15)

The three steps of the mother's journey repeat an earlier three shifts in locale:

He's doen him to the Jew's castell, (3^1)

She's gane till her father's garden, (6^1)

She's thrown him in Our Lady's draw-well, (9^3)

The maker controls the story by arranging the narrative material in repeated trinary patterns.

In a number of ballads the central action is developed in three steps, usually corresponding to a triadic arrangement of the stanzas. The unspelling in 'Kemp Owyne' and the bespelling in 'Allison Gross' both progress in three stages, as do the colloquies between villain and hero's wife in 'Brown Adam' and 'The Bonny Birdy'. The crucial scene of 'Lady Elspat' contains the mother's speech against the hero's release, the heroine's speech for his release, and the Lord Justice's actual granting of the release. 'King Henry' exemplifies how the trinary patterns may, on occasion, multiply. The story deals with the unspelling of a loathly woman after King Henry has granted her a series of requests, that begin with this one:

'Some meat, some meat, ye King Henry,
　Some meat ye gie to me!'
'An what meat's in this house, lady,
　An what ha I to gie?'
'O ye do kill your berry-brown steed,
　An you bring him here to me.'

O whan he slew his berry-brown steed,
　Wow but his heart was sair!
Shee eat him [a'] up, skin an bane,
　Left naething but hide an hair. (32: 7, 8)

The action is patterned as shown in Figure 15. Unfortunately, 'King Henry' is one of three old ballad-stories (the others are 'Thomas Rymer' and 'Clerk Colvill') in which asterisks appear at the point in the story where there is some kind of sexual contact between the characters. It may be that Mrs Brown heard the ballads in a censored state, but as all her other stories (apart from 'The Mother's Malison', which has a confused ending in the full versions of it that have been recorded) are quite complete, it is fairly safe to assume deliberate acts of omission on Mrs Brown's part. When we remember the conditions of recording, her cuts, however regrettable, are entirely understandable. In 1783, she was an unmarried woman dictating to a fourteen-year-old boy, and in 1800 she was a lady of the

Figure 15

		Request	Answer
FOOD	Steed	7	8
	Hounds	9	10
	Hawks	11	12
DRINK		13	14
SLEEP	Bed	15	16
	Clothes	17	*
	Contact	*	*

manse dictating to a Church of Scotland minister. He, an ex-army chaplain, would be unlikely to find his cheeks mantling, but would most certainly prevent the publishing under his wife's name of anything approaching the erotic. In spite of the lacuna, however, the opportunities open to the maker for multiplication of the tripling patterns are quite evident; in this case, two units of the main trinary organization are themselves developed in minor trinary progressions. The maker can expand or contract his development of the story depending on his greater or lesser use of the trinary patterns. This particular story appears with the same trinary interaction of two characters in the Norse tale of King Helgi in Hrólfr Kraki's saga but takes a rather different form in a Gaelic folktale, 'The Daughter of King Underwaves'.[1] In this version, the loathly lady begs admission to the company of the Finn, vainly from Fionn and Oisean, successfully from Diarmaid; after Diarmaid grants the second and third of her requests, she is unspelled. Though the story takes a different colouring in this cultural environment, and the specifics vary, the narrative essence is still there, and still organized by trinary patternings. This can help illuminate the process of dissemination of stories from culture-group to culture-group: the narrative core remains the same, and the kind of oral patterning remains the same, but the specific textual units within these patternings will be those intrinsic to the individual traditions; they will probably be formulaic narrative units. The stability so often remarked upon in internationally spread folk stories comes from the oral insistence on retaining the narrative core, and the sharing by oral man, whatever his language, of the selfsame rhythmic patternings. The variation in internationally spread folk stories derives from the individual maker's re-creation of the story through the units of action that are so common as to be formulaic within his own tradition; in 'King Henry', the specific narrative units are the steed–hound–hawk triad common to Scottish balladry.

Many ballads have a trinary conceptual organization dominating the entire story. In these ballads, the essential narrative pattern is not a central action with three steps, but rather three separate actions. To exemplify: where 'The Gay Goshawk' deals with one ruse whose implementation has three stages, 'Brown Robin' deals with three separate ruses by which the heroine outwits her father and his porter. Likewise, 'Fair Annie' and 'Child Waters' have as their cores three scenes of suffering, three trials undergone by the heroines, while 'Lamkin' progresses from the murder of the babe to that of Lady Wearie to the retributive killing of the villains. The other two revenge ballads, 'Fause Foodrage' and 'Jellon Grame', both have a tripartite base, different elements of which are treated more fully in the respective stories: the unborn hero's parent is killed by the villain; the hero survives the killing; the hero avenges his murdered parent. 'Willie o Douglas Dale' and 'Willie and Earl Richard's Daughter' share the pregnancy/escape/birth-in-the-greenwood progression, which is followed in the one case by the episode of the nourice, and in the other by the king's finding of his grandson. Three ballads, each composed of three scenes— 'Sir Hugh', 'The Baron of Brackley', and 'Fair Mary of Wallington'—possess a more general kind of tripartite structure: the first scene presents the situation-plus-complication, the second contains a death, and the third treats of the aftermath of the death.

An awareness of this kind of construction can increase our understanding of individual ballad-texts and ballad-stories. A key element in the construction of 'Thomas Rymer', for example, is a triad of taboos—those against physical contact with fairy folk, against the eating of fairy food, and against speech with fairy folk. The hero breaks the first taboo, which puts him into the Queen of Elfland's power:

> 'But ye maun go wi me now, Thomas,
>> True Thomas, ye maun go wi me,
> For ye maun serve me seven years,
>> Thro weel or wae as may chance to be.'   (37A: 5)

He is prevented from breaking the second taboo by the Queen:

> O they rade on, and further on,
>> Until they came to a garden green:
> 'Light down, light down, ye ladie free,
>> Some of that fruit let me pull to thee.'

> 'O no, O no, True Thomas,' she says,
>> 'That fruit maun not be touched by thee,
> For a' the plagues that are in hell
>> Light on the fruit of this countrie.   (37A: MS. 8, 9)

Here, of course, the simple proscription against eating fairy food is reinforced by the connotatively more powerful proscription against eating the 'Forbidden Fruit'. Failure to comply with the third taboo would put Thomas in the power of the Fairy Host generally, and not simply that of the Queen:

> 'But Thomas, ye maun hold your tongue,
>> Whatever you may hear or see,
> For gin ae word you should chance to speak,
>> You will neer get back to your ain countrie.'
>>>>> (37A: MS. 14)

The last stanza implies that he successfully avoided breaking this taboo:

> He has gotten a coat of the even cloth,
>> And a pair of shoes of velvet green,
> And till seven years were past and gone
>> True Thomas on earth was never seen.   (37A: 16)

Though the three taboos provide the backbone of the narrative structure, the patterning does not end there. Throughout the ballad there is a series of topographical motifs. Thomas lies on the 'grassy bank' that in Celtic and Lowland Scots folklore is frequently the entrance to the hidden places of the Otherworld folk; he visits an Otherworld garden, where the fruit must not be eaten; he views the three roads that lead to Heaven, Hell, and Elfland (and travels on the last); and he crosses the Otherworld water-barrier. The water-barrier stanza, the famous

> For forty days and forty nights
>> He wade thro red blude to the knee,
> And l.e saw neither sun nor moon,
>> But heard the roaring of the sea.

stands stanza 15 in the manuscript but was relocated by Child, in an aberration from his editorial principles, as stanza 7 of his printed text. When this stanza is returned to its intended place, we can see that it divides the narrative unit of the third taboo into two parts—the warning and the implied avoidance—and consequently that the narrative structure reads as shown in Figure 16. The topographical motifs all refer to points on the

Figure 16

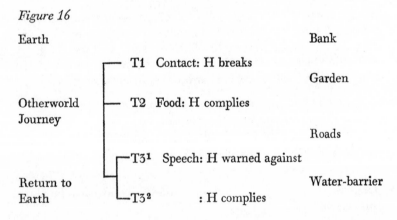

Earth   Bank

         ┌── T1 Contact: H breaks
                                                         Garden

Otherworld   ├── T2 Food: H complies
Journey
                                                         Roads

         ┌─T3¹ Speech: H warned against
Return to   Water-barrier
Earth   └─T3²   : H complies

journey, and emphasize this story's connection with the generic Journey to the Otherworld type. Taken together, the taboos and the topographical motifs show the text's intertwined foci of interest: it is, one, a guide to one's behaviour towards the

Otherworld folk (a branch of traditional *ethea?*), and, two, a geographical guide to the Otherworld.

The diagram presents a narrative structure that is quite efficiently ordered, but closer inspection of the text raises a query about the extreme compression of the version's ending. MS. stanza 15 resumes the journey, and suddenly stanza 16 has Thomas back on earth after his seven years. The stanzaic structure (Figure 17) also suggests an imbalance at the end.

Figure 17

1–(*)–5 :	(?)	triad of balances
6 :		frame
7–9 :		triad
10 :		frame
11–14 :		extended triad including frame
15 :		frame
16 :		frame with stanza 14

From what we know of other stanzaic structures and the principle of *Achtergewicht*, we would expect a much heavier balance at the end. If we turn from these internal question marks to the other—all incomplete—ballad versions, we see that Thomas and the Queen continue their journey to the Fairies' Ha' or Castle, where he avoids breaking the speech taboo during his seven years stint; and in the romance ('Thomas off Ersseldoune') she brings him back to the bank.[2] So, given this story's foci of interest, this text's structural and narrative peculiarities, and the information supplied by the fragmented endings of the other texts, it is likely that the structure of the story that came down to Mrs Brown at one time was as Figure 18 depicts.

It has long been axiomatic that to hunt for the *ur*-text of a ballad-story is to chase a chimæra, but the case of 'Thomas Rymer' would suggest that a knowledge of oral structuring makes possible and legitimate, so long as due caution is observed, the building up of an *ur*-narrative structure for certain ballad-stories.[3] Again, the structurings of 'Thomas Rymer' serve to show not only that the oral poet fashions his artefact differently from the literate poet, but that he is intent on achieving a different kind of aesthetic impact. The oral audience does not receive its pleasure and stimulation from new images and a unique personal vision of the world, but from the narrative reassertion of the motifs of tradition, as they give body and

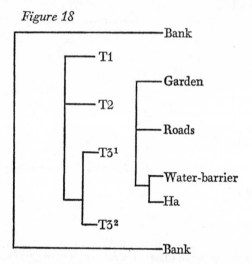

Figure 18

resonance to a story. These motifs carry a powerful reverberative force—at once metaphorical and in the wide sense religious— from the systems of belief and mythology out of which they sprang and from the many traditional contexts in which they have been used. Only someone steeped in the tradition, as we literates are not, can respond fully to the traditional significances and overtones. M. J. C. Hodgart has pointed out that in the ballads there is a kind of symbolic imagery 'referring . . . to a mythology once quite coherent but become fragmentary through the passage of time'.[4] In 'The Maid and the Palmer', for instance, the texts are shot through with allusive imagic references to chastity and its loss, which is the narrative focus of interest.[5] And the story of Thomas's 'Visit to the Otherworld' accrues resonance from the motifs it shares with related stories of the 'Descent into the Underworld' type. It is motif imagery of this kind that provided oral audiences with a distinctively traditional pleasure, that made ballads more densely patterned artefacts

than we often realize, and that distinguishes in kind oral artefacts from written artefacts.

The binary and annular rhythms in the narrative structure
should be considered together because their fundamental relationship, noticed earlier, here becomes explicit. Often in narrative
structures the plain and framed balances are inseparable, as in
'The Lass of Roch Royal'. (Figure 19) The central apposition

Figure 19

S	:	Plaint: laments lack of H
S	:	Journey: goes to sea; sees castle
S + M	:	Rebuff
H + M	:	Rebuff discovered
H	:	Journey: goes to shore; sees boat
H	:	Plaint: laments loss of S

(rebuff/rebuff discovered) is merely part of an integrated balancing
pattern that animates the entire ballad. Few ballads, however,
have the completely chiastic structure of 'The Lass of Roch
Royal'. A number begin with the straightforward balance of the
two parts of a narrative unit. 'Jellon Grame' and 'The Gay
Goshawk', for example, both begin with the 'message sent from
hero/message received by heroine' unit, an episode that occurs
with sufficient frequency in Mrs Brown's corpus for one to class
it amongst the 'themes' that Lord defines as 'the groups of
ideas regularly used in telling a tale in the formulaic style of
traditional song'.[6] The initial scenes of 'Young Bicham' and
'Young Bekie' contain the 'imprisonment of hero/release by
heroine' apposition, and 'Lady Maisry' begins with 'secret stated
by heroine/secret revealed by kitchie boy'. What follows in these
ballads are the balanced framings of the other narrative units.
The thematic strands of 'Lady Maisry' are given in Figure 20.
The relationship of the strands may also be expressed as $a^1 a^2$
$b^1 c^1 c^2 d^1 b^2 d^2$. As frequently happens in the stanzaic and
character structures, the relationship between the final units is
more complicated than that between the initial units. This
derives from the maker's liking for *Achtergewicht*, and his

Figure 20

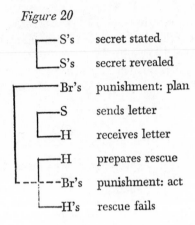

S's	secret stated
S's	secret revealed
Br's	punishment: plan
S	sends letter
H	receives letter
H	prepares rescue
Br's	punishment: act
H's	rescue fails

Figure 21

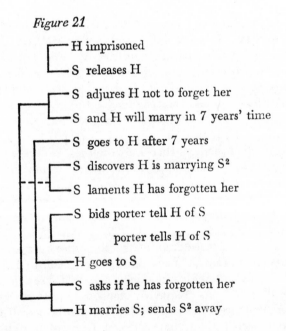

H	imprisoned
S	releases H
S	adjures H not to forget her
S	and H will marry in 7 years' time
S	goes to H after 7 years
S	discovers H is marrying S^2
S	laments H has forgotten her
S	bids porter tell H of S
	porter tells H of S
H	goes to S
S	asks if he has forgotten her
H	marries S; sends S^2 away

consequent attempt to integrate climactically the various strands.

'Young Bicham' and 'Young Bekie' provide an interesting comparison in narrative structures as they are variants of the same story. The narrative structure, in general terms, is this: the hero is imprisoned, but released by the heroine, and they agree to marry after a set number of years; he returns to his own country, and in due course she journeys there; he is about to wed another bride, but spurns her, and marries the heroine. The bare bones, however, are fleshed differently in the two ballads; 'Young Bicham' is shown in Figure 21.

'Young Bekie' is more complicated. In short form, its narrative structure may be outlined as in Figure 22. Each of the three

Figure 22

I	Goal stated	: Wedding
	Obstacle 1 stated	: Bride
II	Obstacle 2 stated	: Journey
	Obstacle 2 overcome	: Journey
III	Obstacle 1 overcome	: Bride
	Goal achieved	: Wedding

Acts has a trinary organization of narrative motifs: in Act I, the release, the hounds, and the vow; in Act II, the cause of the journey, the journey itself, and the result of the journey; and in Act III, the three motifs of Act I are integrated within a triple framing pattern. A fuller narrative structure is depicted in Figure 23. Despite the basic similarities, the story is markedly distinguished in the two tellings. There is much less verbal correspondence between the two than one might initially expect, and this can be partly explained by the maker's using different formulaic patterns for the four beat line of 'Bicham' and the alternating four and three beat lines of 'Bekie'. Partly, however, this can be accounted for by a definite attempt on the maker's part to keep the variants distinct. The major difference is that where Bicham marries another, having seemingly forgotten Shusy Pye, Bekie has been forced into marriage against his love for Burd Isbel. The story of Bekie and Isbel is longer, has a greater wealth of detail, and is compounded of older motifs; it contains, as 'Young Bicham' does not, the helpful spirit, Belly Blin, the magic journey, the token of recognition (the hounds), and a forceful appearance from the spurned bride. 'Young Bicham', on the other hand, plays up the motif of his forgetting.

Figure 23

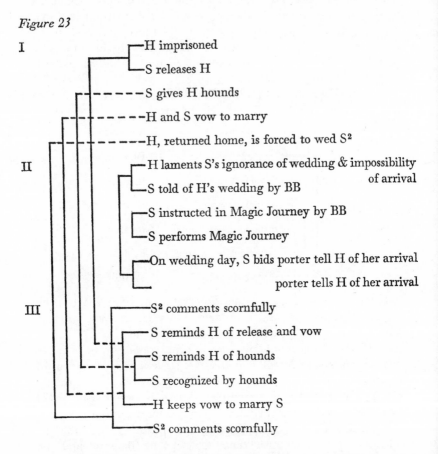

I
- H imprisoned
- S releases H
- S gives H hounds
- H and S vow to marry
- H, returned home, is forced to wed S²

II
- H laments S's ignorance of wedding & impossibility of arrival
- S told of H's wedding by BB
- S instructed in Magic Journey by BB
- S performs Magic Journey
- On wedding day, S bids porter tell H of her arrival
- porter tells H of her arrival

III
- S² comments scornfully
- S reminds H of release and vow
- S reminds H of hounds
- S recognized by hounds
- H keeps vow to marry S
- S² comments scornfully

In both, whatever the individual differences in the content of the narrative units, the relationships between the units are all of the trinary, binary and annular kind.

The mastery that a good maker exercises in controlling the intricate relationships of the narrative patterns shows very clearly in two long ballads—'Bonny Baby Livingston', which has the normal three-character interaction, and 'Rose the Red and White Lily', which has the unusual six-character interaction. Both ballads have three Acts, and have a narrative line which can be expressed in quite simple general terms: Abduction—Letter sent/Letter received—Rescue; and Two sets of Lovers separated—First set reunited—Second set reunited. The elaboration of the narrative lines, however, is not so simple, as Figures 24 and 25 show. These schemas illustrate not only how the oral

Figure 24

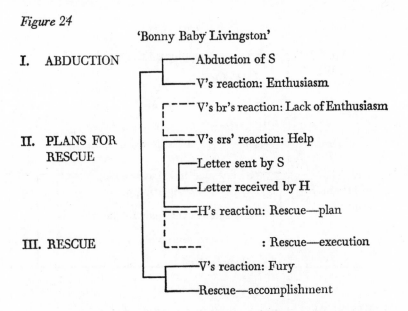

'Bonny Baby Livingston'

I. ABDUCTION
- Abduction of S
- V's reaction: Enthusiasm
- V's br's reaction: Lack of Enthusiasm

II. PLANS FOR RESCUE
- V's srs' reaction: Help
- Letter sent by S
- Letter received by H
- H's reaction: Rescue—plan

III. RESCUE
- : Rescue—execution
- V's reaction: Fury
- Rescue—accomplishment

maker binds his narrative material into Acts, but also how he uses his material in linking one Act with another. In 'Bonny Baby Livingston', though the Acts are distinct entities with their own internal patterns, the maker links Acts I and II and Acts II and III with trinary patterns. The first pair are linked by the three attitudes to the abduction: those of the villain (enthusiasm), the villain's brother (lack of enthusiasm), and the villain's sisters (pity for the heroine). The reactions of the villain and his brother belong to the episodes of the abduction raid itself, while the sisters' reactions occur at Glenlion and belong to the second episode, the events leading up to the rescue. The sisters' scene at the beginning of Act II, which initiates the preparation for

E*

the rescue, balances the scene at the end where the hero completes the preparations for the rescue. And this scene is itself part of the trinary pattern that links Act II with Act III: plans for, execution of, and accomplishment of the rescue. This kind of progression, whereby units function within the internal patterning of scenes and also within patterns linking individual scenes, is one we have already observed operating in stanzaic

Figure 25

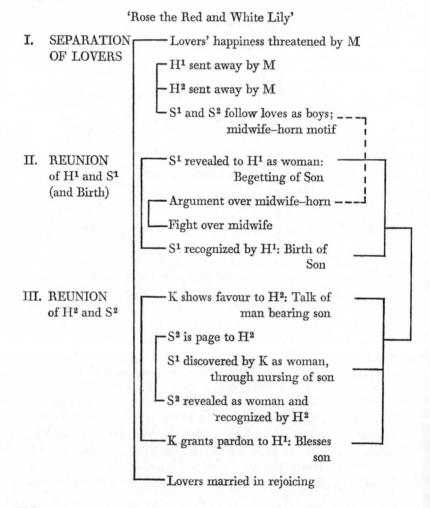

'Rose the Red and White Lily'

I. SEPARATION OF LOVERS
— Lovers' happiness threatened by M
— H^1 sent away by M
— H^2 sent away by M
— S^1 and S^2 follow loves as boys; midwife–horn motif

II. REUNION of H^1 and S^1 (and Birth)
— S^1 revealed to H^1 as woman: Begetting of Son
— Argument over midwife–horn
— Fight over midwife
— S^1 recognized by H^1: Birth of Son

III. REUNION of H^2 and S^2
— K shows favour to H^2: Talk of man bearing son
— S^2 is page to H^2
— S^1 discovered by K as woman, through nursing of son
— S^2 revealed as woman and recognized by H^2
— K grants pardon to H^1: Blesses son
— Lovers married in rejoicing

structure. 'Rose the Red and White Lily' exhibits a different kind of linkage. Here the difficulty of handling six characters prohibits the maker from complicating further an already complex architectonic with linking trinary patterns, and so he uses two linked motifs to bind Acts I and II and Acts II and III: the midwife–horn motif, and the newborn son motif. Just before the sisters separate at the end of Act I, they make a pact:

> Between this twa a vow was made,
>   An they sware it to fulfil;
> That at three blasts o a bugle-horn,
>   She'd come her sister till.   (103A: 15)

It is the blowing of the horn that precipitates the central action in Act II: White Lily requires a midwife and summons her 'brother' with the horn; her argument with Brown Robin over the horn-blowing and his fight with the 'brother' occupy the stage between the begetting and the birth of the son. And it is the son that is the unifying factor in Act III by drawing all the characters together, and providing the focus of narrative interest. In general, then, the maker relies strongly on the binary and trinary narrative patterns both within and between scenes, but the extent of his reliance may be affected by the competing complexity of the patterns in the stanzaic and character structures.

These, however, are not the only patternings at work in the tradition of oral makers. There are other, hidden, narrative rhythms, quite different in kind from the normal literary variety, which help show just how different from the workings of the literate mind are those of the oral mind. Lord has considered this oral kind of patterning when examining[7]

> the complex of themes associated with . . . the return of
> the hero from captivity, although the song itself may
> not necessarily be one of captivity and return. It is a
> curious fact in the Yugoslav tradition, that when a hero
> has been absent for a long period, or even when a long
> war is an element in the story, whether the hero has
> been in that war or not, a deceptive story, or its vestige,
> and a recognition, or its vestige, are almost invariably to

be found in the same song. Some force keeps these
elements together. I call it a 'tension of essences'.

As Lord points out, the *Odyssey* itself contains a grouping of
these themes and hence this tension of essences, and so also do
some ballad-stories. 'Young Bekie' and 'The Kitchie-Boy', for
example, both belong to this class of story, which probably has
its ultimate roots in the archetypal story of the Journey to the
Underworld.[8] The elements that make up the tension of essences
possess what we can only call a symbolic or ritualistic value; at
any rate they are not naturalistic, and possess a different kind of
aesthetic value from the normal narrative elements in written
literature. The deceptive story turns up in 'The Kitchie-Boy':

> O he has blaket his bonny face
>   An closs tuckd up his yellow hair;
> His true-love met them at the yate,
>   But she little thought her love was there.
>
> 'O will you marrie this lord, daughter,
>   That I've brought hame to dine wi me?
> You shall be heir of a' my lands,
>   Gin you'll consent his bride to be.'
>
> She looked oer her left shoulder,
>   I wot the tears stood in her eye;
> Says, The man is on the sea sailling
>   That fair wedding shall get of me.
>
> Then Willie has washd his bonny face,
>   And he's kaimd down his yellow hair;
> He took his true-love in his arms,
>   And kindly has he kissd her there.
>
> She's looked in his bonny face,
>   And thro her tears did sweetly smile,
> Then sayd, Awa, awa, Willie!
>   How could you thus your love beguile?   (252C: 31–5)

The disguise motif is designed to test the love of the heroine who
remained at home. In 'Young Bicham' and 'Young Bekie' it is
the heroine who, after the hero's release from captivity, journeys
to the hero's country. It is conceivable, given the basic parallelism,

that the porter episode in these texts embodies the female
equivalent of the male deceptive story:

> O whan the porter came up the stair,
>   He's fa'n low down upon his knee:
> 'Won up, won up, ye proud porter,
>   An what makes a' this courtesy?'

> 'O I've been porter at your gates
>   This mair nor seven years an three,
> But there is a lady at them now
>   The like of whom I never did see.'

> 'For on every finger she has a ring,
>   An on the mid-finger she has three,
> An there's as meikle goud aboon her brow
>   As woud buy an earldome o lan to me.'

> Then up it started Young Bicham,
>   An sware so loud by Our Lady,
> 'It can be nane but Shusy Pye,
>   That has come oer the sea to me.'   (53A: 15–18)

In this story of course, she is testing not only the love of the hero
but also her powers of attraction *vis-à-vis* her rival, the bride.
Where the disguise would suit a hero's purpose, the arrayal in
finery would suit the heroine's.

Side by side with the deceptive story, or an integral part of it
in some versions, is found the token of recognition. In many
versions of 'Hind Horn' and 'The Kitchie-Boy' this token is a
ring. In 'Young Bekie' the important token is a hound:

> She's gien him a steed was good in need,
>   An a saddle o royal bone,
> A leash o hounds o ae litter
>   An Hector called one.   (53C: 10)

This token is obviously of some significance for it constitutes the
central balance of the ballad's last Act,

> 'I gae you a steed was good in need,
>   An a saddle o royal bone,
> A leash o hounds o ae litter,
>   An Hector called one.'

> It was well kent what the lady said,
>   That it wasnae a lee,
> For at ilka word the lady spake,
>   The hound fell at her knee.   (53C: 33,34)

and it is immediately after this that the hero declares he 'maun marry' Burd Isbel. The token serves to prove irrefutably who the returned wanderer is—to meet, in short, a test of identity. The strong force that this traditional pattern exercises even in a declining tradition (and an aging mind) can be seen in the Old Lady's version of 'Young Beachen', where she remembers the necessity of the motif, but can recall only one line: 'An a lish of gued gray honds'. The motif of recognition by a hound also turns up in Book XVII of the *Odyssey*. These motifs function as tests or proofs of love and recognition, and the number of these that occur in the *Odyssey*, where Books XVI to XXIV are dominated by a series of such tests or proofs of love and recognition, enable us to see that poem as a complex collection of themes and motifs associated with the many variations of the basic theme: the hero's return after long absence.[9] Literate puzzlement over the delaying of the climax in the *Odyssey* is paralleled, on a minor scale, by possible queries over the delaying of the climax in 'Young Bekie'. After the porter episode in the ballad comes this stanza:

> O quickly ran he down the stair,
>   An whan he saw 't was shee,
> He kindly took her in his arms,
>   And kissd her tenderly.   (53C: 31)

Here, we might think, the story would end with the happy reunion of the lovers, but it does not. Three stanzas follow in which she reminds him of his vow to marry her, his release from captivity, and her present of the hounds, before he dismisses the bride and declares he will marry Burd Isbel. The maker obviously feels the aesthetic necessity of including these motifs at this point. In doing so he is responding to the dictates of a traditional pattern handed down over the centuries as 'right' and 'fitting'. Homer in the *Odyssey* was responding to the selfsame pull of these traditional patterns. To wonder why Homer postpones the reunion of Odysseus and Penelope for so long is to ignore the nature of the medium in which he was operating. Oral poetry, whether massive Greek epic or compact Scottish ballad, requires a revised set of aesthetic criteria from those we apply to written poetry.

Chapter 11

The Structure of the Ballads III

The stanzaic, character, and narrative structures together make up the ballad architectonic. When considered together these structures provide an illuminating picture of the overall organization of an oral text. In addition to these major structures, however, there is yet another, minor, structure. This one, since it regulates the tone and emotional temperature of a ballad, we may call the tonal structure.

When discussing a poet's *lexis* (technique of verbal communication) in Book Three of *The Republic*, Plato uses Homer to show how the epic poet employs both 'imitation' and 'simple narration'. In the one he projects himself into a character of the story and speaks as that character, and in the other he speaks, however impersonally, as himself. As Havelock points out, Plato is not so much interested in the formal distinction between epic and tragedy and the other genres as in the poet's methods of verbal communication; he places his emphasis on whether and how the poet uses imitation or simple narration:[1]

> all poetry may be said to be in one of three forms: the
> first, where imitation is employed throughout, is . . .
> tragedy and comedy; in the second, the poet tells his own
> story—the best example of that is perhaps the dithyramb;
> in the third, both imitation and simple narration are
> used—it is found in epic and in several other kinds of
> poetry.

Though our division of written literature into drama, poetry, and fiction stems from this differentiation, the criteria upon which Plato bases his distinctions are those relevant to oral rather than written literature. That they are directly relevant can be seen from the manner in which the oral ballad poet uses the combination of imitation and simple narration in his artistic technique. Below is the tonal structure of 'Lady Maisry' where N stands for simple narration, S for the speech of imitation, and the numeral for the number of stanzas.

In a less complete way, the same balancing, chiastic patterns are at work in this structure as in the others. By alternating

Figure 26

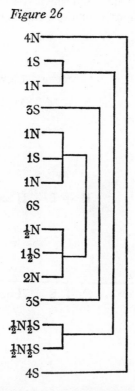

speech and narration the oral maker 'paces' his poem; he is able to raise and lower the dramatic tension in his audience by varying the pitch. And by balancing the rhythmic units of speech and narration the maker not only achieves a coherent and satisfying rhythmic flow but also creates one more strand that works towards the total artistic unity of the poem. This kind of structuring, however, is the least dominant in the creation of the total poem, and the one most likely to be affected, to be pushed out of symmetry, by the pressures of the other major structures.

All ballads contain a mixture of imitation and simple narration, but some concentrate more on the imitation, on the characters' interaction, than others; all ballads tell stories dramatically, but some are more dramatic than others. In fact, it is possible to arrange Mrs Brown's ballads through a dramatic–narrative spectrum. At one pole stand such ballads as 'Kemp Owyne' and 'The Bonny Birdy', which tell their stories primarily through the dramatic confrontation of the characters, and at the other

Figure 27

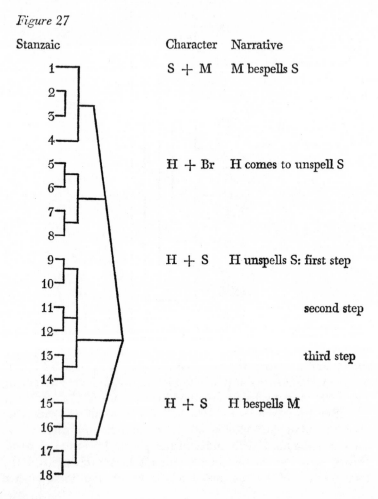

Stanzaic	Character	Narrative
1	S + M	M bespells S
2		
3		
4		
5	H + Br	H comes to unspell S
6		
7		
8		
9	H + S	H unspells S: first step
10		
11		second step
12		
13		third step
14		
15	H + S	H bespells M
16		
17		
18		

stand such ballads as 'Johnie Scot' and 'Bonny Baby Livingston,' which tell their stories with much greater stress on the events of the narrative action. We are concerned here with matters of degree, but grouping ballads in this way does show that those at one end of the spectrum possess, by and large, a set of characteristics antithetical to those at the other end. Those at the dramatic end concentrate on a two-character interaction, while the others have a more evenly spread distribution of characters, and are more likely to have a number of narrative agents. The dramatic ballads tend to have a small number of tightly integrated scenes including one pronounced climactic scene, while the long narrative ballads tend to be in three Acts with some Acts incorporating a number of scenes, and to maintain a general balancing relationship among these scenes and Acts. While both kinds are trinary in their overall architectonics, the former rely less on annular organization than the latter. In short, the dramatic ballads tend to have a simple climbing construction, while the narrative ballads tend to have a more level, complicated construction. Most texts, of course, are ranged along the spectrum, but Figures 27 and 28 give the structurings of two ballads—'Kemp Owyne' and 'Johnie Scot'—which help define the differences.

From these diagrams we can deduce two kinds of architectonic—concurrent and contrapuntal. The ballads at the dramatic end of the spectrum tend to have the former and those at the narrative end the latter. In the first kind the units of the stanzaic, character, and narrative structures all consistently coincide to produce well-defined scenes; in the second the units of the various structures do not always coincide and the structures themselves weave through one another in a kind of counterpoint. An example of the first kind is 'Jellon Grame', whose total structure is represented in Figure 29. Throughout, as in 'Kemp Owyne', the stanzaic, character, and narrative patterns correspond. In Act I, for example, the balance of triads parallels the character balance of hero and heroine and the thematic balance of message sent/message received. In Act II, the triadic coda that follows the climactic death of the heroine apposes her killing with the sparing of the son, who becomes the main actor in Act III. Here the scenes are quite distinct, because a new stanzaic unit always corresponds to a step forward in the narrative and, usually, to a

Figure 28

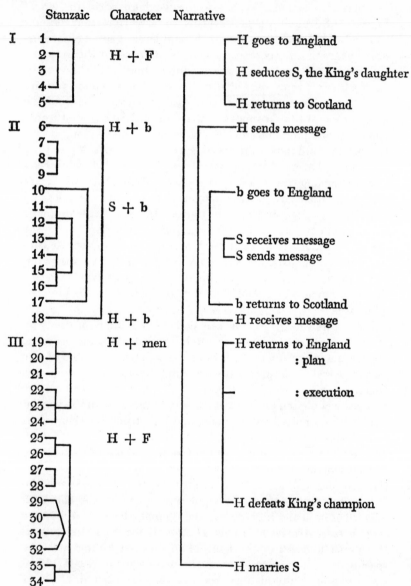

Figure 29

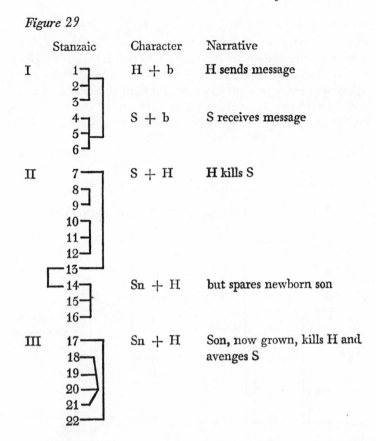

	Stanzaic	Character	Narrative
I	1 2 3	H + b	H sends message
	4 5 6	S + b	S receives message
II	7 8 9 10 11 12 13	S + H	H kills S
	14 15 16	Sn + H	but spares newborn son
III	17 18 19 20 21 22	Sn + H	Son, now grown, kills H and avenges S

new pairing of characters. This is not the case in contrapuntally structured texts.

An example of the latter kind is 'Lamkin', shown in Figure 30. This text has two framing scenes (stanzas 1 to 5, 23 to 27), and a central Act, where the units of the three structures do not correspond precisely. This disparity usually occurs when the maker is dealing with material more complex than the normal and the pressures of inclusion disturb the overall symmetries. 'Lamkin' has, atypically, four characters; one is accommodated by the framing scenes but the other three are all deployed in the central Act. This central Act comprises two scenes, stanzas 6 to 14 and 15 to 22. The first scene leads up to the murder of the baby, has three stanzaic units, and contains two characters; the second

137

scene leads up to the murder of the Lady, has three stanzaic units, and contains three characters. In order to accommodate the extra character the maker does not try to parallel each individual structural unit within balancing scenes but instead maintains a logical symmetry in each structure through the Act. The structures overlap one another; at the conjunction of the two scenes, for example—where the maker uses the crucial event of the

Figure 30

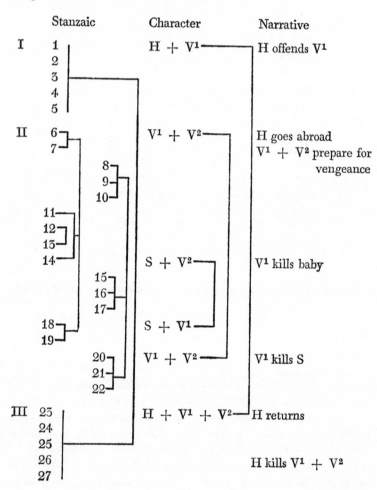

first scene, the murder of the baby, as a bridge to the second— stanza 14 belongs to the stanzaic patterns of the first scene and the character and narrative patterns of the second. The structures do not coincide but, as each one is unified within itself, the Act as a whole is unified. This kind of architectonic is, of course, more complicated and rather less obvious than those of ballads like 'Jellon Grame'.

So far the examples of the oral architectonic have been drawn from quatrain ballads, but the five couplet ballads in the corpus— 'Gil Brenton', 'Willie's Lady', 'The Twa Sisters', 'The Cruel Brother', and 'The Baron of Brackley'—display the same patterns as the quatrain ballads; they have the same three structures organized by the same three rhythms. They also, however, exhibit one or two minor differences.

The shorter couplet ballads are narratively based on a common trinary progression: Situation–Death–Revelation. In 'The Twa Sisters', the hero prefers one of two sisters; the other kills the heroine; the dead girl's hair, strung on a harp, reveals the murderess. In 'The Cruel Brother', the hero asks consent to marry the heroine from all the family but her brother; the brother kills the heroine; in delivering her testament she reveals the murderer. In 'The Baron of Brackley', the villain reives the hero's cattle; the hero, at his wife's urging, resists, and is killed; it is then revealed through an uncharacterized dialogue that the hero's wife welcomed and feasted the villain. While these three texts share the standard three-character situation, they focus on just two characters; the third does not interact in dramatic speech with either of the central pair. On the other hand, 'The Twa Sisters' and 'The Cruel Brother' have in the third scene rather more narrative agents and minor figures than usual: the miller and his son, the harper, the best young man, and the heroine's family; and in 'The Baron of Brackley' the third scene consists of a dialogue between two unidentified, choral voices. In the stanzaic structures, the basic units are still the balances and triads, but the relationships between these units are less complex than in many quatrain ballads. All in all, the structural technique of these ballad-texts is rather cruder and more diffuse than that of many quatrain texts. This would lend weight to the belief that the couplet form antedated the quatrain in British tradition.

The seventy-four stanza 'Gil Brenton', however, stands in some contrast to these three for, despite its length, this text has a quite sophisticated architectonic, shown in Figure 31. This complicated story is organized with a superbly symmetrical coherence. Each Act has five scenes and each scene is integrated

Figure 31

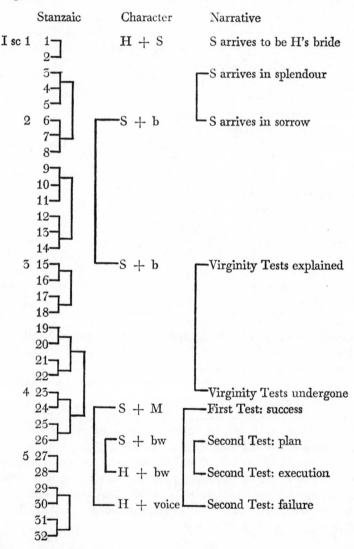

Stanzaic	Character	Narrative
I sc 1 1, 2	H + S	S arrives to be H's bride
2 3, 4, 5		S arrives in splendour
6, 7, 8	S + b	S arrives in sorrow
9, 10, 11, 12, 13, 14		
3 15, 16, 17, 18	S + b	Virginity Tests explained
19, 20, 21, 22		
4 23, 24, 25, 26	S + M	Virginity Tests undergone / First Test: success
5 27, 28	S + bw / H + bw	Second Test: plan / Second Test: execution
29, 30, 31, 32	H + voice	Second Test: failure

Figure 31 —continued

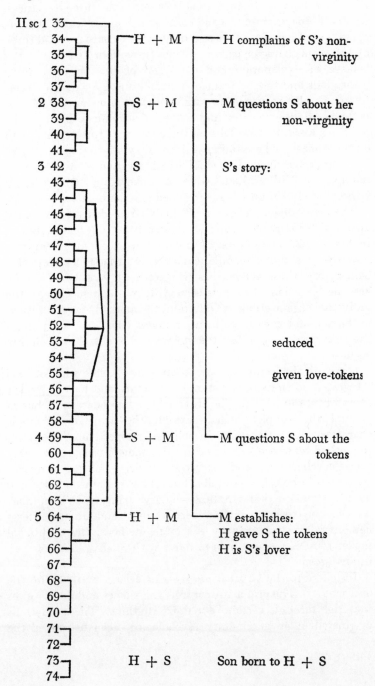

with the others by elements in at least one of the three structures. In Act I, for example, scenes one and two are linked by the apposition of her splendour and her sorrow; scenes two and three by the same character pairing; scenes three, four and five by the balance of explanation and execution of the virginity tests; scenes four and five by framed character and narrative patterns. In Act II, all five scenes are unified by the pronounced annular patterns of the character and narrative structures. Most of the unifying work, in fact, falls on these two structures rather than on the stanzaic, whose units, as in the previous three ballads, are less comprehensively linked. This observation, however, does not apply to 'Willie's Lady' which has, like 'King Henry', 'Kemp Owyne', and 'Allison Gross', repeated clusters of stanzas.

The two versions of 'Willie's Lady', recorded some months apart in 1783, present interesting structural differences, shown in Figure 32. These versions provide an excellent example of how the re-creative technique may affect the structuring of a ballad-story: the a version has two Acts each with three scenes, and the b version three Acts each with two scenes. Though the individual organizations are different, the method of organization, by binary and trinary patterns, remains constant; and though the structures may differ, the story itself is not altered in any essential.

Some of the couplet texts, then, have a less sophisticated integration of units in the stanzaic structure and have a weaker overall concentration on the three interacting characters, but in general the couplet ballads exhibit the same architectonic characteristics as the quatrain ballads. Irrespective of the form, the ballad-texts are organized by the same three structures—stanzaic, character, and narrative—which may be arranged concurrently or contrapuntally, but which are always patterned by the standard oral rhythms—binary, trinary, and annular. As the one corpus contains both couplet and quatrain texts demonstrably structured by the same methods, the traditional maker must have been able to move with relative ease between the two forms.

Insight into the structuring gives us a large insight into the oral method. The oral artist controls and shapes and develops his material through certain dynamic rhythms. These rhythms originated in an elementary psychological need to control the story material and to structure it for aesthetic effect, but they became established within the tradition, both in the storyteller's consciousness and in the stories themselves. So, while the young maker was assimilating the basic rhythms, he was also assimilating a sense of the story-moulds these patterns produce; he

Figure 32

6a	Stanzas	Character	Narrative
	1–4	H + M + S	M arrests S's childbirth
I sc 1	5–11	H + M	First Gift: offer and refusal
2	12–20	H + M	Second Gift: offer and refusal
3	21–28	H + M	Third Gift: offer and refusal
II 1	29–33	BB	BB tells how to discover the spells
2	34–38	M	M reveals the spells
3	39–43	H	H undoes the spells
	44	H + S	Son born

6b	Stanzas	Character	Narrative
	1–4	H + M + S	M arrests S's childbirth
I sc 1	5–12	H + M	First Gift: offer and refusal
2	13–21	H + M	Second Gift: offer and refusal
II 1	22–27	BB	BB tells how to discover the spells : plan
2	28–31	H	: execution
III 1	32–35	M	M reveals the spells
2	36–39	H	H undoes the spells

assimilated a craftsman's feeling for the dynamic rhythms of progression and the more static moulds of overall shape. While he re-creates the story, he fashions the narrative by the rhythms, but is aided in his structural progression by a sense of the basic mould or shape that this story or even other stories have taken in the past.

When we examine the old ballads in the light of their patterned structurings, we can see very clearly that the ballad aesthetic is something quite individual and distinct. It is not unique, because its general features are shared by other genres of oral poetry, but it is crucially different from the aesthetic of written poetry. The principles of aesthetic organization are different, and, as the tension of essences indicates, the kind of aesthetic response aimed at is different. The traditional maker develops and shapes his sung story by certain rhythms and moulds which evolved in response to the circumscriptions of oral performance; and an awareness of these rhythms and moulds is essential for an understanding of the hallmark patternings in the oral ballads, the oral mode of ballad composition, and the spatial rather than linear disposition of the oral sensibility.

Chapter 12

The Sound of the Ballads

Ballad language, like ballad structure, possesses certain formal qualities which render it quite distinctive and which reflect the oral genesis of the ballad. The most striking trait of ballad language is the frequent recurrence of certain phrases, lines, stanzas, and even clusters of stanzas that lend to the ballad a highly stylized air. They are lines such as these:

> She's lookit oer her left shoulder
>
> 'But an my father get word of this'
>
> O she has birled these merry young men
> Wi strong beer and wi wine
>
> Whan bells were rung, an mass was sung,
> An a' man boun to bed
>
> 'O saddle me the black, the black,
> Or saddle me the brown;
> O saddle me the swiftest steed
> That ever rade frae a town.'
>
> O whan he came to broken briggs,
> He bent his bow and swam,
> An whan he came to the green grass growin,
> He slackd his shoone and ran.

The aesthetic effect is pleasing but, to the literate mind trained to set great store by linguistic variety, strangely so. These recurrent lines and part-lines, once referred to as 'the ballad clichés' or 'the ballad commonplaces' or 'the ballad's stereotyped phrases', can now, in the light of Lord, be seen as the formulas intrinsic to the oral mode of composition.

A formula, defined as 'a group of words which is regularly employed under the same metrical conditions to express a given essential idea',[1] grows out of the oral poet's need to fit his narrative ideas to metre while he is re-creating a story rapidly in performance. The problem is solved for the maker by the processes of tradition itself, for, just as he learns from tradition a sense of individual structures and a sense of how to structure, so he learns not only the traditional phrases and lines but also how to create new phrases and lines on the traditional model. As Motherwell wrote in the nineteenth century, these 'commonplaces' are the means 'whereby oral poetry is more firmly imprinted on the memory, more readily recalled to it, when partially obliterated, and, in the absence of letters, the only efficacious means of preserving and transmitting it to after times'.[2] The formulas belong to tradition: they are assimilated by young singers listening to older makers telling the traditional stories and they are used by these singers, when mature, in their re-creation of the stories; and so the process is repeated through the generations, by the only way possible in nonliterate communities.

It is unwise, however, to abstract the formulas from their context, for the ballad language to which they belong is really completely formulaic. Ballad language is a language within a language. This language-within-a-language is created by the restrictions of metre, and composed of word-groups, drawn from the spoken language, which satisfy the metric limitations. The formulas, denoting the most common objects and actions of the traditional narratives, are the most commonly employed word-groups of the specialized language. The young singer, however, learns much more than individual formulas. He learns how to operate successfully within the limitations of his metred language: he learns how to create new formulas on the analogy of the old, and he learns how to combine, split and re-form his formulaic word-groups while maintaining his metrical integrity. In short, the oral maker operates within the patterns of his poetic, metred language very much as we do within the patterns of our spoken language.

Lines from 'Sir Hugh' illustrate the kind of spontaneous adjustment of matter and metre that the oral poet customarily makes. Five times in the story, the singer has occasion to employ the two-part narrative idea: (a) he went to (b) a place. Mrs Brown's standard (a) phrase for a four-syllable (b) phrase is 'He's doen him to':

He's doen him to the Jew's castell	(3^1)
She's doen her to the Jew's castell	(12^1)
She's doen her to the Jew's garden	(13^1)

When the (b) phrase is of five syllables, the (a) phrase alters to 'She's gane till':

She's gane till her father's garden	(6^1)

And when the (b) phrase is of six syllables, the (a) phrase contracts still further to 'She neard':

She neard Our Lady's deep draw-well	(14^1)

These examples illustrate how the singer adjusts the variations of a multiform idea within standard formulaic patterns. The words that carry an idea, however, are determined by more than the accommodation of syllables to metre; they are also determined by patterns of syntax, of melody, and of sound. These patterns obtain in all sung narrative verse, but in the Scottish ballads—as in most Western European folksong—the fact of the stanza provides an aural pattern rarely present in the Eastern European songs studied by Lord, the pattern of rhyme. This pattern exerts a powerful and compelling influence on the making of the texts, and in its workings indicates how the entire formulaic process operates.

The thought of rhyming publicly is a daunting one for the literate person, and yet the nonliterate singer managed this with, on the whole, astonishing effectiveness. To understand how, we must first consider how stanzas are constructed. Normally a stanza contains two essential ideas, one in the first pair of lines, the other in the latter pair. In most cases, the first essential idea is expressed in line one and is reinforced, sometimes by a subsidiary idea but more often by a repetition of its sense and even words, in line two:

She's led him in through ae dark door,	
And sae has she thro nine;	$(155A: 7^{1,\ 2})$

147

The second pair of lines may express the second essential idea
after the same pattern, but here the third line is frequently
subordinated, making the concluding line of the stanza climatic:

> She's laid him on a dressing-table,
>   And stickit him like a swine. (155A: 7³, ⁴)

When, bearing this in mind, we omit from a complete ballad-
text ('Sir Hugh') the second and fourth lines which do not carry
an essential idea, the result is quite illuminating:

1.   Four and twenty bonny boys
         Were playing at the ba,
      And by it came him sweet Sir Hugh,
         . . . .

2.   He kickd the ba with his right foot,
         . . . .
      And throuch-and-thro the Jew's window
         He gard the bonny ba flee.

3.   He's doen him to the Jew's castell,
         . . . .
      And there he saw the Jew's daughter,
         . . . .

4.   'Throw down the ba, ye Jew's daughter,
         . . . .
      'Never a bit', says the Jew's daughter,
         'Till up to me come ye.'

5.   'How will I come up? How can I come up?
         . . . .
      For as ye did to my auld father,
         The same ye'll do to me.'

6.   She's gane till her father's garden,
         And pu'd an apple red and green;
      'Twas a' to wyle him sweet Sir Hugh,
         . . . .

7.   She's led him in through ae dark door,
         . . . .
      She's laid him on a dressing-table,
         And stickit him like a swine.

8. And first came out the thick, thick blood,
    . . . .
    And syne came out the bonny heart's blood;
    . . . .

9. She's rowd him in a cake o lead,
    . . . .
    She's thrown him in Our Lady's draw-well,
    . . . .

10. When bells were rung, and mass was sung,
    . . . .
    When every lady gat hame her son,
    The Lady Maisry gat nane.

11. She's taen her mantle her about,
    . . . .
    And she's gane out to seek her son,
    . . . .

12. She's doen her to the Jew's castell,
    . . . .
    'Gin ye be there, my sweet Sir Hugh,
    I pray you to me speak.'

13. She's doen her to the Jew's garden,
    . . . .
    'Gin ye be there, my sweet Sir Hugh,
    I pray you to me speak.'

14. She neard Our Lady's deep draw-well,
    . . . .
    'Whareer ye be, my sweet Sir Hugh,
    I pray you to me speak.'

15. 'Gae hame, gae hame, my mither dear,
    . . . .
    And at the back o merry Lincoln
    The morn I will you meet.'

16. Now Lady Maisry is gane hame,
    . . . .
    And at the back o merry Lincoln
    The dead corpse did her meet.

17.   And a' the bells o merry Lincoln
            Without men's hands were rung,
        And a' the books o merry Lincoln
            Were read without man's tongue,
        And neer was such a burial
            Sin Adam's days begun.

Four stanzas have no essential idea in lines two and four; in these the singer separates the lines that carry the narrative sense from the lines that carry the rhyme. In all but three of the stanzas the second line is inessential to the narrative: it is 'spare'. Its function is, in fact, primarily aural rather than conceptual, for its purpose is to 'set up' the rhyming pattern of the stanza. In sense, it merely reinforces the first line; in sound, it acts as an important auxiliary to the final line. In two of the other three stanzas, where the second line *is* essential to the meaning, the fourth is not; here the fourth line merely adapts itself to the line which is important in both sound and sense. Normally, then, only one of a stanza's essential ideas is expressed in a rhyming line, and its final sound is what establishes the rhyming sound of the stanza. (Stanza 17 is a static coda, and quite unrepresentative.)

The oral poet integrates the aural pattern and the narrative ideas within the stanzaic form in three ways. To carry the essential ideas, he uses non-rhyming lines one and three; or, more usually, non-rhyming line one and rhyming line four; or, more occasionally, rhyming line two and non-rhyming line three. At no time does the singer have more than one essential idea in the rhyming lines of a stanza; sometimes he has none at all. One should, of course, be careful not to stretch too far any analytic distinction between sense-lines and sound-lines, but it follows from the methods of stanzaic construction that, if the maker has at his creative disposal a familiar stock of rhyming sounds to which the rhyming lines can be keyed, then the difficulties of 'spontaneous' creation in rhyme will have been largely surmounted.

A consideration of the rhyming sounds of Mrs Brown is, however, complicated by the question of orthography. Her language is a kind of *Kunstsprache*, for it is no one dialect, but composite. Basically Northern Scots, it subsumes words from Mid Scots and English. For example, Mrs Brown uses as rhyming sounds no fewer than three words with the same denotation—the Northeast 'g(y)ang', the Mid Scots 'gae', and on occasion the English 'go'; and a number of doublets—the English 'more' and the standard Scots 'mair', the English 'good' and the Northeast 'gweed', the Mid Scots 'twae' and the Northeast 'twa'. The importance of the two foreign elements in her language is, however, greatly exaggerated by the confusing orthography of her texts. Many words are written in English when the context makes it obvious they were pronounced in Scots: to rhyme with 'gang', 'long' must be pronounced 'lang'; to rhyme with 'me' 'die' must be pronounced 'dee'. Some words are written in Mid Scots spelling when they are Northern Scots in sound: to rhyme with 'green', 'alane' must be pronounced, Northeast fashion, 'aleen'. The apparent non-rhyme of English 'dead' and Mid Scots 'blude' rings true when heard as the Northern Scots 'deed–bleed'. These orthographical difficulties, which in one form or another have plagued the writing of Scots to this day, are yet another manifestation of the 'national schizophrenia'. Educated Scots were trained to abjure Scots for English as a medium for writing so that, when necessity demanded they write in Scots, ingrained inhibitions and the lack of a recognized Scots orthography led them to represent Scots sounds with English words. This particular dichotomy between the visual and the aural mirrors the general malaise that infected Scottish culture in the wake of anglicized literacy. With Mrs Brown's Northeast texts, the problem is further compounded because what material was printed in Scots was normally given Mid Scots orthography. Conditioned by this exposure, however slight, to visual Scots, her scribes were liable when they did write in Scots to write in the wrong Scots, giving Mid Scots spellings to incontrovertibly Northeast sounds. The confusions, however, are minimized if the Northeast pronunciation is recognized as the norm throughout the texts.

The rhyming schemes of thirty-four texts were examined, both 'Young Bekie' and 'Young Bicham' being included as distinct variants of the 'Young Beichan' story. These texts have a total of 908 stanzas and 3,342 lines. The 29 quatrain ballads, which will be discussed first, have 713 stanzas and just 57 rhyming sounds. Of these 57, 39 appear five or fewer times, so the bulk of the work devolves on a very few sounds. In fact, 18 sounds carry 73 per cent of the rhymes, six sounds (ee an ane ae air in) carry 53 per cent and one sound (ee) alone carries 28 per cent.

There are in the quatrain ballads two large groups of rhyming sounds, and one smaller group. The first group, the vowel sounds, contains 270 stanzas (38 per cent of the total) and six distinct sounds:

Sound	No. of rhyming stanzas
ee	199
ae	37
a	19
iye	5
ue	3
ou	1

A further six stanzas have slurred vowel rhymes. The second group, rhyming sounds utilizing the consonant 'n', contains 257 stanzas (36 per cent) and 11 sounds:

an/am	44
ane/ame/ang	37
in/ing	31
ine	22
een	14
orn	12
oon	10
un	6
en	4
oan	3
evn	1

A further 73 stanzas have slurred 'n' rhymes. The third group, rhyming sounds utilizing nine other consonants, contains 186 stanzas (26 per cent) and 40 sounds:

	Consonant sound	No. of rhyming stanzas	Consonant sound	No. of rhyming stanzas
R	air	33	ire	2
	eer	9	ore	1
	owr	6	amer	1
	other	4	Slurred	2

	Consonant sound	No. of rhyming stanzas		Consonant sound	No. of rhyming stanzas
D	eed	20		art	1
	ide	12		aft	1
	aid	3		Slurred	3
	ood	3	K	ilk	3
	old	3		ake	2
	ald	2		irk	2
	ard	1		ark	1
	ild	1			
L	ill	5	P	eep	8
	ell	5	TKP		11
	ale	4			
	ile	3	S	ese	3
	eel	2		ace	2
	iddle	1		use	1
	Slurred	1			
			V	eve	2
T	out	6		ave	1
	ite	4		ive	1
	eet	4		Slurred	1
	ate	3			
	ought	1	TH	ith	1

Obviously, the singer relies heavily on a few standard rhyming sounds, but is not confined to them, being able to draw where necessary on a variety of less common sounds. The oral poet also refuses to be restricted only to scrupulously exact rhymes. Particularly with the 'n' sounds, the singer feels free to slur the discrepant vowel and stress the common consonant. In one 'n' sound group, where the vowel remains constant he rhymes words ending in 'an', 'am', 'ang', and words such as 'hand' whose final consonant is normally elided in Northern Scots. What by written literary standards we could call assonance occurs in a number of rhymes all involving the consonants 't', 'k', and 'p': 'sheets' rhymes with 'sleep', 'asleep' with 'speak', 'speak' with 'fruit' (N.S. 'freet'), and so on. These all demonstrate that the eighteenth-century traditional singer possessed a sense of sound values quite different from and much freer than that of the twentieth-century literate reader.

As with the rhyming sounds, so with the rhyming words: a few do most of the work. One word, in fact—'me'—appears in over 13 per cent of all Mrs Brown's rhymes. The following list will indicate the relative frequencies of certain words within the sounds:

> ee (199): me (94), be (37), see (29), thee (28), knee (24),
> three (22), sea (21)
> ae (37): day (20)
> a (19): ha (8), wa (8)
> an (44): han (19), lan (12), gang (10)
> ane (37): hame (16)
> in (31): in (12)
> ine (22): wine (10), dine (7), mine (6), fine (6)
> een (14): green (7)
> orn (12): born (9)
> oon (10): toun (5), broun (4)
> air (33): hair (18), sair (9)
> owr (6): bower (5)
> other (4): mother (4), brother (4)
> eed (20): dead (8), speed (7)
> ide (12): side (8), wide (5)
> out (6): out (6), about (4)
> eet (4): meet (3), sheet (3), sweet (2)
> ilk (3): silk (3), milk (3)
> eep (8): asleep (5), weep (3)

Within the key sounds are key words, and these bear the brunt of the rhyming. In some sounds one could expect one of the two or three most common words to appear in every rhyme. Some of the low frequency sounds have a very limited number of words: the 'eet' sound has three, while 'ilk' and 'other' have each just one pair—'silk–milk', 'mother–brother'. The most popular sound of all, the 'ee' ending, with a theoretical maximum of 398 words, employs only 42 words, 15 words ten or more times, and one word in just under half of all rhymes. It also, however, uses 13 words only once, and the combination of high and low frequency in the word usage provides an insight into the aural processes of tradition. Just as the poet inherits the formulas from tradition but creates new ones on the patterns of the old, so he inherits sounds and words from the tradition, but integrates new words in the rhyming sounds. The low frequency words in the 'ee' sound indicate the kind of word that was assimilated into the later oral tradition: they are mainly tri- or di-syllabic, often abstract and 'English', where the standard words are normally monosyllabic, more concrete, personal and 'Scottish': 'charity', 'liberty', 'solemnly', 'cruelly', as opposed to 'me', 'see', 'knee', 'dee'. A singer such as Mrs Brown who was exposed to a greater diversity of sounds and words than was the rural composer would naturally manifest a greater variety in her rhyming sounds and words, and this is borne out by a comparison of her texts with the texts most nearly contemporaneous in the regional tradition, those of the Old Lady.

The oral composer has at his command a number of rhyming patterns, of sounds and words, which he assimilates through listening time and again in youth and early manhood to other singers. These patterns provide him with certain basic sounds and words and enable him to integrate within the old sounds new words rendered necessary by the demands of a particular narrative. As much of the essential narrative can be accommodated by non-rhyming lines one and three, the strain on a poet's rhyming powers need not be too great. The rhyming words are to a large extent going to determine the formulaic texture of the rhyming lines, and to a lesser extent the other lines, for the necessity of rhyme gives the stanza a basic aural mould, which will condition the singer's choice of formula. (This is not to say, of course, that sense follows sound; it is to say that the choice of rhyme and of formula are interdependent.) The rhyming process, whereby certain words are used often and new words are integrated into old moulds, is itself aural-formulaic, but is also an integral part—perhaps a crucial part—of the larger oral-formulaic process.

Having considered the place of rhyming in the specific processes of composition, we shall now consider its place in the general processes of tradition by examining the relationship of rhyme to text, first, in two re-creations of one story by the same singer made seventeen years apart, and, second, in three versions of one story made by different singers at different times and places. Mrs Brown composed the Jamieson MS. version of 'The Lass of Roch Royal' (76D) in 1783, and the Fraser Tytler

MS. version (76E) in 1800, and a comparison of these texts shows how tradition operates at once conservatively and radically. On the one hand, neither the essential story nor the basic scene structure changes at all, and many individual stanzas remain quite unaltered; but on the other hand, the stanzaic composition of scenes differs and the lexical composition of individual stanzas varies.[3]

Some stanzas retain the sense but replace one regular rhyming sound with another:

> D18 'Sae open the door now, Love Gregor,
>   An open it wi speed,
>   Or your young son that is in my arms
>   For cauld will soon be dead.'

> D19 'Awa, awa, you ill woman,
>   Gae frae my door for shame;
>   For I hae gotten another fair love,
>   Sae ye may hye you hame.'

> E15 'But open the door now, Love Gregor,
>   O open the door I pray,
>   For your young son that is in my arms
>   Will be dead ere it be day.'

> E16 'Awa, awa, ye ill woman,
>   For here ye shanno win in;
>   Gae drown ye in the raging sea,
>   Or hang on the gallows-pin.'

Others retain the sense and sound, but alter the rhyming words:

> D13 'O gin ye be Anny o Roch-royal,
>   As [I] trust not ye be,
>   What taiken can ye gie that ever
>   I kept your company?'

> E12 'Gin ye be Annie of Rough Royal—
>   And I trust ye are not she—
>   Now tell me some of the love-tokens
>   That past between you and me.'

Sometimes, at the same point in the story, the sound remains, while the words and the character involved change:

D23 'I dreamd that Anny of Roch-royal,
    The flowr o a' her kin,
  Was standin mournin at my door,
    But nane would lat her in.'

E19 'Gin it be for Annie of Rough Royal
    That ye make a' this din,
  She stood a' last night at this door,
    But I trow she wan no in.'

Sometimes, at the same point in the story, both sound and words remain while the character involved changes:

D21 O heely, heely gi'd she back,
    As the day began to peep;
  She set her foot on good ship-board,
    An sair, sair did she weep.

E17 When the cock had crawn, and day did dawn,
    And the sun began to peep,
  Then it raise him Love Gregor,
    And sair, sair did he weep.

Sometimes the sound remains, the words differ, and the meaning shifts slightly, though the story is unaffected:

D9 Long stood she at her true-love's door,
    An lang tirld at the pin;
  At length up gat his fa'se mither,
    Says, Wha's that woud be in?

E9 'O open the door, Love Gregor', she says,
    'O open, and let me in;
  For the wind blaws thro my yellow hair,
    And the rain draps oer my chin.'

Again, both sound and words may remain while the meaning of an individual stanza shifts appreciably, though the story remains unaffected:

D6 Her father's gien her a bonny ship,
    An sent her to the stran;
  She's tane her young son in her arms,
    An turnd her back to the lan.

E7   'O row your boat, my mariners,
        And bring me to the land,
      For yonder I see my love's castle,
        Close by the sa't sea strand.'

These compared stanzas illustrate two important aspects of the traditional process. First, although the singer does on occasion change from one rhymed sound to another in his re-creations of a story, in general he keeps to the same rhyming sound, and often the same rhyming words, even though the meaning or tenor of the stanza is considerably altered. The last five sets of examples all show how particular sounds and sometimes particular words are associated by the singer with particular parts of the narrative, despite differences in the lexical context. How tenaciously a sound adheres to a ballad-story may be judged by the incidence of the 'ore' sound. It appears only twice in Mrs Brown's ballads, in stanza 7 of 76D and, seventeen years later, in stanza 24 of 76E. The sound patterns, then, exercise a stronger hold on the oral poet's memory of a story than the minor incidents of line; within stanzas, the rhyming sounds are likely to be more stable than individual words which, in turn, are likely to be more stable than the minor incidents, a scale of priority that has some significance for the study of story variation.[4] Second, the singer does not possess the particular fixation with individual words that comes with literacy, but instead works through sounds and word-groups. The oral poet does not share the print-oriented man's belief that the words *are* the story. For him, the story is a conceptual entity whose essence may be readily and accurately conveyed by different word-groups. He is not so concerned with the minor incidents of the lines as he is with the major events of the ballad; he is not so concerned with truth to the minor facts as he is with truth to the major emotions.[5] Any study of story variation in oral transmission must start, not with a literate belief that the words are all, but with an awareness of the oral poet's sense of priorities.

A comparison of five versions of one story from different singers sheds further light on how the aural patterns function within the general processes of transmission. Here are Child's A–E texts of 'Sir Hugh', all from Scotland, collated according to the rhyming sound:

SOUND	A	C	D	B	E
a	1	1	1	1	
				air	1
ee	2	2	2		2
				ine 2	3
out	3				
ee	4	3	3		4
a		4	4		
				air 4	
ee	5	5	5		
n	6	6	6	3	5
a		7	7		6
				air	7
ine	7	8	8	6	9
in	8	9		5	8
eep	9	10	9	7	10
				n-r	11
ane	10			8	13
an	11	11			
tkp	12	12		9	14
tkp	13	13		10	16
tkp	14	14		12	18, 20
ee		15		11	12, 15, 17
eet	15,16	16		13	21
un	17				
ed		17	10		
				air	22

The general tenacity of the rhyming sound in these five Scottish versions is remarkable; the individual rhyming words may often vary from singer to singer but the sounds themselves stay consistent. The aural correspondence between A (Mrs Brown), C (sent to Percy by George Paton of Edinburgh in 1768 or 1769), and D (collected by Herd before 1776) is particularly close. As these versions are not, so far as is known, from the same regional tradition, the story must have retained fairly constant rhyming sounds over a wide area, in this case probably eastern Scotland. The B version (sent to Percy from Scotland before 1765) and the E version (collected by Motherwell before 1827) maintain a general aural likeness to A, C and D, but introduce a new sound (air), repeat one sound (ine) found else-where in the ballad, and, in E, add a non-rhyme. These versions probably represent the sound patterns of western Scotland. The English, Irish, and American versions of the story in Child contain a number of the same sounds as the Scottish, but, as one would expect from the linguistic difference, show a greater correspondence among themselves; where, for example, the Scottish versions tend to begin a–ee–ee–a–ee, the others tend to begin all–o–ain–all–in.

Some of the aural correspondences are not immediately apparent because they occur at different points in the story. A3, for example, has a favourite pattern of Mrs Brown,

> . . . .
> And walked it round about;
> . . . .
> At the window looking out.

with a sound which does not, on the face of it, appear in the other versions. The 'about' does, however, appear in C12, 13, 14,

> And there ran thryse about

subsumed in a 't-k' rhyming sound.

The rhyming sounds, however, are not all that adhere to a ballad-story; so do certain syntactic patterns, and certain lines, which, like the sounds, do not always appear at the same place in the narrative. C15, for example, possesses the same rhyming sound as A5, and has in lines one and two a distinct syntactic pattern,

> 'How can I speak, how dare I speak,
> How can I speak to thee?

which also occurs in A5:

> 'How will I come up? How can I come up?
> How can I come to thee?

In C4[3] and C5[3] is a syntactic pattern related to that of A5[1] and C15[1]

> 'I canna cum, I darna cum

which also appears at the same point in the story in other versions:

'I winnae cum in, I cannae cum in   (B2³)

'I winna come up, I mayna come [up]   (D4³)

'I mayna come up, I winna come up   (D5³)

'I winna come in, and I canna come in   (E3³)

Certain formulaic constructions also turn up in the story's
versions, and again, not necessarily at the same place. The final
stanzas of C and D

    Whan bells war rung, and mass was sung,
      And a' men bound for bed,
    Every mither had her son,
      But sweet Sir Hew was dead.

    Whan bells was rung, and mass was sung,
      An a' man bound to bed,
    Every lady got hame her son,
      But sweet Sir Hugh was dead.

are related to stanzas earlier in the narrative in A, B and E:

    When bells were rung, and mass was sung,
      And a' the bairns came hame,
    When every lady gat hame her son,
      The Lady Maisry gat nane.   (A10)

    Whan bells wer rung, and mass was sung,
      And every lady went hame,
    Than ilka lady had her yong sonne
      Bot Lady Helen had nane.   (B8)

    When bells were rung, and mass was sung,
      And every body went hame,
    Then every lady had her son,
      But Lady Helen had nane.   (E13)

Sounds, syntactic patterns, and formulaic constructions all adhere
to the ballad-story. They do not necessarily occur in the same
place but, like burrs, they stick to the ballad and appear some-
where within it. The tenacity of these patterns illustrates how
strongly developed is the oral poet's aural memory, and how his
aural sense operates in the process of composition quite differently
from the literate poet's.

Variation from singer to singer in the telling of 'Sir Hugh' is not very great. It is generally of two kinds, largely inconsequential lexical variation and expansion and contraction. Expansion and contraction, let it be stressed, not of a fixed text, but of the linked 'ideas' of a story that has been heard sung; they are purely relative terms, referring to stanzas that appear in one but not in the others. Expansion occurs when an episode or scene is elaborated through doubling or tripling of the basic stanzaic patterns, as in C4 and 5 and E11 to 20, and when a common formula (A3) or floating tag (A17, E22) is introduced, and when a stanza is created on the basis of patterns associated with the ballad, as in C15. Contraction occurs in the coalescing of the sense of two stanzas for dramatic effect, as in A7, or in the forgetting or omission of part of the story, as in the shortened D version. Although the lexical variation is largely immaterial, it could provide a clue to story variation over a period of time. The singer's main priority is to convey the essential story, and in his efforts to convey this in rhymed song he allows himself much greater latitude in the words than in the aural patterns. Consequently, while the rhyming sound may be the same, the sense of the lines may vary. Compare, for instance, A11 and C11:

> She's taen her mantle her about,
> > Her coffer by the hand,
> And she's gane out to seek her son,
> > And wanderd oer the land.

> She's taen her mantle about her head,
> > Her pike-staff in her hand,
> And prayed Heaven to be her guide
> > Unto some uncouth land.

The difference in the third lines may appear inconsequential, but, without A's overt reference to the son, the context of C could conceivably suggest the murderess fleeing the crime, rather than the mother setting out to search for Sir Hugh. From minor lexical variation of this kind could grow, over a period of time, a major change in the conception of a story.

This examination of the aural patterns in the transmission of ballad-stories reinforces what Lord found in his study of the Yugoslav tradition: the primary concern of the traditional singer is thematic, not textual, stability. What matters to him is telling the essential story, not singing the 'correct' words, for, never having read a text, the nonliterate poet has no conception of a fixed text with 'correct words'. What the singer does have is a technique for instantaneous composition. In the study of story transmission, a long time has elapsed since anyone tried to pursue the mirage of a fixed text, but what exactly it is that should be pursued has not been generally clear. There has been a tendency to look at ballads, modern and old, as if they were created by a lesser kind of literate composition, to assume a similar kind of relation between text and narrative essence, and to place the normal emphases of literary criticism on the words. Given the difference between oral and literate methods of composition, it is hardly surprising that this kind of approach has yielded barren results. What has at one and the same time encouraged and baffled this approach has been the stability of the rhyming sounds and words and formulaic patterns. This kind of stability has often been misinterpreted as evidence of groping towards verbal stability as it is known to the literate mind, as signs of attempts at 'memorization', a process quite antipathetic to the oral mind. The inherent stability of the aural and formulaic patterns in traditional ballads should not be misconstrued as conscious attempts to learn by rote a collection of 'correct words'. These attempts come later, in a literate society.

Even Child placed the wrong emphasis on the words for he, with his customary textual scrupulousness, spent much energy trying to trace proper names to an actual source. In the historical ballads this may prove fruitful, but for many stories it is an arid occupation, because the oral poet's concern for the story over-rides any concern for the names of people or places. It affects the story not at all whether the lady is called Maisry or Ellen or Annie, but it does affect the ease of the poet's rhyming. Proper names are likely to be modified to fit a rhyme ending (Bekie, spelt 'Beckie' in the Jamieson Brown MS. could well be a contraction of Becket), or employed because they already possess a common rhyming sound, as in the case of the rivers Clyde, Tay and Tyne, which in the stories have no real geo-graphical significance. The same reason, that they fit very acceptably into a standard rhyming sound, rather than any magical connotation, could account for the frequent appearance of the numbers three and nine, and could explain the retention of such archaic words as 'gare' and 'bower' in the ballad vocabulary.

A high proportion of archaic words is found in the couplet ballads, in whose composition the formulaic patternings again play a vital part. In the aural patterns of the couplet ballads we find the same sounds and words as are in the quatrain ballads, although the relative proportions vary. The 'n' endings are by far the most prevalent, being 36·5 per cent of the total, while the vowel sounds (mainly 'ee', 'ae', 'a') come to only 18 per cent. Apart from the 4 per cent non-rhyme (all in 'Willie's Lady'), the remainder is made up of assorted consonantal endings such as the 'r' endings (17 per cent —almost as much as the vowel sounds), 'd' endings (9 per cent), the 't k p' rhymings, and some sounds which do not occur in the quatrains—'ent', 'ack', 'st', 'ife'. Over all, the couplet ballads are more given to consonantal rhyme endings and disyllabic rhyme words, and, especially in 'Gil Brenton', include both in and out of the rhymes a greater number of old Scots words. As with the structuring of quatrain and couplet ballads, the principles of composition remain the same, but the textual particulars may vary.

The ballad's aural patterns reflect how the larger oral-formulaic process works. When young the singer learns the sound patterns by assimilation: in listening to other singers he assimilates the key sounds and words along with the other melodic, metric, and syntactic patterns. In re-creating the story the singer relies on these basic aural patterns and is helped in doing so by his different scale of sound values: by judicious use of his voice in singing, by elision, by slurring vowels to make the consonant dominant, the singer can produce a vocal equivalence of sounds not immediately observable in print, and this, of course, gives him a fair latitude in his choice of rhyming words. What appears to the literate person a highly formidable barrier, the necessity of rhyming 'on one's feet', is overcome by methods of learning and story-telling that grow organically from the conditions of an oral culture. The aural patterns also exercise an important influence on the formulaic process itself, for they provide the stanza with an aural mould, a basic sound to which the formulaic lines are keyed. An understanding of the significant function of the sound patterns within the oral process helps establish the relative priorities of the traditional singer, and thereby puts the problems of transmission into clearer perspective. It is hardly surprising that a knowledge of the sound patterns is vital to an understanding of the ballads, for where literate, print-oriented man is 'visual', nonliterate man is 'aural'. One could, therefore, expect sound to be of no little significance in oral art.

Chapter 13

The Oral Ballad: A Summing-up

The principles of composition and transmission exemplified by Mrs Brown's texts reveal the essential operations of the oral ballad tradition. The maker learns from older traditional singers not only the individual stories but also the tradition's structural and formulaic patternings, and re-creates the ballad-stories every time he performs. He learns specific structures and formulas but, more important, learns how to expand and create anew on the basis of the old. Behind the maker's creation of individual structures lies his sense of the established rhythms of tradition—binary, trinary, and annular—and behind his individual formulas lies his sense of the aural, melodic, metrical, and syntactic patterns intrinsic to the local tradition's form. Because re-composing marks the essential difference between oral and written poetry, it is natural to emphasize the re-creative element in oral composition, but it is perhaps more necessary, as a corrective, to emphasize that the re-creative method produces story-texts remarkable for stability rather than innovation.

On the subject of stability Motherwell quotes Jamieson approvingly:[1]

> To these peculiarities [the ballad's formulaic char-
> acteristics], in what may be styled the mechanism of
> the ancient ballad, and which appear to be thus common
> to the traditionary poetry of other countries, may be
> attributed the purity and integrity with which a great
> body of it has been transmitted to the present day.

Since the maker has the means to re-create a story afresh each time he performs, one might tend to assume that he could produce, for the same story told at different times, texts with wholesale alterations. The Brown corpus indicates that this is

166

certainly not the case. In fact, it is rather paradoxical that a re-creative technique should produce the degree of narrative conservatism it does. Variation, of course, exists, but it is often made up of verbal minutiae and is frequently unimportant. Stability comes about, first, because the maker normally tries to tell the right and true story, the one he heard, and, second, because each story in a regional tradition carries with it its own inherited patterns—the structural, aural, and other formulaic patterns.

The conservative tendency explains why couplet and quatrain ballads come down in the same tradition and appear in the same corpus: the individual stories retain their basic identity and form. And, as we have already observed, the maker in an established tradition finds little difficulty in moving between forms, because the principles of composition remain the same for both couplet and quatrain. The fact of stability may also shed some light on the evolution of the regional tradition, for oral ballad-texts recorded even in the eighteenth century may display stable characteristics retained from the time of the story's original acceptance into tradition. In the Brown corpus, there is a group of five ballads whose characteristics would seem to illuminate one important stage in the local tradition's evolutionary process.

It has been suggested more than once that the ballads whose stories are told in couplet form have a longer history than those in quatrain form. If the quatrain did at one time supplant the couplet as the common form in tradition, then one would expect textual signs of the traditional singer's adjustment from the patterns of one to the patterns of the other; one would expect stories taken into tradition at the beginning of the quatrain's popularity, before the new patternings had become firmly established, to display vestiges of the couplet's formulaic pattern-ings. The five spell ballads of the Brown corpus—'King Henry', 'Kemp Owyne', 'Allison Gross', 'Thomas Rymer', and 'Clerk Colvill'—do display these vestiges in their metrical, syntactic, and aural patternings. Four of the five texts have four-stress lines throughout so that, metrically, a stanza reads like two couplets. In the couplet ballads, the syntactic unit occasionally extends over two couplets but most often is complete within one; in the spell ballads a quatrain is sometimes made up of two syntactic couplets. Compare the following sets of four lines. Can

167

one, without knowing the stories, confidently ascribe one to
couplet form and one to quatrain?

> O it fell on a Saturday's afternoon,
> Whan a' our langsome wark was dane,
> We keist the cavils us amang,
> To see which shoud to the greenwood gang.

> O a heavier weird light her upon
> Than ever fell on wile woman;
> Her hair's grow rough, an her teeth's grow lang,
> An on her four feet sal she gang.

The first set are couplets from 'Gil Brenton'. Aurally, the spell
ballads tend towards the denser rhyming of the couplet ballads.
No fewer than twenty stanzas in these five texts have rhyming
patterns which correspond more closely to the a a of the couplet
than the a b c b of the standard quatrain: a a b a, a b a b, a a a a,
a a a a b a, a b a b c b. Finally, these ballads have a high frequency
of repeated lines and stanzas, normally in incremental progression, which suggests that the makers were adjusting to a new
form in cautious fashion and were consolidating their sense of
revised formulaic patternings.

These characteristics would indicate that the five ballads are
the earliest stories of the corpus in quatrain form. Other characteristics would bear this out. These texts with their heavy
concentration of magical motifs have narrative material which
stretches its roots some distance back in time; when compared
with the other quatrain ballads, these prove the least modern
in narrative substance. Architectonically, their scenes are
organized, with variations of emphasis, on the principle of the
extended triad, the most basic rhythm of the quatrain itself.
This most elementary of structures—still a popular structure for
today's risqué jokes—seems to have been initially used to
accommodate a two-character confrontation. In both 'Thomas
Rymer' and 'King Henry' only two characters interact, and in
'Allison Gross' the structuring (given in Figure 33) merits
scrutiny. What disturbs the artistic balance of this piece is the
arrival of the Queen out of nowhere, as a kind of *dea ex machina*.
This episode with the third character seems tacked on, and the
compressing of the second and third gifts into the second triad

suggests that the original narrative had been telescoped to make way for this addition. At one time the narrative probably consisted of a two-character interaction, with three offerings and refusals, followed by the bespelling. What this narrative change represents is a special kind of innovation that would occur at a

Figure 33

Stanzas	Character	Narrative
1	H + S	H + S introduced
2–4	H + S	First gift: offer & refusal
5–7	H + S	Second & third gifts: offer & refusal
8–11	H + S	H bespelled by S
12–13	H + Q	H unspelled by Q

formative stage of the tradition's evolution: a maker introduces a third character into what had been hitherto a two-character form in order to expand the narrative potential of his medium. Although the integration of the third character proved rather awkward in this instance, the other two spell ballads show how the makers did successfully expand the capacities of the form. 'Kemp Owyne' and 'Clerk Colvill' maintain a two-character confrontation at their core, but frame a third character in the first and last scenes. This internal evidence, while far from conclusive, would suggest that the archetypal quatrain ballad of the region contained an interaction of two characters in three steps, dramatically stating and finally resolving a central conflict, and that this archetypal structure expanded, initially to accommodate the active participation of a third character and latterly to accommodate more complex story material.

It would appear, then, that the region's earlier ballad form was the couplet which, on the evidence of 'Gil Brenton', the makers came to employ with assurance and sophistication. They must, however, have chafed at the limitations of two short rhyming lines with alternating refrain as a narrative medium, and welcomed the wider scope afforded them by the quatrain. When the quatrain form arrived, it was used at first for simply structured stories but later, as the makers' confidence in the new form developed, for more complicated material, and eventually it superseded the couplet in popularity. The couplet form, however, did not pass out of use altogether, for it recurs in a ballad dealing with events of the sixteenth and seventeenth centuries, 'The Baron of Brackley'. And, as we have seen, the tendency for stories to retain their individual oral patternings ensured that both couplet and quatrain ballads were transmitted within the same tradition. The introduction of the quatrain and the retention of the couplet provides one kind of illustration of tradition's simultaneous capacity for innovation and conservatism; but the major expressions of this lie in the co-existence of lexical variation, a certain stability in oral patterning, and a firm stability in essential narrative. An awareness of the radical and conservative forces may illuminate, as here, the evolution of a regional tradition, but it may also, perhaps, illuminate the transmission of individual stories.

The unusual balance between stability and innovation in ballad transmission underlines once again the distinctiveness of the artistic medium in which the oral maker operates. The ballad poet has a different sense of aesthetic values, a different poetic sensibility, and a different relationship with his audience from the literate poet. The architectonics of the ballad show that where the literate man thinks in linear terms the nonliterate man thinks in spatial terms; the maker places more emphasis on the spatial relationships of parts to parts within the whole than on the smooth linear continuity of consecutive parts. The ballad poet's attitude to language differs from the literate poet's in two ways. Consider the pair of lines in which Fause Foodrage threatens the queen that if her unborn child turns out to be male,

> '. . . as soon as eer he born is,
> He shall mount the gallows-pin.'   (89A: 13)

Obviously the maker does not intend that we should take literally —a significant word—the ludicrous picture conjured up by these lines; he wants merely to convey an emotive impression of the villain's implacable malevolence. Where the literate poet concerns himself with both denotation and connotation, the oral ballad poet is often concerned more with connotative effect than strict denotative meaning. (If it were found that this trait is representative of the oral mind it could explain many of the difficulties in communication and understanding between people from literate and nonliterate societies.) Secondly, where the literate poet strives for originality of expression, the oral poet is content to use his received traditional diction, and not only for reasons of necessity. Through generations of use traditional language accrues a contextual force; it acquires connotative reverberations unrecognized by the ear untuned to tradition and it becomes the 'right' and 'fitting' language of verbal art.[2] Ballads lack the similes and imagery of written literature, but what they do have, we previously noted, is a kind of symbolic imagery whose roots lie in a now fragmented mythology. The maker draws on this mythology of the traditional community not only for the symbolic imagery but also for motifs and episodes. The narrative and linguistic texture of the ballads, then, expresses the texture of thought and feeling in the oral community; what for us may be a prettily decorative conceit could be to the oral mind an essential element in a narrative. Where literary poems express a personal vision, ballads tell stories that express a community's outlook on life. Where the literate poet writes as an individual who may uphold or attack or ignore his society's mores from his personal vantage point, the oral poet tells stories that embody and give expression to the kinds of belief and feeling shared by his community. He is necessarily integrated within his society as the literate poet is not; the literate poet *may* reinforce his society's ethos, but the oral poet *must*. The oral poet, then, differs from the literate in his creative sensibility and in his relationship with his audience, both in the described sense and in the literal sense of actually having an audience.

The polarities of oral and literate composition provide a starting point from which to approach the ballad's relationship to other poetic genres. The relationship to epic is the most straightforward. 'The ballad poets', W. P. Ker remarked many years ago, 'think in the same manner as the epic poets, and choose by preference the same kind of plot.'[3] The most satisfactory explanation of this correspondence is that both the ballad poets and at least the early epic poets were nonliterate composers working within oral traditions that relied on different forms. Other relationships present a more confused picture. In the medieval verse form nearest to the ballad, the *lai*, are texts which have a number of oral characteristics in their motifs, their structures, and their linguistic patterns, but whether all or some or none were orally composed is a question that could only be answered by an intensive study of the genre in the light of the oral technique. Certainly, comments about the *lais* such as 'they were composed originally to be heard' and 'in treatment they had to be dramatic, allowing the maker partly from memory, partly from improvisation to pass quickly from one climactic scene or episode to the next' would indicate that they share with the ballads at the very least an eventual origin in oral tradition.[4] Many of the Middle English romances, which have stories in common with the ballads, exhibit traits of style which would suggest the same likelihood.[5] One cannot, however, on the strength of the oral characteristics in some texts assume that the genre as a whole is a product of oral composition, because oral habits of thought and expression are often carried over into literate contexts. Until comprehensive criteria are established for a genre it is extremely difficult to determine whether a text with some oral characteristics belongs to the end of an oral tradition or the beginning of a literate tradition. When the polarities of the two methods of composition are fully studied and understood, then the difficulty will abate. Until such time one can say with confidence only that the ballads, the *lais*, and many romances draw much narrative material and certain characteristics of style from oral tradition, but that a more precise delineation of their relationships must await a demarcation of the Border Marches between oral and written literature.[6]

The problems of demarcation are likely to remain problems for some considerable time. The basic difficulty in dealing with oral texts is that they were not meant for writing down, but it is only when they have been written down that we have any record of them; and if they have been written down then the probabilities are that the texts have been in some way affected. Paradoxically, it is only because Mrs Brown did not herself belong to the rural folk but to a social group where writing was an accepted practice that we have any record of her ballad repertoire. The rural folk of Allanaquoich, of course, provided the sources for this repertoire; and in the light of the region's history, it is fitting that this valuable ballad stock should be derived from the border country of the Farquharsons and sung by a woman descended on the one side from the Forbeses and on the other from the Gordons.

Again paradoxically, Mrs Brown was herself literate, though she has given us the best examples of the method of ballad composition evolved by nonliterate people. Her texts must inevitably have been affected to some degree by her literacy, but the degree seems to have been insignificant. Her reading provided her with a wider vocabulary than most makers but this she always subsumed within traditional patterns. A line in 'Fause Foodrage' exemplifies the process. This line—'The boy stared wild like a gray gose-hawke'—roused Scott's suspicion because of its similarity to one in Lady Wardlaw's 'Hardyknute' —'Norse een like gray gosshawk stared wild'—but repeated references earlier in the ballad to the boy as 'my gay gose-hawke' explain the correspondence. The literary line had lodged in her memory, and during composition the common element of the 'g(r)ay gose-hawke' led her by association to adapt that line to the ballad patterns. In like fashion, Mrs Brown will use a number of new, English, rhyming words within an old, predominantly Scots, rhyming sound. Although her vocabulary may be more extensive than that of most composers, she is still thinking and creating traditionally. Ideally, of course, one would like to have available the tape-recorded texts of a nonliterate ballad composer, but rather than 'rax for the meen' we should perhaps rest thankful for what we have. And what we have, the Brown corpus, is the earliest known corpus in British balladry and may well be unique in its clear exemplification of the oral method. By illustrating the workings of tradition, the Brown texts provide a frame of reference, first, for considering the possible orality of other ballad-texts, and second—our next concern—for charting the changes in the local tradition after widespread literacy broke on the Northeast. These texts also enable us to construct definitions of folk and ballad applicable to a nonliterate society such as the Northeast. In this context, a ballad is a narrative song created and re-created by a traditional oral method, and the folk are the nonliterate participants in the traditional process of composition and transmission.

Part III

The Tradition in Transition:
the Folk

Chapter 14

The Revolutions

The eighty years from 1750 to 1830 saw the Northeast undergo a startling transformation. During this time there took place an agrarian revolution, an industrial revolution and, consequent upon these, a social revolution. Society was remodelled, and people's ways of working, thinking, and relaxing all recast. This period saw the disappearance of the old 'medieval' Northeast and the emergence of the modern society.

Although the most intensive changes occurred between 1780 and 1820, 1750 and 1830 mark the commonly accepted outer limits of the revolutionary period. The Union of 1707 had at first adversely affected Scottish economic life, but by the middle of the century Scotland was beginning to enjoy the benefits of commerce with England and the Colonies. By 1750 Scotland had also sustained its last civil war, and the measures following the Forty-Five ensured that a more integrated country could take industrial advantage of political peace and the stolid stability of the Hanoverian regime. By 1830, however, the first wave of technological advance had spent itself, and Scotland settled down to assimilate its effects and maintain a steadier development in the second stage of the industrial revolution.[1]

During this period the region lost its comparative isolation with the development of a much superior system of communications. Sir Archibald Grant, one of the first improvers, complained that in the first decades of the eighteenth century there was 'not one wheel carriage on the esteat; nor indeed any one road that would allow it', and that 'I could not, in chariote, get my wife from Aberdeen to Monymusk'. Conditions by the middle of the century were still bad: 'there was no road in this county on which wheels of any kind could be dragged'.[2] Though the situation had improved previously, the really startling developments came in the years between 1796 and 1810, when 300 miles of turnpike and 1000 miles of commutation roads and highways were constructed in Aberdeenshire. One result of this was easier and quicker communication with the rest of the country, as, for example, by the Aberdeen–Edinburgh coach service begun in 1798. Canals, moreover, enabled goods to be transported from within Aberdeenshire to Aberdeen and by sea and the Forth and Clyde canal to Glasgow. And sea trade was further stimulated by the new harbours and piers built all round the coast under the supervision of Thomas Telford. These better transport systems not only linked the Northeast with the rest of Britain more conveniently than ever before but also opened up those communities in the region which had formerly been isolated for much of the year, thus intensifying their exposure to new influences.[3]

The agrarian revolution did not proceed at a uniform pace throughout Scotland, or the Northeast, or even throughout individual estates. Some heritors, such as Sir Archibald Grant, introduced reforms in the first half of the century; others, through conservatism or lack of capital, waited until the last decades of the century when the advantages of the innovations had been conclusively proved. In general, the highland districts reacted more conservatively to the improving ideas than the lowland and so their cultures were less quickly affected.[4]

As the improvements altered not only the economy but also the social patterns of the area, it is necessary to consider them in a little detail. The two seminal innovations were the introduction of that revolutionary vegetable, the turnip, and of sown grasses. An Aberdeenshire tenant-farmer records their impact in his diary under the year 1771:[5]

> But this year gave birth to a work far superior in its
> consequences to this part of the country and likely to be
> of far greater value. Patrick Murray, son of Alex. A.
> Murray, farmer in Slap, built a new town this year
> called New Slap and was the first in this place that
> sowed field turnips and laid down grass. All the neigh-
> bourhood followed his example and I may say with
> safety that it is in a great measure owing to this

improvement in method that these parts have arrived
at such a pitch of opulence as they have now done.

The introduction of turnips gave a powerful impetus to the
stock-rearing industry. Previously, cattle had been killed and
salted at Martinmas or allowed to forage for themselves during
the winter months. When spring came, the remaining beasts
had often been too enfeebled to stand upright, but now the
farmer could maintain them in decent condition with the new
fodder. And after the Forty-Five, he had no fear of losing them
to a spulzie of the caterans. The cattle trade also expanded
because members of families once politically rather than com-
mercially oriented began to interest themselves in it. One such
trader was Patrick Ogilvie, brother of Lord Seafield, Chancellor
of Scotland at the time of the Union. When Seafield expostulated
with his brother over this ignoble trafficking, Ogilvie caustically
rejoined, 'Better sell nowte than sell nations'.[6]

To preserve the new crops, however, the increased numbers
of cattle could not be allowed to wander at will, as they previously
had at all times except the growing season. And so came the
next important stage of the reforms: the enclosing of land by
dykes and fences. Within these enclosed fields, the improvers
could now take advantage of the new crops' capacities for
enriching and cleansing the soil, and institute a regular beneficial
rotation of crops. Enclosing set off further activity: the stones
were cleared from between the old rigs to make dykes for the
fields or new forestry plantations; draining ditches were dug
alongside the dykes; marshes were reclaimed and waste-land
brought under cultivation. The net effect of these changes was
to abolish the co-operative run-rig system which had been in
operation for hundreds of years and which, as we saw earlier,
was a crucial factor in maintaining the region's communal
culture.[7]

The improvements stimulated agricultural technology. Grant's
imported overseer complained bitterly on his arrival that[8]

> should we in England labour our land though the best
> of it after such a careless maner and with such instrew-
> ments wee should get nothing but weeds. Indeed they
> have no instrewments to doe it with, and are fully
> persuaded in them selves that there is no better than

> what they have nor no better way of making use of
> them then what thay practise of which and such-like
> errours I hope to be able to convinse them.

But by the nineteenth century the 'instrewments' had altered
out of all recognition. The scythe replaced the sickle, the
threshing-machine the flail, iron harrows the wooden, and the
cart the currachs—the wicker-work creels slung on either side
of a horse. Most important of all, the two-horse swing-plough
superseded the old clumsy plough, which required an unwieldy
team of ten to twelve oxen and as many as four men to work
it. One of these men was the gaudsman, whose task it was to
encourage the team by whistling, often psalm tunes, or by
prodding with a sharp stick. In Banffshire, the work group
expanded further: 'I have heard it whispered that in the Highlands of our country a proper "plowman" would not drive his
team afield without a piper to play in addition to the more
ordinary "gaudsman".'[9] These leisurely practices soon disappeared when scrutinized by improvers now zealously pursuing
the economical and the efficient. The rural people, understandably, did not take too kindly to the abolition of old practices
and the introduction of new, and heritors had to work hard
'to convinse them'.

The improving movement in agriculture began with a few
enlightened heritors. They exchanged information and discussed
new ideas through agricultural societies, such as the Scottish
'Honourable Society of Improvers in the Knowledge of Agriculture' or the 'Society of Farmers in Buchan'. As the passion
for experiment spread, university professors joined in. The
Gordon's Mill Farming Club, which operated from 1758 to 1764,
numbered fifteen members, six of whom were on the staff at
King's College.[10] Of these six, the 'most outstanding' was the
Club Secretary, Thomas Gordon, Professor of Humanity and
father of Anna Gordon, Mrs Brown of Falkland. It is retro-
spectively rather ironic that just as Anna Gordon was learning
her ballads, Thomas Gordon was directing his efforts to trans-
forming the conditions from which the old ballads sprang. As
the innovations proved increasingly successful, more and more
heritors and prosperous large farmers instituted the reforms,
until by the end of the century 'the real problem was not what

should be done, but how the tenants were to be encouraged to do it'.[11]

In the *Old Statistical Account* the minister for Auchindoir lists a number of obstacles to the swift prosecution of improvements, including lack of capital, inadequate transport facilities, deficient leases, and the retention of feudal services, but heads the list with this comment: '1st, It requires a considerable time to draw men from long confirmed habits.' Grant found that his schemes were hampered by his tenants' unwillingness to abandon the inherited methods and inability to grasp the need for the improvements. Among the tenants' transgressions he notes 'Makeing roads through inclosures & cutting timber & young planting, especially birtch; have no sence of ye crime, even of concealing.' How little some tenants understood the purpose of enclosing is exemplified by the crime of Alexander Downey who 'took stones from Inver dyke to build his dyke'. Unsurprisingly, Grant laments that 'Such of you as are diligent misapply it and won't take advice from those who know better, nor will you follow good example when you see it has good effects, but will keep straitly to the old way.'[12]

Heritors tried various means to encourage their tenant-farmers.[13] When Lord Deskford found his farmers letting their cattle browse in the young plantations, he changed their attitudes by a move which affected their own economic interest: he allowed them at the end of their lease to take, or receive the value of, every third tree planted during that lease. Joseph Cumine of Auchry frequently travelled among his estate tenants 'rousing them to industry by motives suited to their respective tempers', but exhortation alone was not enough:

> He also keeps meeting with his own farmers, entertains them with a glass of the produce of the country in a publick house. All who do not improve are debarred, and go by the name of DRONES. There is a book kept of all improvements worth while, particularly what lime or limestone each has carried, and they are commended accordingly. This excites emulation.[14]

And in the Mearns the Quaker improver, Robert Barclay of Ury, included among his methods of encouragement physical chastisement. Gradually the heritors' efforts, together with better communications and leases, more capital, the abolition of feudal services, and the effects of the bad winters in 1782 and 1783, convinced an increasing number of the tenant-farmers to take up the new ways.

The methods their forefathers had pursued for four hundred years the tenants balked at discarding overnight. But they were not merely being obstinately conservative. They were motivated not so much by a reactionary distrust of newfangled agricultural methods as by a natural reluctance to give up the way of life predicated on the old methods and which, they rightly sensed, would be for ever disrupted by the new improvements. Understandably, they had a psychological blockage: 'They FEEL on many occasions insurmountable difficulties where superficial observers cannot perceive any.'[15] And yet, within a few decades, they had surmounted these psychological difficulties and accepted in positive fashion the dual inevitabilities of agrarian progress and social upheaval. By 1811, Skene Keith divides the farmers into three groups: the old-fashioned farmers, the imported Lothians farmers, and

> the more numerous one of younger farmers, or of men not beyond the middle of life, who have contracted the greatest zeal for agriculture, attend the meetings of agricultural societies, and both endeavour to understand the principles, and pay great attention to the practice of agriculture. . . . Many of them have also a spirit of enterprize, which is not possessed by their neighbours, who have come from the southern counties. Hence the greatest and most expensive improvements have been effected by the better sort of the native farmers, who have spared neither money nor labour. Many of these, who are desirous to excel in agricultural knowledge, read what books they can get on Husbandry, and The Farmer's Magazine, (a most useful periodical performance) is held by them in very general esteem.

These men represented the new breed of professional farmer that emerged in response to the changing conditions. As enclosing, to be economically viable, had to be done on a sufficient scale, all the improved farms were enlarged farms, and required considerable financial outlay, both for rents and the improvements.

182

The professional farmers were the men who had the capital—perhaps earned in previous tenancies or gained through the system of cash credits instituted by the Scottish banks—and the advanced knowledge necessary to run these enlarged farms.[16] As far as the tenant-farmers were concerned, the nettle of progress had been grasped. Where initially they had reacted negatively to the reforms now they actively prosecuted them, accepting the inevitable changes in their way of life and culture. The difficulties that before they 'felt', they felt no longer. They adopted new ways of thinking, and underwent what might be called a psychological revolution.

Evidence of the transformation is provided by the activities of the Farmers' Societies which sprang up at the end of the century. These were not normally composed of heritors like the earlier Agricultural Societies but of tenant-farmers, who took the initiative in prosecuting diverse kinds of improvements. One, the Buchan and Boyne Farming Society, built a large granary near Macduff harbour, but the general aims of a society were more likely to be those expressed by the Farmer Society of Deer, which were to help 'the improvement of agriculture and the relief of the distressed'. This society held quarterly meetings with essays and discussions on agricultural problems, corresponded with like societies, and bought treatises on farming for general use.[17] In Kincardineshire and Banffshire no fewer than four Farmer Friendly Societies pursued the second aim of the Deer Society: the support through a fund of farmers' widows and children.[18] How far societies extended their social reference can be seen from the rules and purposes of the Banffshire Farming Society, formed in 1785. Its aims were:[19]

> To introduce proper regards for carrying friendship and
> social virtue into better practice: to form regulations of
> conduct that might promote good plans of agriculture
> . . . to produce unanimity and social intercourse between
> the proprietors and farmers, . . . to have under their
> consideration the necessary regulations for the police of
> the country, fixing servants' fees, bringing vagrants to
> justice, and as far as possible to prevent litigous pleas
> arising among country people . . . and keeping by the
> rules established. . . .

These rules stipulated that

> the society resolve to discourage all NOCTURNAL MEETINGS
> upon pretence of RAFFLING and PLAYING CARDS, as well
> as house-holders who entertain such diversions, and to do what
> is in their power to suppress such evil practice, which
> often has a tendency not only to debouch the morals of
> the servants, throwing them into scrapes with recruiting
> parties, but to occasion also neglect of duty to their
> masters, as well as improper uses made of the horses under
> their care at untimely hours.

The tenant-farmers had taken not only an initiative in the improvements, but also responsibility for attendant social effects. But however new the situation, their response traced an old pattern, for the societies, in their concern for 'friendship and social virtue' and propensity for group activity, reflect the habits of *vicinitas* and communal co-operation of the old culture. For centuries, within a social structure dominated by the heritors, the tenant-farmers had unthinkingly followed the agricultural methods prescribed by custom. At first slow to accept the need for change, they latterly responded with energy and vision to the demands of the new working world of capital and machine technology. In doing so, they helped destroy the fabric of the old life, but none the less managed to retain something of that life's virtues.

We have seen how the improving ideas spread from the heritors to the tenant-farmers. How, then, did the improvements affect the others in the old fermtoun community? While some tenants rose to professional farmers, others—the lesser tenants, sub-tenants, cottars and grassmen—descended in the new social scale.

The enclosure of land, involving as it did the rearrangement of holdings into enlarged farms run by skilled professionals, marked the end of the co-operative runrig system. Enclosing had two important social effects: it displaced some tenants and most sub-tenants and grassmen; and it created the need for a large pool of casual labour. Grant's solution to these problems was quite straightforward. He resettled the displaced families in 'braetouns', where each was allowed to reclaim and work a small tract of land, and these men provided the labouring force, paid generally on a piece basis, for the new improvements. By the turn of the century, however, solutions were more diverse. Some sub-tenants leased reclaimable land and became independent crofters; some moved to cottouns or braetouns and worked as day labourers; others were converted to hired servants who lodged in the farmer's bothies and chaumers. By 1812 the great bulk of the Northeast's agricultural workforce consisted of unmarried farm servants who fell into the last category. In general, the agricultural reforms did away with the sub-tenant and substituted in his stead the farm labourer.[20]

The reorganization of the land produced a comparable reorganization of rural society. Gone was the group township with its close-knit community of joint-tenants and sub-tenants, corporately working the toun lands. Now there were the enlarged farms, the farms in varying stages of improvement, and the small crofts. On the enlarged farms the farmers employed on a financial basis servants who lived in cottouns or bothies, and these men, the professional farmer and the agricultural labourer, represent the two extremes of the new social range. In between were the tenants of the farms in the process of improvement, amongst whom considerable variation in economic and social status existed, and the independent crofters. In short, the improvements produced a large-scale increase in social differentiation.

When the fermtoun's close community disnitegrated, some tenants had moved up the social scale to the status of professional farmers or factors, others had moved down to labourers. Strains now appeared in a relationship that was not based on a community of interest. When the Revolutionary Wars sent wages soaring, farmers complained frequently that agricultural labourers now regarded themselves as a privileged class:[21]

> They feel, from experience, that, in point of ease, comfort, and independence, the condition of servants is more eligible than that of their masters. The short term of engagement, wages immoderately high, inspire them with pride, insolence and indifference, that would frequently require a meek and patient spirit to brook. Nice in the choice of their food to squeamishness, it must neither fall short, nor exceed that exact proportion of cookery,

which their appetites can relish. Care too must be taken, that no offence shall be offered them. They must sleep in the morning as long and go to bed at night as soon, as their pleasure dictates. Expostulations are opposed by rudeness. If their behaviour is disagreeable, their masters are at liberty to provide themselves with others, against the first term. And seldom do they fail to give scope for this liberty. When the term arrives, then, like birds of passage, they change their residence, or migrate to distant countries.

Conversely, the attitude of the farm servant to the farmer became very much that of a wage-earner to an employer or overseer, and may be exemplified by the sardonic reply of Jamie Fleeman, the 'Laird o' Udny's Feel', when his master wondered what crops to sow in a particular field: 'Saw it wi factors, laird, they aye thrive.' Tensions were appearing in society, but they were no longer political tensions that affected the region as a whole; they were tensions between employer and employee, between the 'haves' and the 'have nots', between people on various rungs of a society that was rapidly extending its degrees of differentiation.

During this period the processes of social change were hastened and intensified by a large-scale increase in population. While, however, the total population of Aberdeenshire grew rapidly, the agricultural population declined: between 1801 and 1841 the numbers of those who lived by the land fell by more than one-third from 38,610 to 25,224. The general increase, together with the unsettling effects of the improvements, produced extensive shifts in population, all of which contributed to the disruption of old ties, communities, and ways of living. The displaced rural worker had three options open to him: he could stay on the land, though this might entail moving to another parish with greater demand for labour; he could emigrate to America and the colonies; and he could migrate to a city, town, or new planned village and there become an industrial worker.[22]

The industrial revolution directly influenced the rural North-east mainly through the expansion of the textile industries, especially the woollen and linen. Until the early nineteenth century these were essentially domestic rural industries, being intimately bound up with agriculture, and as such helped stabilize society in this period of unsettlement.

Once famous for its export trade in fingrams and plaidings, the Northeast turned after 1750 to the manufacture of woollen stockings.[23] These soon achieved a comparable reputation through their hard-wearing qualities and the persuasive powers of the 'Sawnys' portrayed by Fergusson:

> Here Sawny cries, frae Aberdeen,
>   'Come ye to me fa need:
> 'The brawest shanks that e'er were seen
>   'I'll sell ye cheap and guid,
> 'I wyt they are as protty hose
>   'As come frae weyr or leem;
> 'Here tak a rug and shaw's your pose.'[24]

The wool for these stockings was generally imported from the south of Scotland or England by Aberdeen merchants, combed in the city, then sent out by pedlars to the women in the rural districts every four weeks. When the pedlars gave out the new wool on 'Factory Days' they also took in the completed stockings which were then sold by the merchants. Country women, of all ages, provided the bulk of the industry's knitters. They seized every opportunity to prosecute their task, whether on the move— '[they] were to be seen everywhere, walking from place to place busily employed knitting, for which they gave up all other employments'—or at rest: 'the small farmer or cottager's wife, or daughter, could attend to her cow, while pasturing on the BAULKS, . . . and could at the same time enjoy pure air, and carry on the knitting of her stockings'.[25] Boys, and even men, also engaged in this work. In fact, many crofter families who subsisted on the produce of their own land were able to pay their rents only by the knitting, while in the infertile upland districts, it was this alone that paid for the corn or meal that had to be bought from the Lowlands. After 1795, however, the industry declined sharply though it was still carried on in certain remote parishes for some decades of the next century.

The other important textile industry, the manufacture of linen, was also a domestic industry closely connected with agriculture.[26] Flax was raised along with the other crops, mainly by the smaller farmers and crofters. Besides their normal

187

agricultural work these farmers and their womenfolk grew and spun, and even wove and bleached the linen cloth. Spinning was normally done by the women since they could take it up and put it down as the dictates of housework and the agricultural seasons allowed. Weaving was generally the province of men, and as it required considerable skill, there was a tendency for it to become a full-time occupation. Two kinds of weaver developed, the independent 'custom weaver' and the weaver employed by a manufacturer, either at home or, at a later date, in a factory. Some, like William Thom the Inverurie poet-weaver, were a bit of both, as he explains in a letter to Gordon of Knockespock:[27]

> 'MEANS OF LIVING'.—employed seven or eight months yearly in customary weaving.—that is, a country weaver who wants a journeyman sends for me. I assist in making bedding, shirting, and other household stuffs. When his customers are served, I am discharged, and so ends the SEASON. During that time I earn from ten to twelve shillings a week, pay the master generally four shillings for my 'keep', and remit the rest to my family. . . . I eke out the blank portion of the season by going into a factory. Here the young and vigorous only can exceed six shillings weekly. This alone is my period of privation; however it is wonderful how nicely we get on.

Gradually the manufacture of linen decayed as a rural industry: the growing of flax declined because it impeded the other agricultural improvements; and once Kay's spinning machine was widely utilized, spinning became concentrated in the towns. Finally, weaving went the same way. By the fourth decade of the nineteenth century the switchover from domestic to factory employment had taken place.

These rural industries had, by and large, expanded from 1750 to 1800 and contracted from 1800 to 1830. During their heyday, many heritors, particularly in Buchan, founded planned villages —one rather hopefully designated New Leeds—whose inhabitants were to be engaged in textile manufacturing. When the industries atrophied, some of these villages atrophied too, but others maintained their position as rural service centres. By this time workers displaced from the land moved to the factories of Aberdeen and the rapidly expanding rural towns: Huntly,

Peterhead and Banff. And so the simple settlement pattern of burghs and fermtouns was superseded by the more complicated one of city, towns, villages, single farmsteads, and crofts.[28] The diversification of the settlement pattern reflects the changes in social organization. Just as the touns had given way to a number of enlarged farms and many small crofts, so the integrated community of the fermtoun had been split up into a few farmers with capital and a large class of agricultural labourers. With the disappearance of group cultivation went the disappearance of the group settlement unit, which was central to the conditions that nurtured the communal culture. The old picture of the Northeast as a separate well-defined region with the bulk of the population living in self-contained independent fermtouns no longer holds good. The agrarian and industrial revolutions had broken up the old communities and opened up the region. They had effectively destroyed the old integrated society with the communal conditions in which the old culture thrived. In this new society communal co-operation was replaced by social tension and modern competitive individualism.

Chapter 15

The New Society

While the revolutions destroyed the communal elements in the Northeast's culture, their concomitant effects destroyed its oral character. During the transitional period rural society moved from a state of general nonliteracy to a state of general literacy. Obviously we are dealing here not with absolutes but relative proportions of society, which is just as well, for there still exists considerable variation in ideas on what is meant by literacy and how it should be measured.[1] By literacy I mean—and this is not so simpleminded as it sounds—the ability both to read and to write.

The most significant guide to levels of literacy is the existence or nonexistence of schools. In the Scottish context, however, some caution is necessary in using this guide. After the Reformation Knox stipulated that every parish in Scotland should have a school and a schoolmaster, and many generations of after-dinner speakers expatiating on the glories of Scottish education took the stipulation for the deed. Unfortunately for national self-esteem the duty of building the schools and paying the schoolmasters fell on the heritors who, canny men, were reluctant to fulfil such idealistic expectations.[2] In Aberdeenshire by the middle of the seventeenth century, only twenty-eight of the eighty-three parishes are reckoned to have possessed, at some time or another and for however short a period, a parish school.[3] Throughout the seventeenth century the legislation concerning schools and schoolmasters had to be re-enacted, and it was only after the 1696 Act that progress began to be made in Scotland generally. By the end of the eighteenth century, however, every Aberdeenshire parish or united parish had its school, and the prevailing nonliteracy of the previous century was a thing of the past.[4]

At some point in the eighteenth century, the region changed from being predominantly nonliterate to being predominantly literate. Though this changeover, like the agrarian revolution, was probably an irregular process, varying in degree and speed from district to district, the evidence points to its major phase occurring in the Northeast in the second rather than first half of the century. First, the drive for parochial schools initially came from the Presbyterian Kirk, for whom learning to read— with the Bible and Shorter Catechism as textbooks—was a means to the greater spiritual good. The Northeast, however, was a predominantly Episcopalian region until the Jacobite rebellions of 1715 and 1745 made Presbyterianism more politic, and the Episcopalian pastors did not respond favourably to the exhortations of the Presbyterian Kirk.[5] Second, there is a definite Europe-wide correlation between growth of schools and economic expansion and revolutionary social change;[6] these factors, we have just seen, did not obtain in the Northeast until the second half of the century. Third, there is the rapid growth of popular literature, the chapbooks and broadsheets, aimed at the new mass market. The chap industry would have little market before general literacy, but could be counted on to expand greatly when a suitably literate mass market did come into being. This expansion took place towards the end of the century's third quarter, for in the Northeast, as in Scotland generally, the heyday of chap production occurred between 1780 and 1830.[7] The indications, then, point to the arrival of widespread literacy in the northeast only in the second half of the eighteenth century.

It should be emphasized, however, that the literacy achieved by many northeasterners was of a fairly minimal kind, for the quality of education dispensed by many schools in the eighteenth and early nineteenth centuries did not reach a very high standard. There were a number of reasons for this.[8] School premises were often ramshackle and schoolmasters poorly paid. Consequently teachers were difficult to get and of varying abilities; often a teacher's departure was followed by a gap of months before a replacement came. Because of agricultural work and the topography of some parishes, pupils' attendance was intermittent. The two most important subjects, taught to every child, were religious instruction and reading, but as a separate fee was charged for writing, not everyone learned to write. This was especially true of girls, as many fathers thought they would only waste the skill in penning love-letters; and in general, parents justified their refusal to spend the extra fee for writing by quoting a Northeast proverbial phrase: 'Mony ane's deen ill wi vreet' (many a person has done harm through writing).

It was not until the middle of the nineteenth century that both the conditions and the substance of rural education improved considerably. Only then did the schools generally adopt the 'intellectual method', by which pupils were encouraged actually to understand what they read.[9] Previously learning had consisted almost entirely of rote memorization of passages from the Bible and the Shorter Catechism; and a teacher who introduced the modern method was liable to complaints from parents 'for bothering their children by trying to make them understand the meanings of words and the substance of what they read'. Education took long 'to free itself from a belief in the peculiar virtue of the printed word—especially the sacred word—and to realize that words are mere symbols without intrinsic value'.[10] This attitude to the printed word is not uncommon in newly literate societies, and neither is the state of mind it denotes. In his investigation of the ancient Greek culture's changeover from oral to literate, Havelock shows how Plato's attack on poetry, which has embarrassed so many commentators, is an attack on the oral state of mind, as it was epitomized by the practitioners of the (oral) poetry of his day:[11]

> . . . there was a state of mind which we shall conveniently
> label the 'poetic' or 'Homeric' or 'oral' state of mind
> which constituted the chief obstacle to scientific rationalism,
> to the use of analysis, to the classification of experience,
> to its rearrangement in sequence of cause and effect.
> This is why the poetic state of mind is for Plato the
> arch-enemy and it is easy to see why he considered this
> enemy so formidable. . . . *He asks of men . . . that they*
> *should think about what they say, instead of just saying it.*
> And they should separate themselves from it instead of
> identifying with it; they themselves should become the
> 'subject' who stands out from the 'object' and reconsiders
> it and analyses it and evaluates it, instead of just
> 'imitating' it. [italics added]

Obviously the practical skill of literacy does not immediately and automatically bring with it all the fully literate habits of mind. If educational methods are any guide, the oral state of mind took some time a-dying in the Northeast.

The general spread of education helped channel the energies of the people in new directions. The Senecan motto adopted by the Banff Literary Society—*Otium sine Literis Mors Est*—typifies the change, for by the early years of the nineteenth century reading had become a widespread habit. As one would expect, this is most evident in the towns. Not only Aberdeen but even the small towns such as Banff, Peterhead, Huntly and Stonehaven possessed Reading Societies, circulating libraries, booksellers and reading-rooms.[12] But the rural districts did not lag far behind. In the early nineteenth century parishes began to set up local libraries, and the frequent references to them in the *New Statistical Account* would suggest that by the eighteen-forties these parish libraries were established throughout the region. Fiction, however, rarely appeared among their stock, the staple reading being volumes on religion, travel, history and science.[13] The most striking aspect of the countryside's new reading habit was the way in which the farmers turned it to practical account. Because the increasing complexity of agriculture necessitated better communication of ideas as well as materials, many books and pamphlets were written on agricultural subjects, and these the farmers devoured:

> There is an agricultural library in the parish of Grange, of which the farmers in the neighbouring parishes have the convenience. Cheap publications, such as Lord Kaimes's Gentleman Farmer, several of the surveys of the Board of Agriculture, the Farmer's Magazine, and tracts on livestock are everywhere read in the houses of the farmers in Banffshire.[14]

With their recently acquired reading skills, the farmers had set up a new form of leisure activity, respectable in its usefulness.

Not all the available reading material achieved the respectability of the *Farmer's Magazine*. Skene Keith remarks that 'Of the two kinds of knowledge, viz. agricultural libraries, and cheap publications, we do not feel any want' but adds that the latter publications 'are not always the most proper'.[15] These cheap publications were the chapbooks which included a wide variety of productions: 'broadsides of all kinds; humorous sketches, sacred and profane; political and sectarian squibs; histories romantic and narrative; jest-books and manuals of instruction in dancing, cookery, charms and the interpretation of dreams.'[16] The chapbooks were eventually supplanted by the newspapers, though because of the newspapers' relatively high cost, some time elapsed before they attained a wide rural audience. It was the practice of some farmers to form a small consortium where they clubbed together for a newspaper and gathered in a farmhouse on the night of its arrival, when it was read aloud by one member with great solemnity from the first to the last page.[17]

Though important, reading was not the only new means of spending leisure time. The dancing master appeared in some rural lowland parishes and found in the winters many willing pupils. The dances he taught were probably the Country Dances, which originated in England.[18] In a few parishes farmers could attend evening classes on agriculture and land-surveying.[19] Many reports in the *Old Statistical Account* note what on the face of it would mark a further retreat from the old ways: a sharp falling-off in the trade done by alehouses. Many of these accounts, however, may owe more to the ministers' desire to advertise moral improvements in their flock than to any spontaneous turning to temperance.[20] At all events, the people were now spending in new ways much of the leisure time that would formerly have been passed in the song and story of convivial gatherings. The business of agriculture now took up time formerly devoted to more genial social pursuits, through the activities of the societies, the evening classes, and the reading the farmer put in on the subject. In the leisure time beyond that, the farmer could indulge in other reading, informative or entertaining, and in 'modern' dancing. The patterns of leisure as well as of labour were irretrievably altering.

The revolutions also raised considerably the general standard of living. Before the improvements the farmer engaged in subsistence farming was, together with his family, at the mercy of the climate, and in the seventeenth and early eighteenth centuries he suffered many years of scarcity and some years of great distress. The most devastating time was the seven 'Ill

Years' at the end of the seventeenth century; the minister of Montquhitter recounts what happened in the parish:[21]

> One Thompson, wadsetter of Hairmoss, driven from his
> home by want, was found dead, near the shore, with a
> piece of raw flesh in his mouth. Of 16 families that
> resided on the farm of Littertie, 13 were extinguished.
> On the estate of Greens, which presently accommodates
> 169 individuals, 3 families (the proprietor's included)
> only survived. The extensive farms of Touchar, Greenness,
> Overhill, and Burnside of Idoch, now containing more
> than 100 souls, together with some farms on the parish
> of Turiff, being entirely desolated, were converted into
> a sheep-walk by the Errol family, to whom they then
> belonged. The inhabitants of the parish in general were
> diminished by death to one half, or as some affirm, to
> one fourth of the preceding number. When the means of
> saving the living and of burying the dead began to fail,
> natural affection was in a great measure suspended. A
> fellow, George Allan, having carried his deceased father
> upon his back, half way from his home to the church-
> yard, threw down the corpse at the door of a farmer,
> with these words: 'I can carry my father no further.
> For God's sake bury his body: But if you chuse not to
> take that trouble, you may place it, if you please, on the
> dyke of your kail-yard, as a guard against the sheep!'

The worst winters after the seven lean years were those of 1782 and 1783. An Aberdeenshire farmer wrote in his diary how in one storm that lasted four days no beast could stand outside, and how a man kept his cattle alive with the thatch from a new roof, and a woman preserved a cow and a quey for three days on her bed-straw. The storms were succeeded by a severe frost in the first week of October:

> It was a mortifying sight that morning to see the corn
> half shot lying flat and green as at Lammas. At the same
> time, white with frost, the pease was as if a tide of the
> sea had gone over them and the potato shaws against
> 12 o'clock were as bleak as moss.[22]

These years, however, bad as they were, saw very few perish

from hunger; a number of parish accounts record that, despite
the great scarcity and in contrast to the Seven Dear Years,
no one actually died of want.[23] Once improved communications
had opened up the country, measures could be taken to alleviate
distress: heritors imported meal, Kirk Sessions doled out their
funds, and the Government provided supplies. The revolutions
ensured that the farmer no longer faced the yearly possibility of
starvation if the crops failed.

The improvements not only removed the old spectre of
famine but also enhanced the quality of the day to day living,
particularly in the areas of food and housing. Though prices rose
in this period, wages rose a good deal faster, and throughout the
Old Statistical Account ministers compare the old and new
styles of living, especially in diet and dress.[24] Perhaps the greatest
change regarding food was that there was now plenty of it,
however deficient in variety. Little meat was eaten in the
country, the staple diet being oatmeal, served in a number of
ways. The northeast farmer lived up to his reputation for
canniness in his serving of one of these oatmeal preparations,
sowens: 'From its slight degree of acidity, it is used as a dinner
dish, as it prevents the servants from being thirsty.'[25] The oatmeal diet, however, was supplemented by the most important
culinary innovation of the period—the potato. In Kincardineshire they were 'at first such a rare production, as to be reckoned
equally precious with apples and pears, and were distributed on
holydays with the same sparing hand', though elsewhere they
were used as livestock fodder, a function served in Kincardineshire, rather exotically, by yams. Beneficial though it was, the
new crop's widespread acceptance stirred doubts and misgivings:
in Tyrie, the prevalence of rheumatism was 'much attributed
to the disuse of wearing flannel next the skin, and the too great
use of potatoes'.[26] Tobacco and especially tea gained rapid
popularity, though condemned by some ministers as species of
inebriation.[27] In dress, a 'taste for finery' pervaded all ranks,
so that it became difficult 'to distinguish the man from the
master, and still more so, the maid servant from the mistress'.
The minister for Ordiquhill declares that whereas thirty years
previously there had been only three hats and three watches
in the parish, belonging to the proprietor, the minister and the
schoolmaster, 'now almost every labouring servant has his hat,

and watch, his English cloth coat, his white thread stockings, &c.'[28]

The dwellings of the farmers and farm servants also underwent considerable change. For much of the eighteenth century, houses had been built of turf and thatched with straw, and divided into two rooms, the but and the ben, which were separated by box-beds and, perhaps, chests. Their comfort may be gauged from the reply by a farm labourer to a minister who rebuked him for sleeping in church: 'I canna sleep at hame for the rattons and the sklaters.' After the improvements, the use of stone for building gradually became standard. On the enlarged farms, where stone was commonly employed, the steadings were laid out in a new design, with bothies and chaumers, according to the more modern social structure. With the growing use of stone and mortar came the tendency to employ a mason; previously most tenants had built their houses themselves.[29] The time was fast passing when every man 'was his own artisan', for just as society itself was moving towards stratification, labour was moving towards specialization.

The professions of medicine and law, hitherto practised largely in the towns, now began to have an influence on rural living. The beneficial effects of modern medicine were felt particularly after the introduction of inoculation, which sharply reduced the incidence of smallpox. Again, however, old ideas died hard. Despite the fact that medical attention to the poor was sometimes given free, many people, and especially the fishers, would refuse inoculation on the grounds that it was tempting God to bring on a disease of their own accord when they could conceivably have avoided it.[30] On the other hand, many more people than formerly made willing recourse to law. In a series of 1807 'Family Necessities' is listed: '6th Law. This is thought to be a dear commodity, but it is not scarce. The preservation of rights, and the keeping of the people in good neighbourhood with each other, will not cost less than 4000 L.' In one parish a spirit of litigation had been introduced by strangers, 'dignified with the name of gentlemen, but as much entitled to that character as a Russian bear':

Now, at 2 annual fairs held at the village of Tammtoul,
one may see the law-fed vampers walking in consequential

197

> state, attended by their clients, while words sweet as
> honey from their lips distil. But this honey, in the issue,
> never fails to change into gall, to some one or other of
> the contending parties.

The writer goes on to say that doctors were seldom called to the
parish because of its healthy situation, which was fortunate, as
the people could 'ill afford to pay doctors and retainers of the
law at the same time'. In another parish, whereas the dozen
years before 1778 had seen all disputes bar one settled by
arbitration, the years after that date were marked by frequent
lawsuits.[31] Increasing exposure to the law helped alter the fabric
of life in the rural districts. Belief in the law and the legal
profession, that institution of a literate society which, even more
than most, relies heavily on the official word in the written
document, supplanted belief in community arbitration, and in
general eroded belief in the principles of good neighbourhood
which had animated the communal culture.

The revolutions destroyed the social patterns that had existed
in the Northeast for the four hundred years before 1750. In the
eighty years of the transitional period the region transformed
itself into a modern society; it was no longer a nonliterate
homogeneous agricultural society situated in a border region
abounding with feuds and wars. The revolutions altered the
patterns of labour, of leisure, and of day to day living, and put
an end to the communal culture. What the minister of Kirkmichael says of his upland parish applies to the region as a
whole:[32]

> The character of a people never fails to change with their
> changing situation. In contemplating them at the extreme
> points of a period of 70 or 80 years, it would be as
> difficult to recognise their identity, as that of Sir John
> Cutler's worsted stockings, when scarcely an atom of
> their original texture remained. . . . The spirit of
> commerce which, in a certain degree has pervaded every
> corner of the Highlands, . . . has penetrated hither. In
> the private views of the individual, the interests of the
> community are disregarded.

The individual was now a separate unit in society rather than a
joint member of a community, and society itself had evolved

from a simple and relatively homogeneous structure into a more complex and diversified organization. Economic developments produced increased economic differentiation, which in turn brought about increased social mobility and differentiation. The idea of class distinction took firm root, and society's tensions, formerly political, were now social tensions arising from disparities in economic and class status. In brief, the old communal homogeneity gave way to social differentiation and modern competitive individualism.

As was inevitable, the attainment of widespread literacy altered substantially the old oral culture. First, it changed the modes of thought, and consequently slackened people's adherence to traditional belief and custom. Second, it reduced the importance of the oral community's arts and entertainments—proverbs, riddling sessions, tale-telling; the once significant functions fulfilled by these in a nonliterate society were largely usurped by the sophisticated alternatives of literate society. Third, when the verbal artefacts of these arts and entertainments—such as ballads—were carried over to the new culture, literacy ensured that they differed in kind. For literacy both removed the *raison d'être* of oral composition and exposed people to new literary modes and criteria, new kinds of language, and a new method of composition. The results for balladry will be examined in more detail in the next chapters.

William Thom, the poet-weaver, has left a fascinating picture of how some of the habits of the old culture were transformed by an urban industrial environment.[33] Thom and his work-mates led a grim life in the weaving factory where 'the distinctive character of all sank away. Man became less manly. Women unlovely and rude' and where weaving for him 'became at length an evendown waste of life—a mere permission to breathe'. In this depressing existence poetry and song still played a part: 'On a summer's day they'd forsake their labour, and would congregate in the Garden of Gordon's Hospital, talk and read Scott, Byron, Moore.' But more important than the poems were the songs, for the love of song was bred in the bone:

Nearer and dearer to hearts like ours was the Ettrick
Shepherd, then in his full tide of song and story; but
nearer and dearer still than he, or any living songster—

to us dearer—was our ill-fated fellow-craftsman, Tannahill, who had just then taken himself from a neglecting world, while yet that world waxed mellow in his lay. Poor weaver chiel! What we owe to thee! Your 'Braes o' Balquhidder', and 'Yon Burnside', and 'Glooming Winter', and the 'Minstrel's' wailing ditty, and the noble 'Gleniffer'. Oh! how they did ring above the rattling of a hundred shuttles! Let me again proclaim the debt we owe those Song Spirits, as they walked in melody from loom to loom, ministering to the low-hearted; and when the breast was filled with everything but hope and happiness, and all but seared, let only break forth the healthy and vigorous chorus 'A man's a man for a' that', the fagged weaver brightens up. His very shuttle SKYTES boldly along, and clatters through in faithful time to the tune of his merrier shopmates!

Who dare measure in doubt the restraining influences of these very Songs? To us they were all instead of sermons. Had one of us been bold enough to enter a church, he must have been ejected for the sake of decency. . . . Church bells rang not for us. Poets were indeed our priests. But for those, the last relic of our moral existence would have surely passed away!

Song was the dew drops that gathered during the long dark night of despondency, and were sure to glitter in the very first blink of the sun. Yonder you might have seen 'Auld Robin Gray' wet the eyes that could be tearless amidst cold and hunger, and weariness and pain. . . .

For the factory workers, song was the leaven in the bread of life. The act of singing was a communal activity which rendered their work bearable by making it a communal activity too, while the songs afforded opportunities for self-expression otherwise denied by the grim environment. Some weavers were stirred to compose:

It was not enough that we merely chaunted, and listened, but some more ambitious, or idle if you will, they in time would try a self-conceived song. Just as if some funny little boy, bolder than the rest, would creep into

the room where lay Neil Gow's fiddle, and touch a note
or two he could not name. How proud he is! how blest!
for he had made a sound, and more, his playmates heard
it, faith!

But the songs and poems sung and composed were not traditional;
they were modern literary and subliterary productions. Just as
their social conditions changed, so did the taste and the songs of
the displaced rural workers who formed the new industrial
proletariat.

In the rural districts certain factors encouraged the continuation of old cultural habits. Whereas the cotton industry in the
west was rapidly put on a factory basis, the textile industries in
the Northeast remained primarily rural domestic industries for
some decades. The country women engaged in these congregated
most nights at one house in the neighbourhood where they
knitted or span their 'stents' together, and enlivened the evening
by singing songs and ballads.[34] Furthermore, as neither the
standard education nor the volumes available in the local
libraries stimulated the imagination or the emotions, the songs
and ballads would have served this age-old function for men and
women both. But of course the great weight of social change
had subverted the traditional culture, and ensured that where
the traditional forms survived, they would be decisively altered
by the new conditions. One would naturally expect any collection
of ballads published in the Northeast at the end of this period,
in 1828, to show signs of the social upheaval that had taken
place in the previous eighty years.

Part IV

The Tradition in Transition:
the Ballads

Chapter 16

The Peter Buchan Controversy

By far the most productive of ballad collectors in the Northeast during the transitional period was a vain and volatile printer and would-be gentleman from the Buchan area, Peter Buchan. His texts, particularly during the chauvinistic wars between Scots and English folksong collectors, have drawn much adverse comment, some of it as eccentric as the man himself. On occasion these texts have been used as pegs on which to hang weirdly diverse theories about 'the' ballad and 'the' folk. When, however, Buchan's versions are placed in a specific context, that of the northeastern folk and their ballads, and not in the vaguely general context of 'the' ballad, then they can be seen in their true perspective. Although the work of Will Walker and Gavin Greig[1] has helped considerably, if not completely, to rehabilitate Buchan, it is only when his ballads are recognized as products of a particular tradition, subject to the mutabilities of regional social change, that the basic trustworthiness of his texts becomes fully apparent.

Those who have declared Buchan's texts to be untrustworthy have based their attitude on two facts, each incontrovertible in itself. The first of these is that it was common editorial practice at Buchan's time to amend and stitch together ballad fragments in order to publish a reasonably whole and comprehensible ballad-text. In a letter to Motherwell Scott admitted that such was once his practice:[2]

> In fact, I think I did wrong myself in endeavouring to
> make the best possible set of an ancient ballad out of
> several copies obtained from different quarters, and that,
> in many respects, if I improved the poetry, I spoiled the
> simplicity of the old song.

Motherwell, who is normally reckoned the most scrupulous of contemporary editors, reveals his attitude to the amending of texts in a letter to Scott asking for copies of 'Gil Morice':[3]

> I would rather wish to have it in my power to ~~correct~~ [sic] amend by the assistance of other recited copies than trust to my own judgment in doing so. Other copies may possibly supply preferable readings in many places, and contain additions of material moment.

Even for Motherwell, it was not imperative that the ballad editor should abstain from using his 'own judgment' to amend texts. Jamieson also thought along these editorial lines, for Anderson writes in a letter to Percy:[4]

> I objected also to his [Jamieson's] plan of editing the Old Ballads, with interpolated stanzas written by himself, wherever he conceives the narrations defective, or the transitions abrupt, obscure, etc.

In the little he did write of his 'Introduction' Child provides examples from their manuscripts of the early editors' proclivity for improvement and shows that Kinloch used the same methods as the others.[5] Buchan was not included in this company, presumably because Child was waiting for Will Walker's collation of the printed ballads with the 1827 MS., of whose existence Child had remained a long time in ignorance; a letter from Kittredge to Walker explains that Child never lived to see his collation.[6] It was, then, common editorial practice to compound and amend ballad texts, and this need hardly be wondered at, as no publisher would ever have presented his customers with a book, at a guinea and a half per copy, of ballad fragments. For the collector, it was often a choice between compounding the texts and having them published, or not having them published at all. That Buchan followed the current practice is not to be doubted for he expressly speaks of creating the 1828 publication 'out of a chaos of rude materials'.[7] The second incontrovertible fact is that a fair number of Buchan's texts are aesthetically unattractive: many are marred by stretches of artificial poetical English and some by interminably drawn-out formulaic sequences. Some critics put these two facts together, then made the inductive leap into explaining the second in

terms of the first: Buchan, the assumption went, must have
done more than compound the texts, he must have 'improved'
them extensively or even fabricated them. The possibility that
the textual peculiarities of Buchan's versions could be explained
in quite traditional terms was largely ignored.

For all its popularity, the initial assumption had surprisingly
little in the way of evidence to support it. Undoubtedly the
major item of apparently confirmatory evidence was the widespread story of the 'Chil Ether' hoax. Indeed, two Northeast
men who were helpers of Child, Norval Clyne and Charles
Elphinstone Dalrymple, both reversed their ideas about the
genuineness of Buchan's texts solely on the grounds of this story.
Clyne writes of this reversal in a letter to Child which includes
the transcript of a letter from John Hill Burton, whom Clyne
had asked for an account of the hoax:

> The ballad called *Chil Ether* was drafted at my bedside
> by a friend, when I was recovering from an illness. It was
> with the intention to take the measure of Peter's honesty.
> It was sent to him in shattered fragments, but he was
> so successful as to get it completely among the Buchan
> peasantry!

Nowhere, however, does Peter claim to 'get it completely among
the Buchan peasantry'. When Hill Burton's story is reduced to
its essentials, all that it shows is that Buchan, believing the
fragments to be genuine, stitched them together in accordance
with current editorial practice. That he believed them genuine
can hardly be held against him, for, as Hill Burton says later
in the letter—and in this he displays a peculiar ambivalence to
the palming off of forgeries—Scott himself 'with all his skill,
was seriously imposed upon'. Hill Burton continues: 'All Collections of Ballads I believe to be more or less dressed, but for
bungling dishonest patching I would be prepared to back Peter's
against any others to be found. Scott touched his cautiously
and gracefully, but Peter pitched in his rubbish in the mass.'
Given his acceptance of the editorial habit of 'dressing' ballads,
it is difficult to see any justification for his use of the word
'dishonest'; apparently Hill Burton's criterion for dishonesty was
not the *fact* of dressing but the degree of success attained in the

process. Again, it is difficult to see any grounds for his highly coloured assertion that 'Peter pitched in his rubbish in the mass' beyond Buchan's stitching together of Hill Burton's own fabrications. Hill Burton's account of the hoax became a popular joke which was re-told with many an embroidery. Undoubtedly its growth was fostered by Dean Christie's announcement in the prospectus for *Traditional Ballad Airs* that he had discovered the tune 'Chil Ether' was sung to.[8] Child must have remained rather dubious about the whole affair, as he sent Macmath to see Hill Burton, but Macmath's account of the visit can hardly have set his mind at rest:

> I called upon Dr. Hill Burton yesterday, and found him
> quite what your letter had led me to expect on the subject
> of Ballads. He gave me a harangue of which I could
> make neither head nor tail. I caught something about
> his Ballads being all 'in confusion' and certainly if they
> are half as confused as his discourse they will be bad
> enough.[9]

Later that year Child endeavoured by direct correspondence with Hill Burton to get to the bottom of the 'Chil Ether' business, but merely received in return a decidedly unhelpful letter from Hill Burton's daughter.[10] The whole affair reduces to this: Buchan accepted as genuine a fragmented ballad-text which he had no reason to believe manufactured; in keeping with contemporary editorial practice, he then glued the pieces together to form a reasonably comprehensible unit. The real fabricators and villains of the piece turn out to be John Hill Burton and his friend (Joseph Robertson), abetted by Dean Christie.

Before Hill Burton published his account of the 'Chil Ether' hoax in the *Book-Hunter*,[11] the story was already in popular circulation and so could possibly have influenced R. C. A. Prior's claim that Buchan had made wholesale reivings on the Danish ballads. A brief consideration of the close relationship between the entire northeastern ballad tradition and the Scandinavian ballad traditions reveals the baselessness of such a claim.[12] A knowledge of this close relationship would have saved a more recent critic, H. O. Nygard, from the same pitfall. Nygard propounds the theory that the ballad-story of 'Lady Isabel and the Elf-Knight' came to Britain exclusively from France, and dismisses the Buchan texts, which run counter to his theory by exhibiting strong links with the Scandinavian texts, as forgeries.[13] The texts collected in the Northeast by other collectors as well as Buchan would suggest that 'Lady Isabel' is not the only ballad-story which entered Britain both from France through southern England and from Scandinavia through the Northeast of Scotland. Failure to realize that the folk-culture of the Northeast shared material not only with the Scandinavian but also with the Gaelic folk-cultures raised doubts about other lore recorded by Buchan. It was noted, first by A. B. Grosart and then by J. F. Campbell, that the folktales collected by Buchan were also to be found in both Norway and the Scottish Highlands. Campbell, who had already recovered most of the tales from Gaelic speakers, declared that the collection was derived 'directly or indirectly' from the Gaelic, but Hamish Henderson, while allowing that the stories might have been carried over from the Gaelic at an earlier date, has shown that 'Buchan's tales—nearly all of which are identifiable international folktales . . . were in fact taken down from the recitation of tradition-bearers speaking braid Scots, and constitute in the main faithful if somewhat undistinguished recensions of the stories as originally told'.[14] It is noteworthy that the folktales, like many of the ballads, are 'somewhat undistinguished'. Efforts to prove that Buchan's fabrications took the form of plagiary from other cultures all founder once Buchan's texts are placed firmly in the context of the regional culture.

The assumption that the unattractiveness of Buchan's texts could be caused only by deliberate editorializing sometimes led the bloodhounds to a different quarry. Where Buchan himself was not accused, James Rankin was held to be the 'humble but enterprising rhapsodist who has left his trail over so large a part of Buchan's volumes'.[15] In many comments about Rankin one can detect a certain suspicious horror that a collector should employ someone else to collect ballads, and moreover, actually pay him for the collecting. Buchan, however, was not alone among contemporary collectors in hiring a sub-collector, as we learn from Motherwell's Ballad Notebook. In listing his expenses Motherwell makes these insertions:[16]

	£	S	D
To James Macqueen to enable him to go to Ayr in quest of ballads		10	6
To fitting up Macqueen with a pack and dispatching him thro' Ayr & Galloway on the old quest.		2	2

What information we have about the Buchan-Rankin relationship depends on a series of letters written over the period from January 1826 to December 1831 by Buchan to Motherwell and notes on Rankin supplied to Gavin Greig and J. B. Duncan by Bell Robertson.[17] The first mention of Rankin comes in a letter dated 16 February 1827, when Peter sets himself up as a latter-day, but rather impoverished, Maecenas:

> I sent for and brought an old blind man from a great
> distance, kept him in Peterhead for upwards of four
> weeks, and paid all expenses, besides his own charges,
> which were not inconsiderable. Such have been my love
> and enthusiasm for the preservation of the ballads etc.,
> of my native country. He was, however, worthy of his
> reward, great as it was, if I could have afforded it, for
> he was without doubt, a second Homer. He was possessed
> of the best memory I ever knew, and had been travelling
> through the north of Scotland, as an itinerant singer and
> beggar for the last fifty years. I got many pieces from
> him which I had never seen before, and many older
> sets of what I had seen.

This account illustrates vividly Buchan's predilection for hyperbole. The 'great distance' from Strichen to Peterhead is about fifteen miles; according to Bell Robertson's notes the 'four weeks' would be one week, and the 'fifty years' could be no more than two or three, as Rankin did not start begging until after the death of his father in 1824; 'through the north of Scotland' has to be seen in the light of a comment Buchan makes in another letter to Motherwell, dated 24 December 1827: 'My old minstrel has left me, only a few days. I spoke to him of going to Paisley, but he never crossed the Don or Dee in his life, and would not do it for any sum of money.' From Bell Robertson's notes, it would appear that his territory was very circumscribed indeed, being limited to a consortium of farmers in Buchan who gave him food and lodging in return for his songs. Buchan's account of Rankin, some of which he reproduces in the notes to 'Sir Patrick Spens' in the 1828 publication, has, then, to be viewed in the light of the general hyperbolic tone that Peter's vanity frequently led him to adopt. From the letter dated 21 November 1827, we learn that Rankin provided a number of the folktales, which is significant in view of Hamish Henderson's endorsement of their trustworthiness. The last reference to Rankin occurs in the letter dated 24 September 1829:

> My old minstrel has just returned from a voyage of
> discovery laden with honey, but such, I am afraid, will
> not suit our present hypocrites—they are too *high kilted*.
> [Presumably the material in 'Secret Songs of Silence'.]
> He says he has now scoured the country clean; and,
> altho' he is off again, it is without hopes.

Buchan, by his hyperbolic claims, has only himself to blame for much of the opprobrium that has attached to Rankin's name. His statement that Rankin was a 'second Homer', or indeed any kind of statement imputing creative ability to Rankin, must be set against Bell Robertson's comment on the man:[18]

> His memory was very remarkable, he had a large stock
> of ballads and songs, but was distinctly of low intelligence.
> What he heard he picked up readily in a way, but
> lacking intelligence, he would often pick things up in a
> wrong way. . . . Many of his songs and ballads were so
> mixed up as to be a kind of jumble. He just sang what
> he got. Being blind, he learned everything from someone's
> saying or singing, and probably did not know whether
> it was sung from a printed copy or from memory and
> tradition. The idea of Jamie making up anything himself
> was considered absurd.

In short, James Rankin was too stupid to be able to fabricate ballads. Knowing this, one can hardly agree with Child's comment on 'the inventive ability of Buchan's blind beggar', Kittredge's claim that he was a composing 'professional minstrel', or MacEdward Leach's elevation of Rankin to 'folk-poet'.[19]

Many people, of course, did not leap into assuming that the linguistically unappealing or incongruous stretches in Buchan's texts could only be the result of editorial fabrication. As Will Walker points out, all the contemporary collectors who had themselves a first-hand acquaintance with the tradition and who saw Buchan's 1827 MS., pronounced the ballads to be basically genuine.[20] Scott gave his opinion of their genuineness in no fewer than four places—in the letters to Buchan and Kirkpatrick Sharpe which are reprinted by Walker, in the *Minstrelsy*, and in his *Journal*, where for 23 August 1827, he writes of a visit from[21]

> . . . a whimsical party, consisting of John Stevenson, the
> bookseller, Peter Buchan from Peterhead, a quiz of a
> poetical creature, and a bookbinder, a friend of theirs.
> Their plan was to consult me about publishing a great
> quantity of ballads which this Mr. Buchan has collected.
> I glanced them over. He has been very successful, for
> they are obviously genuine, and many of them very
> curious. Others are various editions of well-known ballads.
> I could not make the man comprehend that these last
> were of little value; being generally worse readings of
> what was already published. A small edition published
> by subscription may possibly succeed. It is a great pity
> that few of these ballads are historical, almost all being
> of the romantic cast. They certainly ought to be preserved,
> after striking out one or two which have been
> sophisticated, I suppose by Mr. Buchan himself, which
> are easily distinguishable from the genuine ballads. No
> one but Burns ever succeeded in patching up old Scottish
> songs with any good effect.

Buchan took Scott's advice and left the MS. in the hands of David Laing and Kirkpatrick Sharpe, who were to delete whatever they thought inappropriate to the publication and generally see it through the press. They disagreed violently over editorial presentation, but neither apparently had any doubts about the authenticity of the texts.[22]

One scholar who remained firmly convinced of the genuineness of Buchan's texts was the distinguished Danish folklorist, Svend

Grundtvig. The Grundtvig-Child correspondence, reprinted in Sigurd Hustvedt's *Ballad Books and Ballad Men*,[23] shows how Grundtvig was able, over two years, to force Child to moderate his initial hostility towards Buchan; on one occasion Child even recanted sufficiently to say: 'I must confess that my treatment of his ballads both seems and *was* capricious.' Child distrusted Buchan's versions because of the 'Chil Ether' 'forgery', and the length and 'artificial vulgarity' of the texts. The latter charge Grundtvig counters by drawing on his experience as a ballad collector acquainted with live tradition: 'what you term the "vulgarity" of the Buchan texts is to me the best proof of their material authenticity'. From his perspective on the Scandinavian traditions, Grundtvig also completely reverses Prior's argument by asserting that a comparison 'with undoubtedly genuine Scandinavian ballads' proves the genuineness of Buchan's versions. Child, however, was never quite able to accept Grundtvig's position on Buchan; his ambivalent attitude is epitomized by this statement: 'I shall treat Buchan's ballads as substantially genuine, but I think that I shall put them into smaller type than those of honest collectors.'[24] The Buchan controversy, one cannot help feeling, is one case where Child's lack of acquaintance with live tradition militated against an accurate judgment.

In one letter to Grundtvig Child asks why other ballads gathered in 'the North' of Scotland, Kinloch's ballads, lack the 'artificial vulgarity' of Buchan's.[25] The answer is threefold: first, some do possess this vulgarity; second, Kinloch's northern texts were recorded in large part from an educated family, the Beatties of Stonehaven, rather than from Jamie Rankin and a rural peasantry; and third, his northern texts seem to have been collected mainly in the Mearns, and certainly not in Peter's stamping ground, the Buchan area. The only collector who did work extensively in the Buchan area was Gavin Greig, who recorded some sixty to ninety years later. As Keith demonstrates in the Introduction and Notes to *Last Leaves*, the Greig collection provides a mass of evidence testifying to the strong probability that Buchan's texts were taken from local tradition. It contains not only ballad-stories previously recorded only by Buchan and other examples of Northeast oikotypes, but also passages and stanzas which had been designated 'suspect' by Child when he found them in Buchan's collection. In story and in text, the ballads later recovered from the same area provide strong testimony for the basic authenticity of Buchan's texts.

If, then, the evidence is overwhelmingly against explaining the texts' unattractiveness by assuming that Buchan fabricated as well as stitched, how do we account for the unattractiveness? Why do many of Buchan's texts look tawdry when set against those of Mrs Brown? All-important to the answer is the factor of time. While Mrs Brown learned her ballads by 1759, Buchan collected his ballads in the decade previous to 1828. As was described in the preceding chapters, these seventy years were crucial years for the Northeast. The agrarian and industrial revolutions and the consequent social revolution altered the social structure, the conditions of employment, and the spending of leisure; they brought in their train education, literacy and the spread of printed material. The folk's ways of life, ways of thinking, and ways of linguistic expression were all changed, and inevitably the ballads of the folk tradition were also changed.

The change that occurs when a society passes from a condition of nonliteracy to a condition of literacy is the crucial one for that society's oral tradition. The advent of literacy rings a death-knell for the technique of oral composition, the necessity for which lies in the nonliteracy of its practitioners. But although its decay is relatively swift, the traditional technique is not destroyed at one blow. Lord found in Yugoslavia that the older people remained almost unaffected by the changes:

> Actually older unlettered singers, even when they are exposed to the reading of song books to them, are not greatly influenced. The learning of the song in this way is like the learning of it from a sung performance. Their habit of oral composition is too well inculcated to be changed.

And it takes time for the full impact of literacy to be felt throughout the older generations of a society, as the mental changes that the acquirement of reading and writing brings about do not occur overnight. In fact, the fatal blow to an oral tradition is likely to come 'not when writing is introduced, but when published song texts are spread among singers'.[26]

Unlike the 'arrival of literacy', which is not an event but a drawn-out process, the arrival of the published song texts can be dated with a fair degree of accuracy. Obviously it could not occur before a fairly high level of general literacy had been attained, and this, we reckoned in the previous chapter, happened in the Northeast generally during the last half of the eighteenth century. The dates of the printed songs, however, enable us to chart more firmly a crucial point in the transition of the tradition from oral to modern. Scotland, unlike England, had never built up a trade in printed balladry[27] (a lack which contributes greatly to the differences in Scottish and English ballad traditions), but it is quite surprising how quickly a trade in printed ballads did come into existence once the general level of literacy was sufficiently high to support the production of cheap publications. There is in the British Museum a collection of white-letter broadsheets (B.M. 1346. m.7) which were printed at Aberdeen as early as 1775 and 1776,[28] dates which prove conclusively that the broadside trade was in operation in the Northeast at least fifty years before Buchan's publications. These forty broadsheets were all printed between May 1775 and June 1776, a rate of publication which would indicate that the trade was already thriving. The miscellaneous nature of the items printed provides a clear illustration of the variety of influences which affected the old tradition. The broadsheets include a dozen broadside versions of ballad-stories later printed by Child: 'Lord Thomas's Tragedy' (73), 'Fair Margaret's Misfortunes; or Sweet William's frightful Dreams on his Wedding Night; with the sudden Death and Burial of those noble lovers' (74), 'Gil Morice' (83), 'Barbara Allen's Cruelty' (84), 'Robin Hood and the Proud Pedlar' (134), 'Robin Hood rescuing the Squires' (140), 'Chevy Chase' (162), 'John Armstrong's Last Good-Night' (169), 'The Buchanshire Tragedy; or Sir James the Ross (To the Tune of Gill Morice)' (213), 'Andrew Lammie' (233), 'The Duke of Gordon's Daughter' (237i), and 'The Lowlands of Holland' (286). Nine of these were later collected by Gavin Greig in versions bearing the broadside stamp, so it can be assumed that the broadside ballads were swiftly and firmly accepted in the Northeast. Most of the sheets include songs like the one printed with 'The Gosford Tragedy' and entitled 'A Love-Song. To the Tune of Andrew Lamie'; its first stanza provides some indication of the linguistic incongruity, arising from the mixture of artificial English and more earthbound Scots, that pervades these songs:

> My love is like the Flora queen;
>   surpassing fair Diana:
> By a' the maids that e'er I saw
>   forget my love I canna'.

The incongruities are not limited to language, however, for the productions themselves exhibit a startling diversity. Together with the religious songs such as 'The New Jerusalem. The Mourning Soul for Christ . . . To the Tune of, the Bride's Burial', one can find an earthy version of 'Charly is my Darling', 'The Babes in the Wood', 'Rule Britannia', poems by John Skinner, and songs such as 'The Ravelled Booking of the Ord' that look forward to songs sung in the bothies.

The same influences affecting the taste of the folk are to be observed in another collection in the British Museum entitled 'Curious Tracts, Scotland' (1078. m. 24). An introductory note says: ·

> This Collection was made by me, James Mitchell, at
> Aberdeen in 1828. It may be considered as the Library
> of the Scottish Peasantry, the works being sold by
> itinerant Chapmen about the country, especially at fairs.
> No such collection could now be made, and Chambers
> Edinburgh Journal and similar publications have superseded
> the writings of our forefathers.

Mitchell's reference to the method of distribution and to the customers, the 'peasantry', should dispel any lingering belief that the broadsheets were intended primarily for urban consumption. His collection has four parts. First there is a forty-page chapbook, 'The trial of Richard Parker', published in London, 30 July 1797. Parker was the 'President of the Delegates for Mutiny' at the Nore, but his story held special interest for the Northeast, as Mitchell explains in an added note:

> Richard Parker commonly supposed to be a Scotchman
> was in reality an Englishman. He usually sailed from the
> port of Aberdeen to London, and married a wife from
> Aberdeen. After his execution and his exposure on the
> gibbet, his wife arrived from Aberdeen, and by the
> assistance of her friends, they rescued him from the

ignominious exposure. The Government apprehended
her, but in a few days after they gave her a free pardon.

Alexander Laing's *The Thistle of Scotland* is then followed by
sixteen eight-page chapbooks and twenty-five single songs pasted
on to the leaves of the volume. The mixture is very much as
before. There are seven versions of ballad-stories later printed
by Child—'Captain Wedderburn's Courtship' (46), 'Susie Pye or
Young Beichan's Garland' (53), 'Bonny Barbara Allan' (84),
'Bessie Bell and Mary Gray' (201), 'The Tragedy of Sir James
the Rose' (213), 'The Duke of Gordon's Daughters' (237), 'The
Jolly Beggars' (279Bb), innumerable songs dealing with 'swains'
and 'fairest of soft creations' in groves where 'soft whispering
gales wanton', sentimental ditties such as 'Home! Sweet Home!',
genteel Scottish effusions like 'The Lass of Glenshee', poems
by Skinner and Scott such as 'The Adventures of John o'
Badenyon', 'Blue Bonnets o'er the Border' and 'Young Lochinvar',
and songs like Tannahill's 'The Kebbuckston Wedding' which
look forward to songs sung in the bothies. The published 'Bessy
Bell and Mary Gray' is worth giving in full, for it illustrates
very clearly that the language of the songs now sung by the
folk was in a very unsettled state:

O Bessy Bell and Mary Gray
    They were twa bonny lasses,
They bigg'd a bow'r on yon burn brae,
    And theek'd it o'er wi' rashes.
Fair Bessy Bell I lo'ed yestreen,
    And thought I ne'er could alter,
But Mary Gray's two pawky een
    They gar my fancy falter.

Now Bessy's hair's like a lint-tap,
    She smiles like a May morning,
When Phoebus starts frae Thetis' lap,
    The hills with rays adorning:
White is her neck, saft is her hand
    Her waist and feet's fu' genty;
With ilka grace she can command;
    Her lips, O vow! they're dainty.

217

> And Mary's locks are like a craw,
>   Her een like diamonds glances;
> She's ay sae clean, redd up and braw,
>   She kills whene'er she dances;
> Blyth as a kid, with wit at will,
>   She blooming, tight and tall is;
> And guides her airs sae gracefu' still,
>   O Jove, she's like thy Pallas.
>
> Dear Bessy Bell and Mary Gray,
>   Ye unco sair oppress us;
> Our fancies jee between you tway,
>   Ye are sic bonny lasses:
> Waes me! for baith I canna get;
>   To ane by law we're stented;
> Then I'll draw cuts, and tak my fate,
>   And be with ane contented.

In this song, which is actually reprinted from the works of Allan Ramsay,[29] there are three linguistic varieties; there is poetical English, ordinary vernacular Scots, and in the first quatrain the formulaic language of the old tradition. The language of the songs the folk were singing was in a state of flux. It is in the light of this fact that the linguistic vulgarities and incongruities of Peter Buchan's ballads must be considered.

Further evidence of the type of material printed can be gained from the bibliography of Peter Buchan, for he himself printed thirty-three known song-chapbooks between 1817 and 1826.[30] A number of these were printed for Alexander Keith of Aberdeen, a bookseller and printer who published from 1810 to 1835, and whose 'Robin Hood and the Beggar' is Child's 134a. The Buchan-Keith partnership worked two ways, as we discover from a letter to Motherwell dated 23 August 1826:

> I embrace the opportunity of my honest and worthy
> friend the bearer, Mr. Alexander Keith, copperplate
> Printer, Aberdeen, and of introducing him unto your
> notice as a dealer in and collector of Old Ballads. To him
> I am deeply indebted for many pieces in this way, and
> perhaps he may be useful unto you in the same.

It would appear, however, that by the end of the first quarter of the nineteenth century, the peak years in the production of chapbooks and stall-copies were past. Just as Motherwell in 1824 had himself noted a difficulty in procuring the humorous chapbook,[31] Peter Buchan in a letter to him marked simply April 1827, remarked on the falling off in the printing of the 'Halfpenny ballads':

> It is now sent you, a collection of about two hundred
> half-penny ballads, the gleanings of all the Bookshops
> in Aberdeen and Peterhead, as all of them have been
> searched painfully, by my son and self—I have not
> printed any of this description, (a few for Mr Keith
> Abdn excepted) these few years, and there are none
> printed now in Abdn unless on broadsides, or single
> leafs for the street singers.

The advent of literacy brought in its wake a great burst of activity in song-printing, but after the boom, the fifty years from 1775 to 1825, the printing of songs seems to have been carried on at a much reduced pace.

The end result of the spread of printed songs in a newly literate society is that people, with an awed respect for the authority of the printed word, come to believe that the printed text is *the* text; they lose their acceptance of the textual multi-formity of the oral ballad-story. Once they believe in the fixed text, then it is only a short step towards their memorizing the one 'right' text of a song. As Lord stresses, 'this process is not a transition from an oral to a literary technique of composition. It is a transition from oral composition to simple performance of a fixed text, from composition to reproduction.'[32] But though with literacy the *raison d'être* of oral composition was removed and the oral technique broke down, the ballad-stories still remained. While the oral technique was breaking down, and before the concept of the fixed text and memorization gained a complete hold, the folk still sang these ballad-stories. It is during this transitional period that the spread of printed material, both verse and prose, had its most immediate effect: the linguistic deracination of the folk.

Most of the texts to which the singers were exposed were, in vocabulary and idiom, at variance with both the formulaic language of the traditional ballad and the native dialect of the region. The singers, in fact, were exposed to new *kinds* of language. As has been seen, the folk came in contact with varieties of English poetical language. An extract from a broadsheet—'Last Speech, Confession and Dying Declaration of James Ritchie Who was executed at Aberdeen, on Friday the 5th June, 1818 For the Crime of Sheep-Stealing'—will also provide some indication of the type of English prose to which they were now subject:[33]

> [He] maintained a composure and firmness superior to his years, exciting the astonishment of the very numerous spectators who witnessed the revolting spectacle . . . he made a pathetic address, especially to the young, earnestly exhorting them to an early obedience of the laws of God and precepts of Religion, and warning them to avoid Sabbath breaking and bad company, of whose fatal effects he was now a sad example. He then bowed to the Clergyman and Gentlemen attending, as also to the spectators, when stepping forward with a perfect serenity, and with a mind seemingly exalted by the most happy prospects, he ascended the fatal drop, which fell at ten minutes to three, and he died with but little struggle.
>
> The Rev. Mr. Ward, of the Methodist Connection, then delivered an excellent and appropriate discourse, chiefly on breaking the Sabbath-day . . .

The wide range of publications that were being sold at the time is well illustrated by this account of what a shop-window's wares were likely to consist of at the turn of the eighteenth century:[34]

> When these prints [twopence coloured, penny plain] were not in the window, their place was occupied by those esteemed works, The History of the Holy Bible; King Pipin; The Death of Cock Robin; &c. &c., with cuts; and bound in gilt, price one penny, and above them were the larger volumes of The History of Lothian Tom; Wise Willie and Witty Eppy; The Sayings, Doings and Witty Jests of George Buchanan; Sir William Wallace, &c. &c.; and in the poetical department was to be found

Chevy Chase; The Cherry and the Slae; Sir James the
Rose; The Dominie Deposed; Ajax's Speech to the
Grecian Knabs &c. &c.

The interesting point about the catalogue is that amongst the
staple fare of the chapbook we find also works from a literary
tradition written in literary Scots. Not only was the northeastern
singer exposed to various kinds of English, but also to various
kinds of Scots. It is small wonder that many of Peter Buchan's
ballads are a linguistic *mélange*. Once the essentially oral nature
of the traditional ballad had been broken down, the formulaic
language was mixed with, and replaced by, a variety of other
kinds of language, English and Scots, literary and sub-literary,
artificial and vernacular. That their ballad language was in a
state of flux is an index of the state of mind of a folk subjected
to all the wrenching upheavals of society's swift transition from
medieval to modern.

It is now possible to get a much clearer view of the Buchan
controversy. Buchan was an editor of his time, that is, he
stitched and compounded some of his ballads. That his ekes and
splicings were probably not of very high quality can hardly be
doubted, for, in the first place, he himself did not possess the
most discriminating of poetical tastes[35] and, in the second place,
there is the possibility that he used parts of stall-ballads for the
ekes and splicings.[36] There exists, however, no evidence for the
assumption that Buchan was more than an editor of his time,
that he was a fabricator. His own view of editorial fabrication
he expresses quite forcibly in the letters to Motherwell. In that
marked 31 July 1826, he commends Motherwell for

> your having given the ballads without the disagreeable
> and disgusting emendations and interpolations so frequently
> met with in works of this sort

and condemns Cunningham's *Songs of Scotland*:

> His corrections are too visible; and, altho' not visible,
> why impose upon the public?

Cunningham he attacks again in the letter of 16 February 1827:

> many of our best national pieces are grossly mangld and
> defective. I am personally acquainted wt. Mr. C. but for

all this, I cannot forgive him for the abuse which he has made of our best ballads.

In that marked April 1827, he writes:

> The difference between them [two records of 'False Colin'] is not very material, but as I am a sworn foe to emendations, etc. I would not substitute a single word from Ramsy and you have it in its original purity, wt. all its imperfections, as Ramsay had thought them—I mean its lengthened beauties.

Here Buchan makes very clear his disapproval of editorial 'improvement', and it is highly ironic to set up these statements, with their impeccable sentiments, against those decrying Buchan as the arch-example of the ballad-fabricator.[37]

The most important argument in Buchan's favour, however, is supplied by the evidence of the ballads themselves. When they are placed firmly in the context of the local tradition their peculiarities and incongruities are seen as the inevitable outcome of social change. In the half century which preceded Buchan's publications, the region had undergone a number of social revolutions whose combined effects produced great changes in the folk and in their ballad tradition. It can hardly be the case, as Will Walker suggests, that the folk were 'lower in mental and moral fibre',[38] but rather that their attitudes of mind, like their song-language, were in a state of flux. The folk were now largely literate, but literacy was not an unqualified boon: 'When a tradition or an individual goes from oral to written, he, or it, goes from an adult, mature style of one kind to a faltering and embryonic style of another sort.'[39] What Child calls 'the silliness and fulsome vulgarity' of Buchan's texts is actually a strong indication that the ballads are genuine, for these characteristics reflect the effects of the revolutionary upheavals on the peasantry and on their balladry. The folk had changed, and their ballads had changed.

Chapter 17

The Ballads of James Nicol

The changes that occurred in the tradition may be studied in some detail in the corpus of one of Buchan's contributors, James Nicol of Strichen. His ballads show what happened to the singers and songs of the Northeast in the transitional period; they show, in general, the effect of the new social influences on the stories, and they show, in particular, the effect of literacy on the oral technique of composition. Surprisingly, perhaps, they have escaped the general censure of Buchan's texts. Child, for example, had no doubts about their authenticity as he, while lamenting the 'flimsy and unjointed' condition of 'Young Bearwell' (302), declared that it required 'a respectable voucher, such as Mr. Nicol undoubtedly was, for the other five pieces communicated by him were all above suspicion, and have a considerable value'.[1]

James Nicol of Strichen was no uneducated farmer. Though he received only a basic schooling he was, besides being 'a bit of a character', a well-read and intelligent man, a disciple of Tom Paine, and the author of some pamphlets which set forth views quite advanced for his time: *Letters written in 1816, on infant education, etc., Some few thoughts on the feeing markets, on robbing of kirk-yards, and on begging, Some thoughts on crimes and punishments,* and *Some thoughts on deism and on Agur's prayer*.[2] While a young man he spent three years in America, and on his return worked at his trade as a cooper before setting up in a shop where he dispensed books and ballads along with the groceries. On his death in 1840, he left a bequest of £400 to establish 'a free school in the village of Mormond (Strichen) for the teaching of poor children in the elementary branches of education, reading, writing, and arithmetic'. In 1852 a teacher was engaged, after a nine-hour examination, and she ran Nicol's

Free School until 1889, when it was merged with the local parish school.[3]

Although Child mentions only six pieces in the quotation above, he actually printed seven ballad texts which he marked as Nicol's: 'Kemp Owyne' (34A), 'Hind Etin' (41C), 'The Clerk's Twa Sons o Owsenford' (72D), 'The Knight and Shepherd's Daughter' (110E), 'Archie o Cawfield' (188D), 'Redesdale and Wise William' (246A), and 'Young Bearwell' (302). Of these, six were communicated by Nicol to Buchan who sent copies to Motherwell, and one (72D) must have been communicated straight to Motherwell, for it is found only in Motherwell's MS.

These seven texts, however, are far from constituting Nicol's entire stock. Buchan writes to Motherwell on 17 January 1826:[4]

> 'Lord Salton'—'Bonny John Seton'—'Mary Hamilton',
> and the 'Burning of Frendraugh', were sent by my old
> friend Mr. James Nicol, who resides near this, to Mr.
> David Webster, Bookseller Edinb.—and printed by him
> in 'A North Countrie Garland'.
> . . . It was the same Mr. Nicol who also gave the copies
> to me of the above. In addition to them I have lately
> received a packet from him containing upwards of
> twenty sheets of foolscap, closely written with old Ballads,
> but have not as yet got time to examine them.

If Nicol could send Buchan more than twenty sheets of ballads, his repertoire (even allowing for Buchan's hyperbolic arithmetic) must have far exceeded the handful of acknowledged texts. To the original seven we can immediately add the four mentioned in Buchan's letter, which were published without ascription in his *Gleanings* and, as he notes, were also published the previous year in *A North Countrie Garland*. James Maidment's preface to the *Garland* furnishes a further clue to Nicol's ballad stock: ' "Lord Thomas Stuart"—"The burning of Frendraught",— "Child Vyet",—"Bonny John Seton",—and two or three others, of minor importance, had long been preserved by tradition, in Aberdeenshire; and were procured from an intelligent individual, resident in that part of Scotland.' Two of these four texts were ascribed by Buchan to Nicol, so he must be this 'intelligent individual'. As Maidment writes that the sources of his remaining texts are given, the 'two or three' Aberdeenshire ballad texts turn out, by a process of elimination, to be: 'Lord Saltoun and Auchanachie' and 'Mary Hamilton', also ascribed by Buchan to Nicol; the 'north-country' 'Earl of Errol', a similar version of which is printed next to the other four Nicol ballads in Buchan's *Gleanings*; 'Eppie Morrie', and the 'north-country' 'Katharine Jaffray'.[5] The Nicol corpus now amounts to sixteen—the original seven and these nine: 'Lord Ingram and Chiel Wyet' (66A), 'Mary Hamilton' (173M), 'The Fire of Frendraught' (196A), 'Bonny John Seton' (198A), 'Katharine Jaffray' (221G), 'Eppie Morrie' (223), 'The Earl of Errol' (231D), 'Lord Saltoun and Auchanachie' (239A), and 'Lord Thomas Stuart' (259).

This information clears up a minor mystery concerning Scott's Abbotsford MSS., for eight of these nine Nicol ballads make up the bulk of the Scott manuscript entitled 'North Country Ballads'. We can now safely recognize that the source of the collection was Nicol, rather than, as Child tentatively suggests, Hugh Irvine of Drum, though it is possible, of course, that Irvine acted as middleman between the singer and Scott, as James Skene did with the Old Lady's ballads.[6] The Nicol trail does not end here, however. Charles Kirkpatrick Sharpe owned an independent transcript of Nicol's 'North Country Ballads', and in his 'Second Collection' possessed yet another batch of Nicol's songs. This collection contains two ballad-texts ('Kemp Owyne' and 'Redesdale and Wise William') marked as Nicol's by Buchan and Motherwell; two song texts found also in the 'North Country Ballads' ('There is a talk in Glasgow town' and 'You lasses of Cairn/Cordill Village'); five songs all with a strong northeast flavour ('The Guise at Tyrie', 'The Marquis of Huntly's Retreat', 'The Banks of Ugie', 'The New Buchan Market', and 'When Willy came to the windmill brae'); and five more ballad-texts— 'James Grant' (197), 'Tam Lin' (39D), 'Jellon Grame' (90B), 'Lady Maisry' (65B), and 'Burd Isabel and Earl Patrick' (257C). All five also appear in Motherwell's MSS. though not in his *Minstrelsy*, and one (65B) is noted as deriving from Sharpe; one (197) was printed by Buchan in his *Ballads*; and one (39D), described by Motherwell as 'a North Country version', is published by Maidment in *A New Book of Old Ballads* (Edinburgh, 1844) and turns up in Pitcairn's MSS., having been 'procured by David Webster, Bookseller, from tradition'. The middleman between Nicol and Sharpe was the same David Webster who provided Maidment and, in the one instance, Pitcairn with Nicol's ballads. From a letter written by Sharpe to Scott in the summer of 1824, when Sharpe was contemplating publishing another ballad book, we learn that Webster had provided Sharpe with two 'cargoes' of ballads from a single source: 'I send . . . a cargo which Webster got from the man who furnished the last; and if, at your leisure, you could give me any notices about them, I shall be much obliged. I shall print my second volume of stuff very soon. . . .'[7] All the evidence points to these cargoes being the 'North Country Ballads' and the 'Second Collection', and the man being James Nicol of Strichen.

A reconstruction of Nicol's dissemination of his texts produces a picture along these lines. In the early eighteen twenties Nicol sent a parcel of ballads to David Webster. The year was not later than 1822 as Pitcairn, whose Nicol text of 'Tam Lin' was procured from Webster, dates all three of his manuscript volumes 9 November 1822. At some time before 1824, the publication date of *A North Countrie Garland*, Webster gave out Nicol texts to Maidment. Between 1823, when *A Ballad Book* appeared without any Nicol versions, and the summer of 1824, Webster provided Sharpe with almost the same batch of texts; and in the summer of 1824 he furnished Sharpe with another cargo of Nicol's versions. Both these collections came into the hands of Scott, who had one set copied out, and provided Sharpe with notes on the other. Probably in the same year, 1824, Nicol himself sent to Buchan the texts which were published in the 1825 *Gleanings*, and near the beginning of 1826 sent him the large parcel of more than twenty foolscap pages. Nicol apparently communicated at least one text direct to Motherwell, who received other Nicol texts from both Buchan and Sharpe in time for inclusion in the 1827 *Minstrelsy*, and later on still more from Sharpe, who by this time had obviously given up the idea of another ballad book.[8]

Nicol's ballad corpus, then, is quite sizeable. There may be more unascribed texts in print, but at least twenty-one ballad versions are certainly Nicol's. This tripling of his known ballad repertoire raises some interesting points. The twenty-one ballad-stories sung by Nicol are represented in Child by no fewer than sixty noted 'versions'. Given this inflation, it is legitimate to wonder, first, whether the number of variant texts recorded by Child is actually much smaller than it at first seems, and, second, whether the number of singers represented in the early nineteenth-century Scottish ballad collections is also much smaller than it at first seems. Certainly the case of Nicol would suggest that many collectors were poaching in the same pools. Again, it would suggest that some of these 'collectors', Maidment, Sharpe, and Scott, were, at least in later life, hardly field-collectors, but rather retailers who relied on correspondents or a middleman like Webster to provide their ballad stocks. David Webster, who himself published only one slim ballad volume, *A Collection of Curious Old Ballads and Miscellaneous Poetry*,[9] now bulks large as a key figure in the ballad transactions of the Scottish eighteen twenties.

From a regional viewpoint, we find that just as Mrs Brown contributed considerably to the two important collections of the first decade—Scott's and Jamieson's—so Nicol in the third decade contributed to four important collections, those of Buchan, Motherwell, Sharpe and Scott, only one of which is reckoned a local Northeast collection. Of the other editors of this decade, Maidment drew heavily on Nicol for his *Garland*, Laing gleaned Aberdeenshire for his *Scarce Ancient Ballads* and *The Thistle of Scotland*, and Kinloch, himself born in the Mearns, relied on a Number of Northeast singers and correspondents for his *Ancient Scottish Ballads* and *The Ballad Book*. The Northeast tradition, then, supplied ballad-texts to both local and non-local collectors and made no little contribution to the remarkable outpouring of Scottish ballad books in the early nineteenth century.

Although Nicol's texts retain many of the old oral elements they also reflect the inroads made by literacy upon the folk's consciousness. Most bear evident signs of the oral architectonic, but in general they have lost the dramatic yet disciplined coherence of structure that characterized the oral texts. In the stanzaic structure, there are still balances, triads, and occasionally frames, but these units are often not organized in the old firm fashion. Sometimes a sequence of balances is merely a string of paired stanzas rather than an organic scene whose units are intricately related. Sometimes the triads are spun out to inordinate lengths, as in 'Lady Maisry', stanzas 1 to 10, or 'Redesdale and Wise William':

'Come down, come down, my lady fair,
    A sight of you give me;
And bonny are the gowns of silk
    That I will give to thee.'

'If you have bonny gowns of silk,
    O mine is bonny tee;
Go from my yetts now, Reedisdale,
    For me you shall not see.'

'Come down, come down, my lady fair,
    A sight of you I'll see;
And bonny jewels, brooches and rings
    I will give unto thee.'

'If you have bonny brooches and rings,
    O mine are bonny tee;
Go from my yetts now, Reedisdale,
    For me you shall not see.'

'Come down, come down, my lady fair,
    One sight of you I'll see;
And bonny are the ha's and bowers
    That I will give to thee.'

'If you have bonny ha's and bowers,
    O mine are bonny tee;
Go from my yetts now, Reedisdale,
    For me you shall not see.'

'Come down, come down, my lady fair,
    A sight of you I'll see;
And bonny are my lands so broad
    That I will give to thee.'

'If you have bonny lands so broad,
    O mine are bonny tee;
Go from my yetts now, Reedisdale,
    For me ye will not see.'

'Come down, come down, my lady fair,
    A sight of you I'll see;
And bonny are the bags of gold
    That I will give to thee.'

'If you have bonny bags of gold,
  I have bags of the same;
Go from my yetts now, Reedisdale,
  For down I will not come.'

'Come down, come down, my lady fair,
  One sight of you I'll see;
Or else I'll set your house on fire,
  If better cannot be.'

Then he has set the house on fire,
  And all the rest it tuke;
He turned his wight horse head about,
  Said, Alas, they'll ne'er get out!   (246A: 12–23)

This kind of logorhoea, the result of a deteriorating structural sense, is a much remarked upon characteristic of many texts collected by Buchan. The third stylistic trait of oral structuring, the annular device, appears with comparative infrequency in Nicol's texts. It is hardly surprising that this device should rapidly atrophy, for it constitutes the clearest artistic mark of the nonliterate mode of spatial apprehension. Its disappearance reflects the change in mental consciousness—from spatial to linear—that is brought about by literacy. The singers' adoption of linear ways of thinking slackened their overall sense of ballad construction and the first sign of this is their omission of the frame.

In the character and narrative structures the same tendency towards diffuseness is apparent. Although the triangular interaction of three characters remains the basis of most stories, the development of the basic situation tends to include an enlarged cast of minor personae who detract from the once tautly dramatic interaction. The minor characters not only appear in greater numbers, but also take a greater part in the action, thereby blurring the distinction between the actors who are essential and inessential to the story, and, in general, dissipating the oral concentration of effect. Another kind of diffuseness results from the opposite tendency, that of emphasizing just one character throughout, as in 'Bonny John Seton' or 'Katharine Jaffray'. In the latter only Lochinvar of the three major characters actually speaks. What is lacking in these texts is the tightly organized dramatic interaction of a close-knit group of characters. The oral narrative structure with its balances and triads is still observable in many ballads, such as 'Lord Ingram and Chiel Wyet', as shown in Figure 34. In some ballad-texts, however, the sense of narrative proportion that was built into the oral

Figure 34

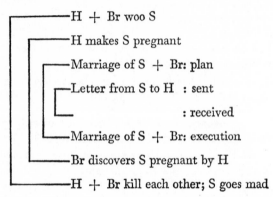

technique has disappeared, as the story has shifted its focus. In the other versions of 'The Clerk's Twa Sons o Owsenford', the story's emphasis lies in the attempts to save the lives of the students, but in Nicol's text they are killed off by stanza 6, and the emphasis shifts to the reactions of the Clerk and his wife to their deaths. Likewise the main concern of Nicol's 'Hind Etin' is now the 'gude kirking' for the heroine and her children rather than the conflicting claims of the earthly and the elfin worlds. This kind of change would indicate that the aesthetic sense of the folk, their conception of what constituted a good story well told, had itself undergone a shift in emphasis.

Although many elements of the oral structures remain, hardly any text retains a fully integrated oral architectonic. The change in the folk's consciousness from spatial to linear resulted in their losing the ability to construct in the old way the same organically unified wholes. They lost their sense of the ballad as a spatially related entity and began to see it as sequentially related. Instead of seeing the ballad as one coherent dovetailed piece, where the individual scenes, characters, and narrative strands are integrally welded together by the binary, trinary and annular patterns into an overall narrative conception, they began to view it as a story where simply one thing follows another. It was as if a three dimensional view of the ballad were succeeded by a two dimensional view. The oral technique ensured that the ballad-stories were retold in such a way that the organic relationship of the parts contributed to the total aesthetic unity. In Nicol's texts, however, the stories may be fragmented into two isolated scenes, as in 'Mary Hamilton', or have a series of once clearly defined scenes run together, as in 'Tam Lin', or have an un-balanced, disproportionate relationship between the scenes, as in 'Lord Saltoun and Auchanachie'. In short, the folk's ability to conceive of the ballad-story as a spatially related entity and to reconstruct it on that basis atrophied with the advent of literacy. Once the folk lost their sense of the necessary relationships between the parts and the whole and their sense of proportion, the architectonics of the oral ballad began to disintegrate.

In the verbal and aural patterns of the ballad, there occurred the same kind of breakdown in the oral aesthetic. Many formulaic words and episodes remain, but the necessity for composition by formula had gone. Consequently ballad language lost its former homogeneity and developed incongruities. English, the language of literacy for Scots, made ever-increasing inroads into the old formulaic style. Everywhere in the texts we can see the results of the new education: in words like 'espied' (188D: 11^3), in phrases like 'this witty lady fair' (110E: 60^5), in lines such as 'Lay gasping on the ground' (198A: 8^4), or ' "I'm not deceived," Queen Marie said' (173M: 3^1), or

> And underneath, there strangled lay
> A lovely baby sweet.   (173M: $4^{3,4}$)

or

> And were supported from time to time
> By what he made of prey.   (41C: $5^{3,4}$)

or such stanzas as

> The gentlemen all wondered
>   What could be in his mind,
> And asked if he'd a mind to fight;
>   Why spoke he so unkind?   (221G: 14)

or

> 'O woe is me,' the clerk cried out,
>   'This dismal sight to see,
> All the whole comfort of my life
>   Dead hanging on the tree!'
>
> He turned his horse's head about,
>   Making a piteous moan,
> And all the way to Oxenfoord,
>   Did sad and grievously groan.   (72D: 10,11)

The folk's exposure to poetical and polite and sentimental English produced not only stretches of doggerel but also lamentable drops into bathos. The revenger of 'Jellon Grame' upbraids the murderer

> 'For killing of my mother dear,
>   And her not hurting thee.'   (90B: 22)

While being burnt alive, Lord John laments:

> 'My eyes are seething in my head,
>   My flesh roasting also,
> My bowels are boiling with my blood;
>   Is not that a woeful woe?'   (196A: 18)

His lady is grief-stricken:

> Sophia Hay, Sophia Hay,
>   O bonny Sophia was her name,
> Her waiting maid put on her cloaths,
>   But I wot she tore them off again.   (196A: 25)

Not only the English of chap literature but also the English of the Bible infiltrated ballad language. After the battle at the Bridge of Dee John Seton is stripped of his armour by his enemies:

> Yea, they have left him naked there,
>   Upon the open field.   (198A: 12[3, 4])

There is, however, another tendency apparent in the ballad's linguistic changes. It is a tendency for the rhythms of the everyday vernacular of the Northeast, as distinct from the stylized rhythms of the formulaic language, to break through the traditional patterns. This can be seen very clearly in the last line of the following stanza,

> Syne rode the water with great speed,
>   And merrily the knows;
> Then fifty to the bridal came—
>   Indeed it was nae mows—   (221G: 20)

or in the arguments put forward by Jeannie Gordon's father in favour of her ugly suitor:

> 'Though he's bowed on the back and thrawin
>   on the knee,
> The bonny rigs of Salton they're nae
>   thrawin tee.'   (239A: $7^{3,4}$)

In his introduction to 'The Clerk's Twa Sons' Child comments that Nicol's version has 'some amusing dashes of prose, evidently of masculine origin', and goes on, 'We have here a strong contrast with both the blind-beggar and the housemaid style of corruption, something suggesting the attorney's clerk rather than the clerk of Owsenford, but at least not mawkish'.[10] The lines he cites are these:

> They thought their father's service mean,
>   Their mother's no great affair;   (72D: $2^{1,2}$)
>
> When he was certain of the fact,
>   An angry man was he,   (72D: $6^{1,2}$)

and

> 'O saddle a horse to me,' he cried,
>   'O do it quick and soon,
> That I may ride to fair Berwick,
>   And see what can be done.'   (72D: 8)

What we have here, however, is not clerkish corruption, but rather signs of a speaker of the Northeast vernacular adjusting to English and trying to re-create in English the broad-vowelled strength of his own dialect. In doing so, he reproduces the 'aff-takin', literal and unemotional characteristics of the dialect. These linguistic characteristics of the region were perfectly suited to the impersonal and objective tone of the oral ballad, but when they are transmuted into English and turn up in texts where sentimentality supersedes drama, then the results can be somewhat incongruous.

The aural patterns contain the same mixture of old and new. In general Nicol's rhyming sounds belong to the same groups as Mrs Brown's and contain the same key sounds and key words within sounds, although the frequency of use varies to some degree. The vowel rhymes make up 44 per cent of the total, the 'n' rhymes 30·5 per cent, and the consonant rhymes 25·5 per cent, as compared with Mrs Brown's figures of 38 per cent, 36 per cent and 26 per cent for the quatrain ballads and 18 per cent, 36·5 per cent, and 41·5 per cent for the couplet ballads. Nicol shows a predilection for the vowel rhyme, the vowel most often used being the standard 'ee' sound, which appears in 31 per cent of all Nicol's rhymes—more frequently than all the 'n' rhymes or all the consonant rhymes. The figures would suggest a swing over the centuries from the consonant rhymes, which are so common in the couplet ballads, to the vowel rhymes, and particularly the 'ee' sound. Nicol's texts, however, also reflect how the old patterns were breaking down under new pressures. They contain a greater variety of sounds and a higher proportion of slurred sounds than Mrs Brown's. Often Nicol is forced to rhyme on the same word; often the last line of a stanza is merely padding for the rhyme. Many rhymes are awkward because the singer attempts, not too successfully, to fit new words, frequently disyllabic, into the rhythms, as in the 'bower–honour' pairing of 'Lord Ingram and Chiel Wyet' (66A:1). English words now crop up regularly, sometimes coupling with a Northeast sound ('grenadiers–meares', 188D:4), and sometimes constituting a complete rhyme ('sell–well', 66A:8). These points all indicate that the singer was moving away from the traditional formulaic habits of the region.

In general the language of Nicol's texts is shot through, normally for the worse, with the new language of education, English. English not only transformed the formulaic verbal patterns but also helped to break up the formulaic syntactic patterns. Exposure to the rhythms of written English led the folk to imitate the poetaster ('And underneath there strangled lay,/A lovely baby sweet'), and to forego the basically paratactic method of oral construction in favour of the co-ordinated syntax of the prose writer:

And ere the porter could open the gate,
  The boy was in the hall,

In presence of that noble lord,
  And fell down on his knee: (65B: 14[5,6], 15[1,2])

And she would meal you with millering,
  That she gathers at the mill,
And make you thick as ony daigh:
  And when the pan was brimful

Would mess you up in scuttle-dishes,
  Syne bid us sup till we were fou,
Lay down her head upon a poke,
  Then sleep and snore like ony sow.   (110E: 42, 43)

In both cases, the co-ordinated syntax spans two stanzas. Just as the folk's grasp of the ballad as a structural unit slackened, so did their grasp of the stanza. The effects of their exposure to English and the available material in English were pervasive. English, the language of education and the language of literacy, exposed the local folk to new patterns of thought and linguistic expression and new conceptions of what constituted 'poetic' expression. There grew up a conception of English as the language of propriety and the language of poetry. English was 'poetic' because it was distanced; the more distanced and the more stilted, the more poetic. Nineteenth-century Scottish taste in Burns's poetry, which invariably favoured the sentimental and the stilted English poems, is a parallel indication of the national schizophrenia.

The breakdown in the oral technique of composition resulted in one large change in the aesthetic nature of the ballad. The aesthetic hallmark of the oral ballad is that it welds together into a perfectly unified whole dramatic, lyric, and narrative elements. In telling his story the maker concerns himself with what the characters do, how the characters feel, and how the characters interact with one another. He varies his scenes of narrative action, of emotional release and of dramatic confrontation to achieve a smooth blending of tones in the complete ballad. As the irreducible core of a ballad-story is the interaction of a few characters, we may say that the dramatic element is the predominating one and that it subsumes the narrative and lyrical elements. In the transitional texts, this is no longer the case. They manifest a distinct lack of subtlety in the tonal variation from scene to scene, because the singer now tends to think in terms of individual scenes or individual stanzas rather than the overall relationship of stanza to stanza and scene to scene. The binding dramatic element decreases in force and effect, and the narrative and emotional elements assume a greater prominence. Many versions begin dramatically and forcefully, then tail off because the singer thereafter concentrates on telling the story in flat sequential narrative, or concentrates on the emotions aroused by one event within the entire story. Such Nicol texts as 'Katharine Jaffray' and 'Lord Ingram and Chiel Wyet' suffer considerably from long stretches of flat narration. In the former, only one scene could be called effectively dramatic. The singer has lost not only the unifying dramatic conception of a ballad-story, but also the compulsion to re-create the action in dramatic terms; this is reflected in the steadily decreasing number of scenes in dialogue. Where in some ballad-texts the focus on the dramatic is replaced by a focus on the narrative, in others it is replaced by a focus on the emotional. In Nicol's corpus such texts include 'The Clerk's Twa Sons o Owsenford', 'Mary Hamilton', 'The Fire of Frendraught', 'Bonny John Seton', 'Lord Saltoun and Auchanachie', and 'Lord Thomas Stuart'. In all these versions, the main focus of interest is no longer on the dramatic interaction of characters but on the emotions connected with the death or dying of hero and heroine. The emphasis now given to the death-bed scenes and the gallows-foot speeches clearly betrays the influence of the new society's chap literature, with its 'Dying Confessions', 'Last Words', and the like. These by-products of literacy, however, merely intensified the process begun by literacy itself, when it removed the *raison d'être* of the oral mode of composition. The consequent decline of the oral-traditional technique resulted in not only a breakdown of the structural and formulaic patterns but also a fragmentation of the aesthetic and conceptual patterns that unified the oral ballad.

Although literacy was the crucial factor in altering the ways in which ballad-stories were told, the singers and their songs were also much affected by other forces at work in the new society. Nicol's transitional texts reflect the growth of two kinds of realism—a realism of detail and a realism of attitude. Where the oral texts derived no little imaginative power from the tension between the distancing and the localizing processes, the transitional texts rely much more heavily on localizing. Along with the references to the rural world,

> Wi plough-culters and gavellocks
> They made the jail-house door to flee;   (188D: 10[1,2])

appear references to the environment of the Industrial Revolution:

> As I cam in by yon canal
> And by yon bowling-green.   (231D: 3[1,2])

The growing prominence of law, medicine, and education in the new society is mirrored in the texts. The introduction of the law to rural districts and the consequent litigiousness that the minister of Kirkmichael comments on so ironically is reflected in 'The Earl of Errol':

> Now she is on to Edinburgh,
> For to try the law.   (231D: 6[1,2])

In like fashion, the arrival of medical practitioners results in this stanza:

> He did him to the doctor's shop,
>   As fast as he could gang,
> But ere the doctor could get there
>   Bird Isabel bore a son.   (257C: 5)

which is a far cry from Mrs Brown's traditional

> O he's bent his bow, an shot the deer,
>   An thro the green wood has he gane,
> An lang or he came back again
>   His lady bare him a son.   (101A: 24)

In another Nicol text, however, occurs a stanza with a leech rather than a doctor:

> 'O leech is come, an leech is gane,
>   Yet, father, I'm aye waur;
> There's not a leech in Edinbro
>   Can death from me debar.'   (259: 7)

The mixture of old and new in the style of that stanza parallels the mixture of old and new in these lines:

> And when he did grow up a bit,
>   She put him to the lair,
> And of all the youths was at that school
>   None could with him compare.
>
> And it fell once upon a day
>   A playtime it was come,   (90B: 15, 16[1, 2])

The ancient motif that has the hero overshadowing his fellows in youth is here relocated in the new environment for youths, the schoolhouse. Education and literacy also bring with them a new awareness of documents. This perhaps accounts for the new form of blandishment proffered one heroine by her suitors:

> The very charters of their lands
>   Into her hands they pat.   (302: 10[3, 4])

Education undoubtedly contributed to the other kind of realism, a logical, prosaic realism of attitude. Chiel Wyet responds thus to the news that his brother is going to marry his love:

> 'But I'll send to my brother's bridal—
>   The bacon shall be mine—'   (66A: 15[1, 2])

The details of Lord Thomas's illness are spelt out:

> When steeds were saddled an weel bridled,
>   An ready for to ride,
> There came a pain on that gude lord,
>   His back, likewise his side.   (259: 4)

May Margerie does not respond like other ballad heroines to her lover's command:

> Word has come to May Margerie,
>   In her bower where she sat:
> 'You are bid come to good green-wood,
>   To make your love a shirt.'
>
> 'I wonder much,' said May Margerie,
>   'At this message to me;

> There is not a month gone of this year
>   But I have made him three.'   (90B: 1, 2)

These lines all point to the development of a plodding rationalism. The motives of characters are also made more 'rational' by
being altered to accord with the conditions and probabilities of
the new society. Where the villain of Mrs Brown's 'Jellon
Grame' murders the heroine for this reason,

> 'O shoud I spare your life,' he says,
>   'Until that bairn be born,
> I ken fu well your stern father
>   Woud hang me on the morn.'   (90A: 11)

the villain in Nicol's text advances this explanation:

> Says, take you that now, May Margerie,
>   Just take you that from me,
> Because you love Brown Robin,
>   And never would love me.   (90B: 9)

The tendency towards a modern kind of rationalism undoubtedly helped provoke the replacement of the marvellous ballad
birds by the talking parrots found in the texts of Buchan and
other contemporary collectors. Altogether, education and the
sequential logic that comes with literacy blunted the folk's
appetite for the marvellous and the supernatural. In 'Hind Etin',
for example, Nicol's hero, now called 'Hastings the Groom',
retains only one attribute that would indicate his elfin origin, and
the story as a whole has lost its supernatural element and with
it most of its power.

The reading matter of the new society that reached the rural
districts affected both the substance and the style of the transitional texts. The influence of the broadside is particularly evident
in the initial stanzas of some ballads. 'Bonny John Seton' begins
with the heavy concentration on detail that is quite alien to the
oral ballad but common to the broadside:

> Upon the eighteenth day of June,
>   A dreary day to see,
> The southern lords did pitch their camp,
>   Just at the bridge of Dee.   (198A: 1)

'The Clerk's Twa Sons' opens with the kind of attention-catcher favoured by minstrels and hawkers:

> Oh I will tell a tale of woe,
>   Which makes my heart richt sair;   (72D: 1[1,2])

'Young Bearwell' and 'Burd Isabel and Earl Patrick' both begin with the kind of moralistic-proverbial tag that appears frequently in the broadsides:

> When two lovers love each other well,
>   Great sin it were them to twinn;
> And this I speak from Young Bearwell;   (302: 1[1-3])

and

> All young maidens fair and gay,
>   Whatever your station be,
> Never lay your love upon a man
>   Above your own degree.
>
> I speak it all by Bird Isabel;   (257C: 1, 2[1])

The first person comment is not confined to opening stanzas, however, for, as in 'Katharine Jaffray', it sometimes intrudes into the later action:

> 'But if I were young Lochinvar,
>   I woud not care a fly
> To take her on her wedding-day
>   From all her company.   (221G: 6)

This kind of personal intrusion is, of course, quite alien to the oral ballad.

As with the style so with the substance. The stories in which the singer makes much emotional capital out of a death nearly all exemplify the growing sentimentality of the transitional texts. An unappealing preciousness characterizes the deaths of the hero and heroine in 'Lord Saltoun and Auchanachie':

> Then ane of her maidens they loosed aff her gown,
> But bonny Jeanie Gordon she fell in a swoon;
> She fell in a swoon low down by their knee;
> Says, Look on, I die for my love Auchanachie!   (239A: 12)

and

'Some of you, her maidens, take me by the hand,
And show me the chamber Miss Jeanie died in;'
He kissed her cold lips, which were colder than stane,
And he died in the chamber that Jeanie died in. (239A: 15)

Just as the sentimentality derives from the new literature of popular entertainment, the religiosity that now incongruously appears in the ballad-texts may be traced to the spread of devotional literature. Evangelical terminology accords ill with the ballad context:

'O waken, waken, Rothiemay!
    O waken, brother dear!
And turn you to our Saviour;
    There is strong treason here.' (196A: 7)

'So I cannot loup, I cannot come,
    I cannot loup to thee;
My earthly part is all consumed,
    My spirit but speaks to thee.' (196A: 20)

Other odd changes in diction indicate how exposure to the new reading material affected the folk's attitudes. Where Nicol's text of 'Lord Ingram and Chiel Wyet' reads

'For a bit I'll beg for Chiel Wyet,
    For Lord Ingram I'll beg three;
All for the good and honourable marriage
    At Mary Kirk he gave me.' (66A: 31)

the Old Lady's version reads

'[For]ae mile [I wad gae] for Gil Viett,
    For Lord Ingram I wad hae gaen three;
An a' for that in good kirk-door
    Fair wedding he gave me.' (66B: 18)

The difference between the traditional 'fair wedding' and the modern 'good and honourable marriage' says much about the influences acting upon the folk. Hints of a growing class consciousness, and perhaps of exposure to polite literature, occur in the singer's emphasis on modes of address when, in 'Burd Isabel and Earl Patrick', the great-grand-aunt converses with heroine and hero:

And Isabel styled her madame,
　　And she, her Isabel dear.　　　　　　　　(257C: 11³,⁴)

And she has styled him, Patrick,
　　And[he] her, aunty dear.　　　　　　　　(257C: 15³,⁴)

Apart from the disintegration of the oral patternings, the alterations that have been noted in these Northeast texts bear a strong similarity to those noted by Tristram Potter Coffin in his study of ballad variation in North America.[11] Nineteenth-century ballad singers throughout the British-American world, it appears, were influenced by much the same forces. The widespread changes that occurred do not, however, in themselves constitute 'Ballad Variation'. They are the changes that affected the ballads after the advent of literacy, and do not explain ballad variation of the oral period. But as most of the recorded ballad versions in both Britain and America are transitional texts, a knowledge of the transitional period's changes is essential in determining the oral predecessors of these transitional versions.

Nicol's texts argue for the existence of a transitional mode of ballad reproduction in the transitional period. If Nicol's stories had been reproduced by the oral method, then his texts would be fully oral-traditional. If the modern method of reproduction by rote memorization had immediately succeeded the oral, the texts, again, would be fully oral-traditional. His texts, however, are not; there must therefore have been a transitional mode of reproduction. Like the oral, this mode was re-creative, for it is apparent that Nicol re-created his stories. The stanzaic variation in his different texts of 'Tam Lin', 'Lord Ingram and Chiel Wyet', 'The Earl of Errol', and 'Lord Saltoun and Auchanachie', and the frequent lexical variation all demonstrate that he was not bound by the literate fixation with stability of text. Moreover, his texts reflect his own society. But though Nicol re-created his stories, he did not re-create them in the oral manner, through the traditional structural and formulaic patternings. Some of his texts, such as 'Kemp Owyne', are strongly oral-traditional in cast, but in general his versions are not constructed according to the unifying oral principles. The transitional method of reproduction is re-creative, but it is rather haphazardly so, for the singer is not governed by the same organic necessities as was the nonliterate maker. In relation to the fully re-creative texts of an oral-traditional singer such as Mrs Brown, Nicol's texts may legitimately be described as loosely re-creative. In short, Nicol's method of reproduction is transitional because it represents the medial stage between the full re-creation of the oral maker, and the memorization by rote of the modern singer.

Nicol's ballads help to put Buchan's texts in their proper perspective. The defects for which Buchan's versions have been assailed also permeate Nicol's versions. This is hardly surprising, for the influences that acted upon Nicol, this respectable voucher, also acted upon Buchan's other informants. Differences in the degrees of vulgarity found in Buchan's texts can be accounted for by differences in the degree of intellectual power possessed by Nicol, an intelligent man, and others less fortunately endowed. It is possible that the Northeast folk, with their sheltered isolation and their innate conservatism, were more profoundly shaken by the upheavals of the crucial eighty years than were people more in the mainstream of Scottish life, and that their consequent struggle towards mental re-orientation showed more clearly in their ballads. At any rate, the very incongruities and vulgarities that provoked the accusations of fabrication actually present strong testimony for the basic genuineness of Buchan's collection, for Buchan's texts are transitional texts, recorded from a people newly and bewilderingly exposed to machine technology, education, and, above all, literacy.

Part V

The Modern Tradition

Chapter 18

The Ballads of Bell Robertson

After the upheavals of the various revolutions, the Northeast settled down into the social and economic patterns which, in the main, still obtain today. The modern period begins round about 1830. By this date the switchover from domestic to factory employment had brought about the final decay of the woollen and linen industries; and with the disappearance of these rural industries, the Northeast became once more a predominantly agricultural area. The development of communications, however, had broken down for good the old isolation, as the building of roads, canals, harbours and railways opened up the area and brought it into closer contact with the rest of Britain. Within the region, the simple settlement pattern of burghs and ferm-touns was superseded by the modern pattern of city, towns, villages, farms and crofts. And this diversified pattern of settlement reflects the diversified nature of society as a whole; it was no longer a simple, homogeneous society, but a complex, diversified, modern society.

In this society the developments which most strongly affected the regional tradition were growing in importance and influence: education increased its scope, and finally became available to all; literacy became the normal condition, for women as well as for men. Following upon the spread of education and literacy came the spread of printed material. It has already been noted that the wide popularity of chap literature was a phenomenon largely peculiar to the transitional period; that it was not completely confined to this period can be seen in the success of the Fintray Press, which flourished about the middle of the nineteenth century, and published innumerable reprintings of all its twenty-one chapbooks.[1] In the modern period, however, the old-style chapbooks were replaced in a number of ways. The modern equivalents of the old chapbooks were the slip-songs, printed for and sold at the feeing markets, but the replacements were not always in kind.[2] People were now reading newspapers consistently, and taking advantage of the numerous parish libraries that existed by the eighteen-forties. Almost all the reading material in this modern period is, of course, in Standard English.

The great collector of northeastern ballads in the modern period was the dominie at Whitehill, New Deer, Gavin Greig. Although only part of his huge folksong collection has yet been published, *Last Leaves* contains all the versions of the old ballad-stories and *Folk-Song of the North-East* gives a representative idea of the collection in all its heterogeneity. By Greig's time the effect of print on the ballad tradition is quite pronounced. Numbers of texts collected by Greig are obviously of broadside origin, and among them are even traces of blackletter versions. Almost the entire stock of one of his contributors, Mrs Gillespie, comprises ballad-texts derived from broadsheet or chapbook. Her version of one ballad-story, 'The Rantin Laddie', is like three of the other four Greig texts in resembling closely the version in Alexander Laing's *Thistle of Scotland*, a provenance that indicates how printed texts were often introduced into the tradition, for Laing not only published ballads but also hawked his own printed texts round the rural districts of the Northeast.[3] The extent to which the printed ballad-texts had permeated the tradition may also be gauged by the ballads which Walter Gregor picks out as examples of those likely to be sung of an evening in the farm kitchen: 'The Haughs of Cromdale', 'The Duke of Gordon's Three Daughters', 'Sir James the Rose', 'Gregor's Ghost', and 'Andrew Lammie'.[4] This list retails not the old ballads but the favourite chap ballads of the Northeast. 'Sir James the Rose' provides an interesting example of what happened within the tradition, for while Peter Buchan in his *Gleanings* gave two versions of it—the 'old way' and the 'modern way'—Keith in *Last Leaves* was forced to print the modern poem, which had supplanted the older version in the regional tradition. The singers, however, not only learned printed ballad-texts from the broadsheets but also learned other texts which they had written down in their own MS. books. A number of ballad versions in *Last Leaves* came from the MS. books of

John Garioch of Cushnie, James Walker of Alford, Sam. Davidson of Tarves, and Mrs Beaton of Turriff; the earliest date given
for one of these books is 1858. By this stage in its development
the regional tradition was thoroughly permeated by literary
influences.

Greig's most important contributor was Bell Robertson, who
provided him with just under four hundred items of folksong.
She received most of her ballads from her mother, a well-known
singer in Strichen; others she picked up from an aunt, a girl-
friend, a tinker-boy, and a blacksmith she heard at a meal-and-ale.
It is worth remarking that both Nicol's and much of Bell Robertson's ballads come not only from the same regional folksong
tradition, but even from the same village folksong tradition.
Bell Robertson, besides being a reciter of folksong, was also a
poetess in a minor way. Her verses were mainly poems of
conventional piety, as might be gathered from the passage
written with such unselfconscious condescension by Mrs Frank
Russell of Aden:[5]

> It is remarkable what beautiful, spiritual thoughts one
> sometimes gathers from the working classes. In a small,
> two-roomed cottage at one of the lodges at Aden lived a
> one-armed, invalid man who had a very interesting
> maidservant called Isabella Robertson, who wrote
> beautiful poems and hymns. Her wages were only two
> pounds a year and her keep, but she was perfectly
> contented. She liked being of use. Her conversation was
> a mine of beautiful and original thoughts. I only wish I
> had written some of them down. I helped her to publish
> a small volume, called 'Lays of Buchan', and a few
> pieces have been printed in local papers and periodicals,
> but these only give a faint idea of this self taught genius.
> She was a perfect mine of local traditions, and many a
> tale she told me and my children of smugglers and
> pirates, and strange happenings in days gone by, which
> have never found their way into print.

From this, one can perceive in the paradox of Bell Robertson's
situation a parallel to that of Mrs Brown's; both were innately
religious and highly respectable women, yet both were the most
important transmitters, in their times, of the folk's ballads,

which were not religious and were sometimes quite dis-reputable.

On the title page of a volume among the Will Walker MSS. entitled *Scottish Ballads and Songs* is written that the volume contains 'The traditional texts of Popular Ballads, taken down from Miss Bell Robertson & other singers in Aberdeenshire by Mr Greig.—Useful to show the various stages by which traditional lore descends from higher to lower forms in the course of time.' Although Walker does not particularize, this is exactly what Bell Robertson's ballads do; they show the descent from higher to lower forms, for they are modern renderings of the old ballad-stories. Their modernity depends not just on their chronological context, but on their method of reproduction and transmission. They illustrate how ballad-stories transmitted within a modern, literate society were reproduced by the literate method of rote memorization.

The effects of this method of reproduction on the old balladry are most evident in the defectiveness of many of her texts; only one-third of the eighty-four ballad pieces she gave Greig could be called complete. It should be remembered, however, that Bell Robertson did not sing her ballads but recited them, and the absence of the musical aid to memory might well have contributed to the fragmentary nature of many of her songs. Further evidence of memorization can be seen in her attitude to the texts. In stanza 23 of 'The Knight and Shepherd's Daughter' appears the word 'impet', which was the word she learned, but which she had never heard anywhere else, and which she looked on as a mistake for 'mintit'. In stanza 12 of 'Tam Lin' she gave the phrase 'an elfin rae' as she heard it from her mother, but queried its correctness. In her C version of 'Lord Thomas and Fair Annet' appears the word 'moss' which, she said, should perhaps be 'mass'. She did not understand one line in stanza 10 of 'The Gardener', but gave it just as she had heard it. The fourth line of stanza 2 in 'Proud Lady Margaret' is, as the notes have it, 'clearly corrupt, but B. R. explained (charac-teristically) that though she could have put this right, she must give it as she received it'.[6] It is clearly evident from this that Bell Robertson memorized her ballads. Her attitude to the texts, when compared with Mrs Brown's positive, re-creative approach, was negative, even to the extent of her refusing to make sense out of lines that were patently nonsense. Not only was it a case of her memorizing texts sung by other singers but also of her learning by rote off the printed page. Her E version of 'The Cruel Mother', for example, which is very close to Scott's version, was 'learned from a chapbook', and as her principal source, her mother, was fond of chapbooks, it can be assumed that many more were of chap origin.[7]

Literacy wrought far-reaching effects on ballad tradition. The most significant, and in the long term most destructive, change concerned the method of reproduction. Where a nonliterate ballad singer learned both a method of ballad composition and a number of ballad-stories and thereby created ballad-texts, the literate singer merely learns ballad-texts. In the oral period the process of reproduction involved creative composition; in the modern period it involves only memorization. Although the ballad versions of such literate singers and reciters as Bell Robertson are reproductions of oral ballad-stories, they are modern reproductions, that is, they are transitional, and in some cases oral, texts caught in the amber of memorization. The memorized texts do not remain rigidly fixed, of course, but further changes result largely from the negative causes of forgetting, omission, and conflation.

Most of the versions memorized by Bell Robertson are transitional texts, but a few are oral. For example, her versions of 'Child Waters', 'Brown Adam', and 'Bonnie Baby Livingston', though much shorter than Mrs Brown's versions, bear the same oral hallmarks of structure and formula. In these instances, presumably, no transitional singer had intervened in the process of transmission, and a fully literate person—either Bell Robertson or her source—had memorized directly the texts of a nonliterate singer. In general, however, her versions exemplify the changes introduced during the transitional period by singers employing the loosely re-creative mode of reproduction; the characteristics of Nicol's texts repeat themselves. The oral patterns in structure and language have disintegrated. The oral aesthetic pattern, in which the narrative and emotional elements were subsumed within a unifying dramatic conception, has broken down under the pressures of modern concern for sequential narration and indulgent emotionality. The latter tendency occurs more frequently than the former in Bell Robertson's ballads, where emotion has often degenerated into sentimentality. The loss of hard objectivity produces some unprepossessing results, such as the ending to her 'Lass of Roch Royal':

> Love Gregory tore his yellow hair
>   An' rent his clothing fine,
> An' threw himsel' in [   ] Park
>   Among the wild wood swine.
>
> When Lord [   ] heard o' that,
>   That sic a man was there,
> Then he put him in strong prison
>   For full six months an' mair.
>
> When his love Janet she heard o' that,
>   That her true lover was there,
> Then she gart build a bonnie ship,
>   An' set her to the faem,
> An' she's gane an' borrowed her true love,
>   An' safely brought him hame.   (xxx: B26–8)

As in Nicol's corpus, a certain religiosity colours a number of texts: in 'Tam Lin' a bible appears in the pagan rite; in 'Sir Patrick Spens' the ladies wait 'Wi their bibles in their han' '; and in 'Young Allan' the sailor boy, with an equal regard for grace and gear, asks the captain:

> 'What wid ye gie, my master dear,
>   What wid ye gie to me,
> That wi the help o my Maker
>   Wid bring ye safe fae sea?'   (lxxxv: 17)

The tendencies towards realism of attitude and realism of detail also permeate Bell Robertson's versions. The concern for prosaic rationality produces the 'pretty parrot' of 'Lady Isabel and the Elf Knight' and the emphasis on the logic by which Robin discovers Rose to be a woman in 'Rose the Red and White Lily'. The increasing preference for setting the story in a known world manifests itself in such a ballad as 'The Twa Sisters' where the sisters are in love, not with a lord, but with the local 'miller lad'. Despite the change in social ambience, many of the old aristocratic trappings—the lover's land, brooches and rings—still remain to produce a peculiar incongruity. Ironically, the primary cause of these modern characteristics is itself recorded in 'Fair Annie', where the heroine claims proudly for her fifth son that 'he can read an' vreet'.

The linguistic consequences of the folk's ability to 'read an' vreet' pervade Bell Robertson's versions, those of traditional as well as chap origin. Throughout her texts one comes across lines and stanzas whose language shows the extensive influence of sub-literary productions:

Ye're impudent an' insolent — (xxii: B21³)

An' he's seduced my ae daughter — (xxvii: 12³)

I wish it may no proceed — (xxxix: 1²)

Though ye hae reveal'd yoursel in shame — (xxxix: 24³)

They sent for [   ] who instantly came — (li: 2¹, 4¹, 6¹)

They rendezvous'd on Calie's banks — (lxxi: 12¹)

It was nae leal virgin that ye did wed — (lxxxviii: B15⁴)

'O what can I do, nerice,' he said
'To induce her to come down?' — (xxxiv: 3¹, ²)

A pox on you, Logie, now since it is so,
A lady's love laid on you, must she die in her woe?
— (lxxxi: C14)

and

In sorrow then she rent her gown,
    In anguish tore her hair:
'Gin onything ail my bonnie love,
    Father, I will despair.' — (lxxxvii: 12)

As in Nicol's ballads, the old formulaic language is also breached by the vernacular rhythms of the Northeast:

An' my father winna eat a bit gin I be missed awa
— (xix: c2⁴)

But the lassie she's gotten the laddie that she liket
— (liv: 18³)

An' I'm sae fat an' fu' o flesh,
I'm fell feart for mysel. — (xv: 23⁵, ⁶)

My heid's the thing 'at I canna weel want,
My lady she loves it dearly. (lxxxiii: $9^{1,2}$)

These linguistic changes, however, are merely the most visible
of the changes which occurred in the ballad tradition during the
transitional period. The alterations are retained in Bell Robertson's versions because her transitional texts are products of the
modern method of reproduction by literate memorization. With
the arrival of this method, the old tradition passes into its final
stage. Although the ballads of the tradition can be kept as
specimens by modern recording methods, the tradition itself, as
a living body of song sung by the folk, decays. The power, once
inherent in the tradition, of constant revitalization through
constant re-creation dissipates once the concept of the fixed text
takes root and memorization by rote becomes the standard
method of reproduction. The creative energies of the folk are
generally channelled elsewhere; but if the regional tradition is
strong enough, these energies can go towards extending the old
tradition in a new direction. This, as can be seen from the next
chapter, is what happened in the Northeast.

Chapter 19

The Bothy Ballads

From 1830 onwards agriculture was once again paramount in the Northeast, unhampered by the demands of the rural industries. But now, after all the improvements of the agrarian revolution, the agricultural industry stood on a modern footing. New crops and rotations, improved tools and machines, all generated greater productivity. New methods of communication such as the railways and the steamboats enabled cattle to be shipped directly to southern markets and gave a huge impetus to cattle-rearing, one outcome of which was the development of the Aberdeen-Angus breed. As we have seen, the improvements had a pronounced effect on the organization of rural society. Just as the growth of capitalist farming ensured that the farming units were split up into large farms and small crofts, it ensured that rural society was divided into a small group of wealthy farmers and a large group of farm labourers. Those farm-servants who were married generally lived in cottages near the farm, and those who were unmarried—the greater majority—lived in the bothy. This building lent its name to the new type of ballad which grew out of the modern rural conditions.

The breaking down of the old homogeneous class, the small tenantry, into the extremes of gentlemen-farmers and farm-servants had unfortunate social results. Hugh Miller, the geologist, who had himself experienced life in more northerly bothies, wrote an incisive article in 1841 on the iniquities of the bothy system, in which he referred, in a phrase of Burns, to the gentleman-farmer as having passed from the 'head of the commonalty to the tail of the gentry', and to the farm-servant as having sunk 'into a mere ploughing and harrowing machine'. Humane values depreciated; to the farmer, writes Miller, the farm labourer[1]

represents merely a certain quantum of power purchased
at a certain price, and applied to a certain purpose; and
as it is, unluckily, power purchased by the half-year, and
abundant in the market, there is no necessity that it
should be husbanded from motives of economy, like that
of the farmer's horses or of his steam-engine; and therefore little heed is taken though it should thus run to
waste. The consequences are in most cases deplorable.

For much of the nineteenth century, the farm-servant had little
chance of improving his conditions. Before the passing of the
Master and Servant Act of 1867, the individual farm labourer
could expect little help from the law in any dispute over conditions with the farmer.[2]

It was the conditions of employment rather than an increase
in wages that primarily concerned the labourers. Many complaints were laid against the method of engagement, by which
labourers were fee'd to certain farms for six-monthly or yearly
terms. As the farm-workers rarely stayed longer than one term
at any one farm, their life was a roaming one, rooted temporarily
at Whitsun and Martinmas by an agreement made at a feeing
market. This institution came in for much adverse comment; one
Aberdeenshire man, James Allan, who bothied in the eighteen-
sixties, writes:[3]

On the subject of feeing markets and six monthly
engagements I am convinced that, if these were done
away with, then that restlessness and that shifting among
farm servants would disappear also. Wages should be
paid monthly with a month's notice on either side.
Masters and men would get to understand each other
better. Feeing markets always remind me of the old
days when slaves were bought and sold by their general
physical appearance, as one would buy a horse at St
Sair's Fair. I myself have had my wrists examined by
farmers, to see what appearance of strength there was
about them.

The grievances of the farm-servants of the Northeast found
expression in the three attempts made after 1870 to establish
a union of agricultural labourers. The first two attempts, in
1872 and in 1880, came to nothing, but the objectives of the

1872 meeting at Longside provide a fair idea of the farm-servants' grounds of complaint: 'a shorter working week to be secured by the elimination of the "suppering" of horses; increased wages; better sleeping accommodation; the subsidizing of emigration to relieve the overstocked labour market; and the abolition of the hiring fairs and their substitution by the payment of monthly wages'.[4] Although the initial attempts to form a union failed, the third attempt did achieve a certain measure of success, for by 1886 there were established branches of the union, known first as the Scottish Farm Servants' Union and later as the Scottish Ploughmen and General Labourers' Union, which lasted until 1900. The reasons for the relative failure to build up a strong union in the late nineteenth century lay largely in the peripatetic nature of the ploughman's life, and the lack of efficient leaders; to this can be added the innate conservatism of the northeastern farm-servant, which was accentuated in the case of the bothy inhabitant by what Miller calls his 'indifferency and lack of care', results of his 'general discomfort'.[5] In the nineteenth century, then, tensions existed between farmers and farm-servants, and the strained relations resulted in the main from the farm-workers' conditions of employment.[6]

These conditions were far from comfortable, yet they were the conditions which produced a new type of ballad. The bulk of the farm-servants lived in the bothy, or the 'men's hoose', a building which was sometimes part of the steading square, and sometimes an outhouse beside the stable, swinehouse, and byre.[7] In this room the servants cooked, ate, slept, sat, and sang. Although the bothy became common only after the improvements, before that time its prototype could be found on the larger farms. In the 1738 'Accompt of Goods and Gear belonging to the Deceast Morgan in Kirktoun of Monymusk', a list headed 'In the Men's House' retails its multifarious contents: two open beds, two chaff beds, three feather bolsters, three feather cods, a pair of linen sheets, three single sheets, a chaff bolster, six pairs of blankets, and an old covering, together with a malt granary, one pair of curricks, one pair of muck creels, one pair of peat creels, a horse, and two cows.[8] Sometimes some of the men slept in a chaumer, which was often, but not always, a loft above the stable. James Allan's experiences of chaumers were of a mixed variety:[9]

My first 'chaumer' (French chambre, a bedroom) at Tullos was a hut resembling a pighouse, the floor of which was eighteen inches below the ground level. In rainy weather the water came in at the door, and ran out under the wall at the other side of the hovel. There was no fireplace. I had planks to walk on to get to my bed with dry feet. Any modern pighouse is infinitely superior. And I was a boy and alone. My next home was on the west side of Monymusk, and there with another fee-ed man, I slept in a loft above the stable, in the atmosphere which the horses had first used below. The roof was of the common type, rafters, divot lath, divots, and thatch of broom. The stable rats burrowed regularly in this roof. We had to acquire the habit, in the morning, of refraining from opening our eyes until first we shook our heads face downwards over the bedside to clear the dust which fell overnight from the rats upon our eyelids! At other farms, I found the 'chaumer' reasonably good, in some cases, very good.

It is Allan again who provides a concise account of the hours of work:

We worked ten hours a day in two 'yokins' of five hours each; from six to eleven and from one to six with no half holiday on Saturday. In addition, we got up at five or earlier to feed and clean our horses before breakfast at five-thirty; and the horses required attention in the evening. In harvest we worked an eleven hours' day from six to ten, from eleven to two, and from three to seven. All our food was brought to us in the field.

For leisure, there was courting, singing, drinking, and the ploughing matches. The first three may be accounted standard occupations, but the latter were also extremely popular, as the presence of 19,000 spectators at the 1872 national championships at Inverurie might testify. All these goings-on, even the ploughing matches, are reflected in the ballads sung in the bothies.

Food is another favourite subject of the bothy songs. The staple diet of the ploughmen was oatmeal, which can be prepared in a number of ways but which was normally consumed in the bothies as brose. Robertson, writing in 1807, says of the lads of the Mearns bothies[10] that they

> live entirely on oatmeal. Nor are they very nice in the cooking of it. With a little warm water poured over a handful of meal in a dish, their dinner is made in an instant. I have known them use cold water for this purpose, when in a hurry.

By the sixties, however, some diversity had crept into the diet of the farmhouse-fed labourer:[11]

> Regarding our food in farm service, I had no complaint to make; it was clean and wholesome. At five-thirty we had water brose and milk, and oatcakes ad libitum. At noon we had perhaps vegetable broth, or milk broth, potatoes stoved or chappit, or milk brose, whey brose, ale brose, cabbage brose, kale brose or turnip brose. Seldom or never did we have meat. . . . For our third and last meal, we had a plate of porridge or some kind of brose, with oatcakes and skimmed milk to fill any void . . . On this diet, I weighed 14 stones 4 lbs at eighteen years of age. . . . [but in the bothies] we had time only to make brose. On Sundays we pooled our resources, and bought something extra, and the kitchen 'deem' came and helped to cook. Bothies should be made illegal; I did not like them. On some farms on Sunday morning we got each one cup of tea, a small pat of butter and sometimes as a great treat, a red herring.

It is said that a southern visitor, on enquiring whether the monotony of the oatmeal diet ever palled, received as reply from a farm-servant, 'Fat, wad a man iver tire o's maet!'.

The business of living in the bothy is frequently described as 'gey roch', but Miller's account of tempers erupting at the slightest provocation because of the workers' 'bitter discontent' seems to be rather on the lurid side. His experience of bothying under a bad master does provide, however, some indication of what the bothy system at its worst could be like:[12]

> It seems natural for men in such circumstances to be careless of themselves, and equally natural for them to

avenge on the cause of their general discomfort the
irritating effects of their own indifferency and lack of
care. There was a large amount of rude sarcasm in the
bothy, and strange as it may seem, a great deal of
laughter. It has been remarked by, we think, a French
writer, that the people of despotic governments laugh
more than those of free States. We never heard the
name of the farmer mentioned without some accompanying
expression of dislike; we never saw one of them manifest
the slightest regard for his interest. They ill-treated his
horses, neglected his cattle, left his corn to rot in the
fields. Some of them could speak of his approaching ruin
with positive glee.

Life was hard, but not always as hard as this. It has to be
remembered, of course, that the bothy community, like the
cowboy and lumberjack communities of America, was a masculine
community, and was inevitably fairly rough in its style of living.
Yet for the bothy community, and in this it is again like the
others, song played a vital part in its life. Like their forebears,
the men of the bothy both composed and sang, and though
many of the bothy ballads have little aesthetic merit, they do
show how folksongs grow naturally out of the life of the folk
who composed and sang them.

Although the bothy ballad draws its narrative material from
the ploughman's life in the middle and late nineteenth century,
traces exist before then of elements which contributed to its
emergence as a distinctive kind of ballad. We have already seen
how the localizing of the oral ballad led in the transitional period
to a greater realism, and this tendency in the modern period
came to full fruition in the bothy ballad. Among Child's 'Rejected
Pieces' is a ballad, 'The Baron turned Ploughman' (or 'The
Hireman Chiel' or 'The Hind Childe'), apparently indigenous
to the Northeast, whose title is symptomatic of the process.[13] Its
story links the baron minstrelsy, the oral ballads, to the ploughman minstrelsy, the bothy ballads, by reflecting the gradual
shift in focus from baron and baron's life to ploughman and
ploughman's life. The shift in focus must have established itself
by the beginning of the modern period, for some fragmented
stanzas collected by Alexander Laing of Brechin between 1829

and 1835 would indicate that the new ballad was beginning to evolve at that time.[14] One of the stanzas, Fragment III, has a very familiar ring:

> Maggie Mackie made the broth
> An Oh! But they did ill wi me,
> Here a groat an there a groat
> An aye the wearie dribble bree.

It is of course first cousin to the stanza in 'The Barnyards o' Delgaty':

> Meg Macpherson mak's my brose,
>   Her and me we canna gree;
> First a mote an syne a knot,
>   And aye the tither jilp o' bree.   (st. 7; *FSNE*, art. iv)

Influences from outside the folk tradition also affected the development of the bothy ballad. In the eighteenth-century chapbooks appear songs such as 'The Ravelled Booking of the Ord' which are precursors in tone, style and content of the ploughman ballads, and tales which in incident and method of description are also remarkably akin to later bothy songs. One cornkister, 'The Weddin' o' M'Ginnis', illustrates the diversity of possible influences. On the one hand it exhibits striking similarities to the first part of the chapbook tale 'Jockey and Maggy's Courtship'.[15] On the other hand it resembles a popular chapbook song, Tannahill's 'The Kebbuckston Wedding', which is related to the seventeenth-century piece by Francis Sempill, 'The Blythsome Bridal'; this in turn belongs to that long line of poems in the Scottish literary tradition which are devoted to communal revelries and which include, for example, 'Peblis to the Play', 'Christ's Kirk on the Green', 'Leith Races', and 'The Holy Fair'. By the modern period, the folk tradition, the popular tradition, and the literary tradition all overlapped.

The term 'bothy ballad' can be used in two ways: it can be used in the wide sense, to refer to all those songs which were sung in the bothies, or in the more specific sense, to refer to those narrative songs which deal directly with the life of the men who inhabited the bothies. The latter acceptation is the more common and is the one employed here, for these songs of the ploughmen are, as Gavin Greig says, 'the most characteristic kind of folk-song' of the Northeast. He continues:[16]

> folk-song tends to seek the lowest social level. It follows
> that, as the farm-servant class represents this ultimate
> stratum in our rural districts, where alone practically
> traditional minstrelsy survives, we may expect to find
> among them the greatest amount of authentic folksong.
> They are now in fact pretty much its custodians. As a
> class our ploughmen have got the hereditary ear and
> taste for this kind of thing.

The bothy ballads are also known as 'cornkisters', from the habit the ploughmen had of dunting the heels of their tacketty boots on the cornkists (corn-chests) in time to the tune.

The central bulk of the bothy ballads are concerned with the work, leisure, and people encountered during a term's feeing at one particular farm. They number between twenty and thirty: 'The Barnyards o' Delgaty', 'Drumdelgie', 'Guise o' Tough', 'Lamachree and Megrum', 'Cameloun', 'South Ythsie', 'Between Stanehive and Laurencekirk', 'O Charlie, O Charlie', 'The Scranky Black Farmer', 'The Ardlaw Crew', 'Sowens for Sap', 'Newmill', 'Oor Fairm Toon', 'The Woods of Rickarton', 'John Bruce', 'Darrahill', 'Sleepy Toon', 'Swaggers', 'The Barns o' Beneuches', 'Benton', 'The Praise o' Huntly', 'Mullnabeeny', 'Auld Luckie', and 'Nethermill'.[17] The first two are probably the best known, and between them they exemplify the two basic patterns of development that are found, either separately or intermingled, in nearly all of the others. 'The Barnyards o' Delgaty', for example, deals with one term: the feeing, the promises of the farmer, then the bleak actuality of the farm as it shows itself in scraggy horses and poor cooking. In many of the songs this is followed by an account of the farm personnel, each individual being given a stanza. 'Drumdelgie', on the other hand, is basically concerned with the details of a day's work at the farm, recounted in a way that leads naturally to the stalwart valediction:

> Fare ye weel, Drumdelgie,
>   I bid ye a' adieu;
> I leave ye as I got ye,—
>   A maist unceevil crew.   (14; iv)

'The Barnyards o' Delgaty' ends in similar fashion, with another well-known stanza:

> My can'le noo it is brunt oot,
>   The snotter's fairly on the wane;
> Sae fare ye well, ye Barnyards,
>   Ye'll never catch me here again.   (10; iv)

As can be gathered from this pair of final stanzas the tone of the bothy ballads is broadly satirical. Generally it is the farmer who comes under the lash, as in 'Swaggers':

> He'll be aye lauch—lauchin',
>   He'll be aye lauchin' there;
> And he'll hae on the blithest face
>   In a' Porter Fair.
>
> Wi' his fine horse and harness,
>   Sae weel's he'll gar ye true;
> But when ye come to Auchterless,
>   Sae sair's he'll gar ye rue.   (2–3; cxxxviii)

These stanzas illustrate well how the bothy songs, in the same quatrain as many of the old ballads, are very often built up by the same repetitive and antithetical rhythms that characterize the stanzaic constructions of the old ballad. Sometimes the conditions of work are the object of the ploughman's complaint,

> For the Braes o' Broo are ill to ploo,
>   They're roch and reesky a', man.   ('The Braes o' Broo':
> $1^{3, 4}$; lxv)

and sometimes the tools:

> My ploo she wisna workin' weel,
>   She widna throw the fur,
> The gaffer says 'There's a better ane
>   At the smiddy to gang for'.
>
> When I got hame the new ploo
>   She pleased me unco weel,
> But I thocht she wid be better
>   Gin she hid a cuttin' wheel.   ('Guise o' Tough': 8, 9; iv)

The farmer's wife is often portrayed as bad-tempered, affected, and mean, particularly where food is concerned. This latter subject is a favourite one, and has inspired some choice lines,

> The breid was thick, the brose was thin,
>> And the broth they were like bree;
> I chased the barley roon the plate,
>> And a' I got was three.　　　　('Newmill': 3; xcii)

and

> We get beef bree whiles weel seasoned wi' reek
> Wi three seeds o' barley and the smell o' a leek
>> ('The Barns o' Beneuches': 6[1,2];
>> cxlii)

The bothy ballads attack the homely targets of their satire in a wryly good-humoured fashion. For more radical expression of discontent one has to go outwith the bothy ballads to the bothy songs, to such a song as 'Depression', which probably reflects the depressed state of agriculture in the late eighteen-seventies:

> But this cursed gentry they walk oot on sentry,
>> They coont ilka plack an' bawbee that they won;
> Walks oot at their leisure, lies up at their pleasure,
>> Like Solomon's lilies they card not nor spin.

> But we'll fill up a nappie, an' tak' a wee drappie,
>> An' aye be contented wherever we go;
> Nae langer this nation will thole the oppression,
>> The laird an' the factor will get an o'erthrow.
>>>> (4–5; cxlvii)

Other indications of social disturbance are to be found in a fragmentary song dealing with the Fraserburgh Meal Riots of 1846 and in 'The Bothy Lads of Forfar', the heroes of which are sent to Botany Bay for sixteen years. The militant class-consciousness that marks 'Depression' is, however, comparatively rare, and for balance must be considered in conjunction with the lauding of a kind-hearted landlord in 'Lord Fife':

> When to Lord Fyfe his tenants go,
>> Their misery to tell,
> Go home, possess your farms again,
>> I'll pay the rent mysel'.　　　　(8; clx)

Some of the bothy ballads concentrate on specific aspects of the ploughman's life and work that are covered more cursorily in the main group. The subject of 'Ellon Fair' is the feeing, while those of 'Harrowing Time', 'The Dalmuir Ploughing Match', and 'The Plooin Match' are self-evident. The largest group in this category is composed of the harvest songs: 'Johnnie Sangster', 'The Boghead Crew', 'The Hairst o' Rettie', 'The Lothian Hairst', 'The Kiethen Hairst', and 'The Harvest Song'. Here again, the initial pair exemplify the two basic patterns of development, the first song being concerned with the details of the work, the second with the harvest hands.

Another category of the bothy ballads consists of songs which deal with a humorous incident from farm life. Some, such as 'The Courtin in the Stable', 'Tam Gibb and the Soo', 'The Straw Man', and 'Kissin in the Dark' deal with the humours of courtship; some, such as 'Davie and his Kye', and 'Be kin' to yer Nainsel', John' deal with the humours of character; while 'The Tarves Rant' deals, like 'Tam o' Shanter' but more prosaically, with an evening's revelry and its retribution.

The authors of many of these songs can be traced. Indeed, while Greig was writing his articles for the *Buchan Observer*, a friend sent him a ploughman song along the standard lines, 'The Northessie Crew', which had been written the previous year, 1907, by Francis Massie, and William Forsyth, then in his eighties, sent him a copy of 'South Ythsie' which he had composed, along with 'Nethermill', when a young man. The practice of composing songs about the farms they were fee'd to was fairly general, according to Gordon M'Queen, author of 'The Ardlaw Crew',

> For rhymin's grown sae common noo,
>   That the like o' me maun try
> To get a verse or twa to clink,
>   To gar the time pass by.   (3; xcii)

though it is doubtful if the conditions of composition were always those of 'South Ythsie':

> When this few lines I did compose,
>   To haud me on thocht lang,
> I was harrowin' in the Chapel park,
>   Amongst the turnip land.   (26; xxi)

The ploughmen not only composed their own songs but also adapted poems to known tunes and added them to their repertoire. Two such poems are William Anderson's 'Jean Findlater's Loon', and 'Tipperty's Jean', which was composed by Dr Patrick Buchan, Peter Buchan's eldest son. The readiness with which these literate poems were accepted by the folk is one indication that the new ballads of the folk were no longer a genre apart, but merely literate productions ranking low on the literary scale. They still belong to tradition, of course, because they were normally transmitted by word-of-mouth, but the method of transmission was, modern fashion, memorization. Textual variation, consequently, is minor, though the singers seem to have allowed themselves more verbal latitude with the modern ballads than with the old. It is conceivable, however, that modern ballads of other cultures may have been composed and transmitted during the transitional period, and as a result may manifest rather greater variation.

In his notes to 'The Ardlaw Crew', Greig writes that[18]

> these ditties of farm life constitute the most genuinely native part of our popular minstrelsy. They may not amount to much as poetry: but there is an air of sincerity and conviction about them that makes for force and vitality. Further, they illustrate local life and language better than any other kind of song or ballad which we have.

This is a very fair summing-up of the bothy ballad, but it would be impossible to leave the subject without remarking on the writer who worked within the bothy tradition, and yet transcended it. The writer is George Bruce Thomson, a native of New Deer, and the author of 'The Weddin' o' M'Ginnis' ('Sheelicks'), 'M'Ginty's Meal-an'-ale', 'Johnny, Kiss yer Auntie', 'Pirn-taet Jockie', and 'Macfarlan o' the Sprotts'. His impeccable grasp of the Buchan vernacular, his earthily metaphysical imagery, and his sense of humour, so representative of the Northeast, are all to be seen in such a song as the last-named:

Macfarlan o' the Sprotts

Afore that I'd be tyraneest as I this file hae been,
I'd raider rin fae here tae Birse wi' piz in baith my sheen,

I'd raider dee for want o' breath than pine for want o' love;
An it's a' becus Macfarlan's mairret Susy.
Susy's cankert fader wi' mine could never gree,
An' aye fin I gaed ower that gait he'd hun' his dog at me;
I sent my freen Macfarlan doon tae try fat he could dee,
Macfarlan o' the Sprotts o' Birnieboosie.

Cho. I dinna like Macfarlan noo, I'm safe aneuch to state,
His lugs wid cast a shaida ower a sax-fit gate;
He's saft as ony gorblin, bit he's sliddery as a skate,
Macfarlan o' the Sprotts o' Birnieboosie.

Macfarlan spak nae word for me, bit plenty for 'imsel;
He reest the lassie's barley scones, her kebbick an' her kail;
Her fader cried oot, 'Sprotts, ye shid try yer luck yersel,'
Tae Macfarlan o' the Sprotts o' Birnieboosie.
Macfarlan he's the grimmest chiel for twenty mile a' roon,
They buy his fottygraf tae fleg the rottans fae a toon;
He kyttlt up his spunk at this, an' speert gin she'd come
doon
An' be mistress o' the Sprotts o' Birnieboosie.

Cho. I dinna like Macfarlan, etc.

He said that he was able baith tae play at coup-the-ladle,
Wi' a laidder ower a tricle cask, an' ca the churn forby;
Anidder o' his win'ers wis that sawdust mist wi' cin'ers
Wis their spice for feedin' hens at Birnieboosie.
An educatit ostrich fae the wilds o' Timbuctoo
He hid for scrattin' up his neeps, an' hidna them to pu';
I never heard the like o' that come oot o' ony mou'
But Macfarlan's o' the Sprotts o' Birnieboosie.

Cho. I dinna like Macfarlan, it's awfu', bit it's true;
A pewyter speen wis tint in Jock Macfarlan's mou';
He couldna weel be grimmer, an' they feed him wi' the
skimmer,
Macfarlan o' the Sprotts o' Birnieboosie.

Oh, a dirl o' the teethic's nae particularly sweet,
Bit love's the only pine on earth that ever gart me greet;
It's like kyttly chillblains roon yer hert instead o' on yer feet,
They war aggravatit by the sicht o' Susy.

> Noo freens an' kin' philosophers, ye've heard fat me befell;
> Never lippen tull a middleman, bit dee yer wark yersel,
> Or I'll bet my winter sarket ye're a day ahin the market,
> Like fin I sent Jock Macfarlan doon tae Susy.

> *Cho.* I dinna like Macfarlan noo, I'm fairly aff o' Jock,
> I dinna like Macfarlan, nor Macfarlan's folk;
> May his Susy be nae turtle, bit the tyangs aran the spurtle
> Bring oot ower the heed o' Jock o' Birnieboosie. (cxlv)

In the nineteenth century, while the old-style ballad was decaying, the new-style ballad grew and flourished; from the old dying trunk there sprang, for a time, a sturdy new branch. Heredity asserted itself among the rural folk of the Northeast, and the literate descendants of the oral-traditional singers created and sang ballads which have traces of the old style, and which, like the old ballads, grew organically out of a certain set of social conditions. The most striking feature of the new social pattern is the extent to which it is a weaker reflection of the old. The folk were still the rural peasantry; their nucleus, however, was no longer composed of the large homogeneous class of tenant-farmers, but of the ploughmen, those at the foot of the social ladder. The homogeneity of the agricultural community at large was replaced by the predominantly masculine atmosphere of the bothy communities, while the bothy itself was a modern reflection of the old fermtoun, in so far as the inhabitants of both lived and worked together communally. And the political tensions that formerly animated the region were now replaced by the social tensions between master and men that animated the bothy. Again, the psychological function of the ballad for the folk had changed. The oral ballad was distanced from everyday life, and was set in a glamourized and unknown outside world, but by the nineteenth century the outside world was no longer unknown, for it impinged upon almost every aspect of their daily life. Now, the new ballad dealt with that everyday life. Instead of escaping from the hard realities of everyday life by singing about another life, the ballad singer relieved his feelings by commenting directly and sardonically on the life he led, day in, day out.

Although the bothy ballads belong distinctively to the Northeast and its regional song tradition, they present a striking parallel to other groups of ballads which evolved contemporaneously elsewhere. The ballads of the North American cowboys, lumberjacks, miners, and sailors often resemble the bothy ballads in structure, style, attitude, and content. Many are developed in loosely sequential, chronicle fashion and employ the standard stanzaic forms of sub-literary productions. Many have the same broadly satirical approach and the same targets, sometimes attacked in very similar terms. The catalogue of men and positions in the American whaling song 'Bark Gay Head', for example, may be likened to that in, say, 'The Boghead Crew', while the lumberjacks' comments on food in 'Drill ye Terriers' and living quarters in 'Now I Lay Me' may be compared to parallel passages in a number of ploughman ballads.[19] One well-known song that satirizes a region, 'An Arkansas Traveller' (Laws HI has the same concerns—a hard master, ill-paid work, poor food—as most bothy ballads, and the same wryly absurd tone as George Bruce Thomson's songs. In general, however, the songs represent what one might call 'The Occupational Ballad'; they are narrative songs whose subject matter is the result of modern social formations, and whose style derives primarily from literate—but largely sub-literary—productions.

In the modern period, then, the standard method of ballad transmission is rote memorization. Not surprisingly, after the innovations of the transitional period, we find in modern tradition a variety of kinds of memorized texts: derived ultimately from the old tradition are the memorized reproductions of oral ballad-stories in both transitional and oral texts; derived ultimately from the Grub Streets of song are the memorized reproductions of chap ballad-stories in both printed texts and texts which, by virtue of the traditional re-working of the printed originals, may be called transitional texts. These texts are reproduced by what is essentially a negative process of transmission, since the texts at best remain static but more normally are chipped away and fragmented. Also reproduced by literate methods are the modern texts of modern ballad-stories, but these have been created by literate minds within the tradition. Dammed at one place, the creative energy of the folk was diverted in another direction; as they could no longer compose old ballads in the old style, they composed new ballads. Where, however, all singers of the oral period were composers, actively involved in the creation and constant re-creation of oral ballads, in the modern period only the initial writer of the song could legitimately be called a composer. Literacy had not only ensured the atrophy of the old balladry, but also greatly reduced the possibilities for the folk's creative participation in the new balladry. Inevitably, the songs of the folk were to become increasingly peripheral to the lives of the folk.

Chapter 20

Conclusion

To the folklorist there are two kinds of literature: the literature of print and the literature of tradition. As the two kinds have influenced one another, the borderline between them can at times be hazy, but the guiding criterion for differentiation is quite clear: the means of transmission. The literature of tradition comprises material transmitted by word-of-mouth; and since this material is transmitted in different ways in nonliterate and literate cultures, it is necessary to distinguish further between the literatures of oral and verbal tradition.

Not surprisingly, the literatures of print and tradition require different critical emphases and methodologies, largely because of the distinct character of oral tradition. When examining a work of print literature one does not assume automatically an importance for its method of composition and transmission, and neither does one assume that the particular text under scrutiny may be just one of a theoretically infinite number of texts of the work. When examining a work of traditional literature, whether oral or verbal, one has to make these assumptions as a matter of course although, relatively, they are of greater significance for oral tradition. The re-creative mode of oral composition and transmission demands that one thinks in terms of both ballad-story and ballad-text rather than ballad, because any ballad-story may have innumerable ballad-texts, each one unique. Where, however, stability of story is the overriding concern of oral transmission, stability of text becomes the overriding concern of verbal transmission. This shift in attitude, of course, does not happen overnight, and in the first stage of verbal tradition a transitional method of transmission exists whereby the singers adopt a loosely re-creative attitude to their texts. In verbal tradition, then, word-of-mouth transmission still produces textual variation, but its significance decreases in inverse proportion to the acceptance of textual stability as the aim of transmission. As one would expect of a literature whose very difference lies in the fact of transmission, the methods of transmission and their varying consequences for stories and texts are going to be crucial considerations in any defining or analysing of that literature's genres.

One of our original questions was 'What is a ballad?'; the point has now been reached where an answer—or rather answers— can be attempted. The word 'ballad', between popular and scholarly usage, is attached to a wide range of referents. From this range we exclude from consideration literary ballads and pop music ballads. To the folklorist the word 'ballad' refers in general to a narrative song transmitted by tradition, that is, by word-of-mouth rather than print; but at various times different methods of composition and reproduction have obtained in tradition, and hence tradition has transmitted narrative songs that vary both in the kind of story and in the treatment accorded the story. From our study of the Northeast regional tradition we can distinguish, initially, three kinds of ballad according to the conditions of composition. First, and artistically most interesting, there is the oral ballad, or what we normally think of as 'the' ballad or 'the' ballad of tradition; it is a narrative song composed and re-composed by a traditional oral method. Second, there is the chap ballad, a narrative song composed or re-worked in sub-literary style by commercial entrepreneurs expressly for traditional singers. Third, there is the modern ballad, a non-commercial narrative song composed in sub-literary style generally by singers within the tradition. The outlines—as distinct from the details—of this division are not new; they are, for example, implicit in the demarcation of the three books that together cover the traditional narrative song of North America: *The British Traditional Ballad in North America*,[1] *American Balladry from British Broadsides*,[2] and *Native American Balladry*.[2]

This general classification, however, marks only the first step. What necessitates further definition is that we can distinguish different kinds of texts for these ballads according to the different conditions of transmission. In oral tradition the method of transmission is one of disciplined re-creation, and in verbal tradition the transitional, loosely re-creative, method is later followed by the modern memorizing method. Consequently, oral ballad-stories appear in oral and transitional ballad-texts and in modern reproductions of oral and transitional texts. Chap ballad-stories appear in transitional texts, and also in modern reproductions of these and the printed originals. By their very existence, of course, the chap ballads promoted the idea of the fixed text and so helped bring about the third method of transmission by which modern ballad-stories appear in modern memorized texts that have little variation. Although the broad lines of differentiation are clear enough, two areas where distinctions between texts could be blurred remind one in timely fashion of Child's comment that 'Ballads are not like plants or insects, to be classified to a hair's breadth'.[3] First, an oral ballad-story that appears in a transitional text so re-worked as to include many sub-literary characteristics may quite closely resemble in kind the transitional text of a chap ballad-story so re-worked as to include many traditional characteristics. Second, some modern ballads that do not deal directly with the life of the folk come very near the chap ballads in both story and style. In summary and with allowance made for these blurrings, the ballad-texts may be classified thus: oral texts, oral-transitional texts, chap-transitional texts, chap texts, modern texts, and modern reproductions of all these.

The various distinctions we have drawn between stories and texts on the basis of their composition and transmission enable us to chart the evolution of the Northeast ballad tradition. The development falls into three stages: first the oral stage of tradition, then the transitional and modern stages of verbal tradition. For the region as a whole these three stages correspond broadly to the periods 1350–1750, 1750–1830, and 1830 to the present day, though it would be unwise to make too strict an equation, as there must have been considerable overlapping of stages and periods. The defining feature of each stage is, in social terms, the level of literacy and, in literary terms, the consequent methods of composition and transmission. In the first stage, there are oral texts; in the second, oral-transitional and chap-transitional texts; and in the third, modern reproductions of oral, oral-transitional, chap-transitional, chap, and modern texts. The unwisdom of equating the stage with the chronological period becomes apparent when we remember that at a certain time, say the turn of the nineteenth century, it is theoretically possible for all three stages to co-exist within the three generations of one family, with the nonliterate eldest generation providing oral texts, the middle generation providing transitional texts, and the fully literate youngest generation providing memorized reproductions of these and printed texts. Only by a supposition of this kind can we explain the turning up in the modern stage of memorized oral texts. Certainly in the broad outlines if not necessarily all the details of its development, the regional tradition of the Northeast establishes a paradigm for the evolution of other regional ballad traditions.

One important aspect of ballad tradition which lies outside the scope of this work, because it really demands a work of comparable size, is the music.[4] It is, however, possible that the history of the music parallels the history of the texts in passing through the three stages of disciplined re-creation, loose re-creation, and auditory memorization. That many traditional singers adopt a re-creative attitude to their tunes has been frequently noted by musicologists; that this attitude may have been, or in certain areas may still be, akin to the oral maker's attitude to his texts has been implicitly suggested by George Herzog[5] and directly stated by Samuel Bayard:[6]

> if, as Professor Entwistle says, 'ballad language is formula' then we may also say 'ballad music is formula'—and with the same reservations that we should expect to be applied to the verse. For neither folk songs nor tunes are simply chance collections of formulae; and like the ballads, the several separate folk melodies are distinguished by strongly imprinted features. They are, in fact, quite individual musical creations, with varying content and message, just as folk ballads are individual poems telling different stories. But in the case of poems and airs alike, the messages are conveyed to a great extent by the help of formulae.

In this connection it is worth remembering that in the letter Thomas Gordon sent to Alexander Fraser Tytler in January 1793, he remarks that his daughter's ballads 'proceded upon a system of manners, and in a stile of composition, both words *and music*, very peculiar, and of which we could recollect nothing similar' (italics added). In time the degree of inventiveness exercised by the traditional singer declined; Cecil Sharp's famous blind singer, Henry Larcombe, who would 'habitually vary every phrase of his tune in the course of a ballad', was unique in Sharp's experience.[7] In general, however, because music was less quickly affected by print and the notion of the fixed tune, it seems that re-creative attitudes to the tunes remained in force longer than re-creative attitudes to the texts.[8]

The second of the questions we started out with was 'Who were the folk who sang the ballads?'; and as with the ballad question there is no one answer. In folkloristic terminology, of course, the word 'folk' refers simply to the participants in tradition; but for a socially more specific understanding of the folk we must again distinguish between the participants in oral and verbal traditions. In the oral period the folk are defined by nonliteracy rather than by class, though inevitably there is a certain correlation between the two; they are the nonliterate inhabitants of the region. In the Northeast they consisted for the most part of the tenant-farmers, sub-tenants, tradesmen, and families of the fermtoun, the dominant settlement type of the region for four hundred years. Presumably people in the burghs sang ballads as well but since in Europe generally 'Two cultures developed side by side: an urban culture that was essentially literate, and a rural culture that was essentially illiterate',[9] the likelihood is that the burghal tradition, though it may have begun on an equal footing with the rural, became comparatively attenuated quite early on. As the region possessed a certain degree of social homogeneity, those lairds who were nonliterate—and especially in the earlier centuries of the period they must have been fairly numerous—would also have participated in the oral ballad tradition.

After the advent of literacy, however, class does become an important factor in demarcating the folk. In a society where growing industrialization, commercialization, and urbanization demanded increasingly the skills of literacy, ballad-singing remained a common practice with those whose mode of life and work asked least in the way of literate skills. Ineluctably the ballads descended in the social scale, passing from the tenant-farmers to the ploughmen to, nowadays, the 'travelling folk' and the keeping of such a superb singer as Jeannie Robertson. In general, then, 'folk' remains a convenient short term for the participants in both oral and verbal tradition, and though the social referents of the term will naturally vary from one regional culture to another, the folk of oral tradition will be characterized by nonliteracy, and the folk of verbal tradition will be distinguished by occupation and environment. The real importance of the question 'Who were the folk?' however lies in its forcing us to investigate the kind of life led by the anonymous generations; it requires that we consider how the folk's way of life provided both subjects for story and occasions for the telling, and how social changes altered that way of life and the character of the tradition.

The key to an understanding of the folk's ballad tradition is an understanding of oral composition, for it is the source of the ballad's difference from other, non-oral, poetry, the source of its hallmarks, and the source of its aesthetic appeal. The oral perspective eases the solution of many ballad problems. It answers the problem of 'authorship'; it enables us to establish definitions that in turn establish guidelines for a classification of texts; and it provides a contributory answer to the problem of ballad origins. Gerould dispersed the mists that had previously shrouded this problem when he reduced The Question to three questions: the origin of the narrative form, the origin of the poetic and melodic form, and the origin of individual ballads.[10] The reply normally accepted for question three is, a wide variety of sources, and for question two, probably the northern France of the early medieval period. The answer to the first question is that the ballad's narrative form evolved from the exigencies of nonliteracy and shares its strategy, if not always its tactics, with the other genres of oral literature. Oral composition, however, also brings its own problems; it produces ambiguities in current terminology, and requires, besides a new unambiguous terminology, new emphases in critical methodology. For the literate student of ballads, it requires no little effort to adjust to the notion of composition by inherited formulaic and structural patternings, but the results should repay the effort as a study of oral literature can lead to an understanding of the oral mind and its differences from the literate mind. Study of oral structure, for example, need not result in the more boring aridities of structuralism, but can illuminate how the oral mind coped with the nonliterate state, that is, how without the aid of documents it stored and transmitted its material.

Finally, an awareness of the ballad's oral genesis clarifies the status of the Child collection of ballads. In recent decades Child has come under increasingly heavy fire from some critics for having tried to establish what they scornfully call a 'ballad aristocracy'. 'The' ballads, this school maintains, cannot be meaningfully distinguished from all other kinds of narrative folksong, because, in their experience, the folk—by whom they mean the singers of the verbal tradition of a literate culture— draw no distinctions between them. A Child ballad, they say, means no more than one given a subjective imprimatur by Professor Child. No view of Child's work could be more mis leading. Child possessed a remarkable capacity for distinguishing the stylistic traits of oral—or as he would call it, popular— balladry, even when these traits existed in texts that had also sub-literary characteristics. And in separating the oral or popular from the chap ballads he was simply following the practice of the folk of eighteenth- and early nineteenth-century Scotland. Child never published an analytical exposition of the premises upon which he based his discriminations, probably because he died before he could write the projected Introduction, the obvious place for such an exposition, but among the few manuscript jottings for this Introduction is one tantalizingly bare directive: 'Remark on the differences between Mrs Brown's earlier & later versions'.[11] It is, of course, fruitless to speculate on what he would have made of the differences but, even so, it seems typical of the man's unerring instinct that in his last recorded sentences he would focus on such a crucially revealing characteristic of those ballads which epitomize the old balladry. But whatever the Introduction might or might not have said, Child's capacity for discriminating the traits of the old balladry ensured that the collection contains almost all the ballad-stories which had at one time or another been composed and transmitted by the oral method; for good measure, they are accompanied by those, otherwise composed, which had been transmitted by the transitional method. His collection does, in short, embody a ballad aristocracy, with retainers. And with our growing awareness of oral culture, and its differences from print culture, we can hardly cavil at his demarcation of the major literary products of that culture which have cast for so long over so many their own enigmatic glamourie.

Appendix

Northeast Collectors and Collections

(a) The ballad MSS. entirely of Northeast origin are those of
Mrs Anna Brown, the Old Lady, the Rev. Robert Scott (the
Glenbuchat MSS.), Peter Buchan, Joseph Robertson, John
Hill Burton, William Christie, James Gibb, Mrs A. F.
Murison, Gavin Greig, the Rev. James Bruce Duncan, and
Will Walker. Child also received individual communications
of ballads from Dr Thomas Davidson and Charles Elphin-
stone Dalrymple.

(b) The ballad MSS. which contain material recorded in the
Northeast are those of David Herd, Sir Walter Scott, George
Ritchie Kinloch, William Motherwell, and the Rev.
William Findlay. Herd left no record of his sources, but as
he himself came from Kincardine and as some of his texts
bear distinct resemblances to known Northeast versions, he
can safely be placed in this category. Like Herd, Kinloch
hailed from Kincardine, and drew many of his ballads from
the Mearns, while volumes V and VI of his MSS. are in
the handwriting of three other northeasterners, John Hill
Burton, Joseph Robertson, and James Beattie. Scott's MSS.
and Motherwell's MSS. contain transcriptions of Northeast
ballad-texts—as do Sharpe's—but Scott also obtained versions
directly from Hugh Irvine of Drum, James Skene of
Rubislaw, and Williamson Burnet of Monboddo, and
Motherwell recorded from Margaret Black of Ayr and
Widow Michael of Barrhead, who were natives of the Northeast. Findlay, himself born in Angus, procured ballads from
both Deeside and Banffshire.

Full descriptions of the Scottish Ballad MSS. are given in William Montgomerie's Ph.D. thesis (Edinburgh, 1954), 'Bibliography of the Scottish Ballad Manuscripts 1730–1825', and in his continuing series of articles in *Studies in Scottish Literature*, from IV (1966), onwards. In the last twenty years the research fellows of the School of Scottish Studies, in particular Hamish Henderson, have recorded in the Northeast much valuable folksong now deposited in the School's archives.

(c) Books which contain entirely or primarily Northeast material are Alexander Laing, *Scarce Ancient Ballads* (Aberdeen, 1822), and *The Thistle of Scotland* (Aberdeen, 1823), Peter Buchan, *Gleanings of Scotch, English, and Irish Scarce Old Ballads* (Peterhead, 1825), and *Ancient Ballads and Songs of the North of Scotland*, 2 vols (Edinburgh, 1828; reprinted Edinburgh, 1875), George Ritchie Kinloch, *The Ballad Book* (Edinburgh, 1827; reprinted in Thomas Stevenson, ed., *Four Books of Choice Old Scottish Ballads*, Edinburgh, 1868, and at Edinburgh, 1883), [Joseph Robertson], *The New Deeside Guide* by James Brown (Aberdeen, 1832), William Christie, *Traditional Ballad Airs . . . procured in the counties of Aberdeen, Banff and Moray*, 2 vols (Edinburgh, 1876, 1881), Gavin Greig, *Folk-Song of the North-East*, 2 vols (Peterhead, 1909, 1914—articles contributed to the *Buchan Observer* from December 1907 to June 1911; reprinted in one volume together with Greig's 'Folk-Song in Buchan' by Kenneth Goldstein and Arthur Argo, Hatboro, Penn., 1963) and *Last Leaves of Traditional Ballads and Ballad Airs*, ed. A. Keith (Aberdeen, 1925), and John Ord, *The Bothy Songs and Ballads of Aberdeen, Banff and Moray, Angus and the Mearns* (Paisley, 1930).

(d) Books, other than anthologies, which utilize material recorded in the Northeast are David Herd, *Ancient and Modern Scots Songs* (Edinburgh, 1769; 2nd ed., 2 vols, Edinburgh, 1776), Sir Walter Scott, *Minstrelsy of the Scottish Border* (vols I and II, Kelso, 1802, and vol. III, Edinburgh, 1803; 2nd ed., Edinburgh, 1803; 3rd ed., Edinburgh, 1806; 4th ed., Edinburgh, 1810; ed. J. G. Lockhart, Edinburgh, 1833; ed. T. F. Henderson, Edinburgh, 1902), Robert Jamieson,

Popular Ballads and Songs (Edinburgh, 1806), James
Maidment, *A North Countrie Garland* (Edinburgh, 1824;
reprinted in Stevenson and at Edinburgh, 1884), William
Motherwell, *Minstrelsy, Ancient and Modern* (Glasgow,
1827; reprinted Paisley, 1873), George Ritchie Kinloch,
Ancient Scottish Ballads (Edinburgh, 1827), Ewan MacColl,
Personal Choice (New York, n.d.), Ewan MacColl and
Peggy Seeger, *The Singing Island* (London, 1960), and
Norman Buchan, *101 Scottish Songs* (Glasgow, 1962).

Glossary

a: all
aboon: above
ae: one, only
aff-takin: wry, sardonic, satirical
ails: troubles, afflicts
alluterlie: utterly
an: and; if
aneuch: enough
athort: across
ba: ball
bairn: child
balkes, baulks: unploughed ridges between the rigs
barn-well: 'the well has no sense; and has probably been caught
     from 9, at the far well washing' (Child)
bawbee: halfpenny
bere: coarse barley
bing: bin
birl: ply with drink
boll: an old dry measure
bore: crevice
borrow: release, ransom
boun: bound (for), ready to start
bouted flowr: sifted flour
braw: handsome, handsomely dressed
bree: liquid in which something has been steeped or boiled
broust: a brewing

buts: ridges or strips of ploughed land

byk: nest, hive

byre: cattle shed

ca: call; keep in motion

caird: travelling tinker

cateran: Highland marauder

chappit: mashed

chiel: man

clink: clasp, rhyme

cod: pillow

coffer: box, chest

cordiner: shoemaker

coup-the-ladle: see-saw

craigs: cliffs

creach: Highland cattle-lifting foray

currick, currach: wicker-work creel slung on a horse; rough kind
of cart

daigh: dough

dane: done

dee: die

deem: kitchen-maid

dirl: tingling pain

divot: turf, sod

*do to (with reflexive
pronoun):* betake

draff: malt refuse

dree: suffer, endure

durkes: dirks, daggers

fa: fall

fae, prep., n.: from; foe

faem: ocean

falds, folds: that part of the outfield manured by folding cattle
upon it

fat: what

fatts: tubs

faugh buts: pieces of cultivated land not forming a proper rig
faughs: unmanured, intermittently cropped part of the outfield
fause: false
feed: child, man
file: while
fin: when
fingram: a kind of woollen cloth
fleg: scare
forby: as well
foreby: nearby
freely: noble
fur: strip of earth turned over in ploughing
gaed, gid: went
gaire, gare: triangular piece of cloth inserted in a garment;
         gusset
gait: way
gar: make
gavellock: iron crowbar
genty: dainty, neat
gey: as in 'gey roch', pretty rough
gie: give
gin: if
gorblin: unfledged bird
goud, gowd: gold
greet: weep
groats: hulled grain
guise: frolic
ha: hall
had, haud: hold
hae: have
hairst: harvest, autumn
harrages and
   carriages: services (e.g. carting) due to the heritor
haughs: river-meadow land
heely: slowly, gently

Glossary

heirschippis,
    herschip: harryings, devastation
hyeuk: reaping hook; reaper
ilka, ilkane: each, every; each one
impet: see *mintit* and text
jack: martial jerkin
jee: move to and fro
jilp: splash, spurt
keall yeard,
    kail-yard: vegetable plot
kebbick: cheese
keist the cavils: cast lots
ken: know
(a') kin kind: all sorts
kirking: ceremonial kirk attendance for, e.g., the first time
        after a wedding, birth, or funeral
kist: chest
knopsknai: metal skull-cap
knot: lump, esp. of partially cooked oatmeal
know: hillock, knoll
kyttlt up his spunk: raised his spirits
kyttly: tickly
lair: learning
langsome: wearily long
lauch, leugh: laugh
lee: lie
leel and feel: loyal and faithful
leem: loom
leman: mistress
lint-tap: bundle of dressed flax put on a distaff for spinning
lippen: trust
lith: joint in a limb
loon: boy
loup: jump
lout: bend down

284

lugs: ears

lymmaris: scoundrels

mair: more

mane, maun: must

meal, v.: thicken (soup) by adding meal; feed

meare: mare

meikle: greatly

mess: measure out portions

millering: waste meal

mintit: feinted towards

mot: may

mote: a particle of vegetable matter

mows, (nae–): no laughing matter, uncanny

nainsel: own self

nappie: drinking-cup

neep: turnip

nicht: night

nocht: not; nothing

nor: than

nourice: nurse

nowte: cattle

pawky: roguish

philabeg: kilt

pine, n., v.: pain; waste away

pirn-taet: with turned-in toes

piz: peas

plack: small Scots coin

plaiding: coarse woollen twilled cloth

poke: sack, bag

pose: purse, secret hoard, savings

puttin-stane: stone impelled from the shoulder in athletic competition

pykit: with a spike

quhil: till

quey: heifer

rae: roe (-deer)

rattons: rats

redd up: tidily dressed

reef-tree: roof-tree, beam in the angle of a roof

reek, reiking: smoke, smoking

reese: praise

reesky: coarse-grassed

reiffis: plunderings

reive: rob, pillage

roch: rough

routh: plenty

rowd: wrapped

rug: pull, tug

sae: so

sair: sore, sorely

sal: shall

sark, sarket: shirt

sat: salt

scleat: slate

scranky: scraggy

scrattin: scratching

scuttle-dishes: serving dishes

seckes: sacks

shaws: leaves and stalks

sheelicks: husks of oats

sheen, shoon: shoes

sklater: slater, wood-louse

skyte: move skimmingly

smedy, smiddy: smithy

snotter: wick of a candle

souming: pasturing

speer: ask

spulzie, v., n.: to plunder; a plundering raid

spunk: see *kyttlt*

spurtle: stirring-rod

sta: stall

stappit: stepped

steeked: fastened

stent: work-portion

stented: limited

stickit: killed

stovies: a potato stew, hence *stoved*

sucken: legal territory

sue: sew

syne: then

tacketty: full of hobnails

tane—tither: the one—the other

theek'd: thatched

thocht lang (to haud
   me on – –): to keep me from wearying

thole: suffer patiently, endure

thrawin: twisted

tint: lost

tirl at the pin: rattle at door-fastening or early form of knocker

tocher: dowry

tricle: treacle

trow (I –): I can assure you

true: believe, trust

twinn: separate

tyangs: tongs

unco, adj., adv.: uncommon, extraordinary; very

uncouth: unknown

wad, wid: would

wae: woe

wan: dark-coloured

wark: work

waur: worse

weal: welfare

weird: destiny
weel-faurd: well-favoured, pretty, handsome
weyr: wire
wight: strong, lively
wile: vile
win in, up: get in, up
wyle: lure
wyt (I –): I assure you
yate, yett: gate
yeard-fast: fixed firmly in the earth

Notes and References

Chapter 1   Introduction (Pages 1 to 10)

1 Sigurd B. Hustvedt, *Ballad Books and Ballad Men*, p. 4.
2 G. H. Gerould, *The Ballad of Tradition*, p. 3; see also M. J. C. Hodgart, *The Ballads*, pp. 10–11.
3 3 vols, Cambridge, 1932–40; Cambridge, Mass., 1960; Toronto, 1962.
4 For the relevance of oral studies to the humanities at large see Walter J. Ong, 'The Expanding Humanities and the Individual Scholar', *PMLA*, LXXXII (Sept. 1967), 1–7. These studies hold significance for more than literature alone. They can, for example, illuminate Biblical Studies (probably between one-third and one-half of the Bible is orally composed) and the development of the Greek philosophic mind: see Aage Bentzen, *Introduction to the Old Testament*, 2nd ed. (Copenhagen, 1952), pp. 102–8, Eduard Nielsen, *Oral Tradition*, Studies in Biblical Theology no. 11 (London, 1954) and Eric A. Havelock, *Preface to Plato*. For a bibliography to 1964 of critical works on oral literature see Bruce Beattie, 'Oral-traditional Composition in the Spanish *Romancero* of the Sixteenth Century', *Journal of the Folklore Institute*, i (1964), 92–113. For a bibliography of Milman Parry see Albert B. Lord, 'Homer, Parry, and Huso', *American Journal of Archaeology*, lii (1948), 43–4.
5 Lord, pp. 134–5.
6 'Folklore and Dialect', *California Folklore Quarterly*, iv (1945), 151.
7 *European Balladry*, p. 9.
8 *Peter Buchan and Other Papers*, pp. 9, 10. See also D. K. Wilgus, *Anglo-American Folksong scholarship since 1898*, pp. 141–2; Wilgus advocates the reduction of Keith's figure of 108 to 107.
9 For a brief account of the collection, at present being edited for publication, and the first full Scottish version of 'The Maid and the Palmer' (21), see Buchan, 'The Maid, the Palmer, and the Cruel Mother', *Malahat Review*, no. 3 (July 1967), pp. 98–107.
10 Lord, pp. 49, 289 n. 11; Wilgus, pp. 340–3.
11 *The English and Scottish Popular Ballads*, i, vii; G. L. Kittredge and Helen Child Sargent, eds, *English and Scottish Popular Ballads*, p. xxiii; Gerould, p. 67; Bertrand Bronson, 'Mrs. Brown and the Ballad', *California Folklore Quarterly*, iv (1945), 129.

12 Letter of 22 July 1895, *Letters on Scottish Ballads from Professor Francis J. Child to W. W.*, *Aberdeen* (Aberdeen, 1930), p. 24.

13 Albert B. Friedman, *The Ballad Revival*, p. 28. But see Entwistle, p. 229; Hodgart, pp. 17, 134; Sir Edmund Chambers, *English Literature at the Close of the Middle Ages*, p. 182.

14 William Montgomerie, 'A Bibliography of the Scottish Ballad Manuscripts: 1730–1825: Part I', *Studies in Scottish Literature*, iv (1966), 22–4, and 'Sir Walter Scott as Ballad Editor', *Review of English Studies*, vii (1956), 158–63.

15 M. R. Dobie, 'The Development of Scott's *Minstrelsy*', *Edinburgh Bibliographical Society Transactions*, ii: 1 (1940), 72–3. See also William Montgomerie, 'William Macmath and the Scott Ballad Manuscripts', *Studies in Scottish Literature*, i (1963), 94.

16 E. K. Wells, *The Ballad Tree* (New York, 1950), pp. 63, 67, 58.

17 Wilgus, p. 314.

18 Alex. Keith, 'Scottish Ballads: Their Evidence of Authorship and Origin', *Essays and Studies*, xii (1926), 105–6. See also *Last Leaves*, pp. xxii–xxv, 4, 9–10, 29, 47, 52, 57, 197, 213; *Acts of the Parliament of Scotland*, i, 421; W. C. Dickinson, G. Donaldson, and I. A. Milne, *A Source Book of Scottish History* (Edinburgh, 1958–61), i, 94–5; Entwistle, pp. 197, 230; Hodgart, p. 85; Knut Liestøl, 'Scottish and Norwegian Ballads', *Studia Norvegica*, i (Oslo, 1946), 6–9, 14–15; R. Th. Christiansen, 'Scotsmen and Norsemen: Cultural Relations in the North Sea Area', *SS*, i (1957), 15–37; *SHR*, xlviii (April 1969), a number devoted to 'Scotland and Scandinavia'.

19 James Ross, 'A Classification of Gaelic Folk-Song', *SS*, i (1957), 126–7.

20 Hamish Henderson, 'The Green Man of Knowledge', *SS*, ii (1958), 82; Buchan, 'A Lughnasa Piper in the Northeast of Scotland', *Journal of American Folklore*, lxxxi (1968), 262. For Northeast folklore see Walter Gregor, *An Echo of the Olden Time from the North of Scotland*, and *Notes on the Folk-Lore of the North-East of Scotland*; Joseph M. McPherson, *Primitive Beliefs in the North-East of Scotland*; F. Marian McNeill, *The Silver Bough* (Glasgow, 1957–68).

21 P. xliv.

22 *FSNE*, pp. 57–8. On the general lack of contact between Gaelic and Lowland Scots music, see Francis Collinson, *The Traditional and National Music of Scotland*, pp. 32–5.

23 Herschel Gower, 'The Scottish Palimpsest in Traditional Ballads Collected in America', *Reality and Myth*, ed. William E. Walker and Robert L. Welker (Nashville, 1964), p. 123.

24 Child, v, 309.

25 'Local Dialects', *The Northeast of Scotland*, ed. A. C. O'Dell and J. Mackintosh, p. 202. See also Eugen Dieth, *A Grammar of the Buchan Dialect* (Cambridge, 1932), and Walter Gregor, *The Dialect of Banffshire* (London, 1866).

Chapter 2   The Land and the People (Pages 13 to 16)

1 John R. Allan, *North-east Lowlands of Scotland*, p. 17. Written by a master of local linguistic rhythms, this book is the best single introduction to the region.
2 W. C. Dickinson, *A New History of Scotland, Vol. I: From the Earliest Times to 1603*, pp. 34, 104–5.
3 P. Hume Brown, ed., *Scotland Before 1700 from Contemporary Documents*, p. 149.
4 *A History of Greater Britain*, p. 36.
5 'Some [English] lawyer express[ed] to Lord Elibank an opinion, that at the Union the English law should have been extended all over Scotland. "I cannot say how that might have answerd our purpose," said Lord Patrick, who was never nonsuited for want of an answer, "but it would scarce have suited *yours*, since by this time the *Aberdeen Advocates* would have possessd themselves of all the business in Westminster Hall" ' (Sir Walter Scott, *Journal*, eds J. G. Tait and W. M. Parker, Edinburgh, 1950, p. 133).
6 W. D. Simpson, 'The Reg ionbefore 1700', ed. O'Dell and Mackintosh, p. 71.
7 I. F. Grant, *The Social and Economic Development of Scotland before 1603*, p. 122; John Davidson and Alexander Gray, *The Scottish Staple at Veere* (London, 1909), p. 4; W. Douglas Simpson, *The Province of Mar*, pp. 130–1; William Watt, *A History of Aberdeen and Banff*, pp. 37–9. Despite many local traditions of Danes settling in the fishing villages of Buchan, there seems to have been no effective colonization of the Northeast by the Norsemen. Plenty of raids, such as the one in 1151 when Eystein looted Aberdeen, are recorded, but the Vikings concentrated their settlements on the far north and west of Scotland. The Norse influence on the area was extensive for only a short period in the eleventh century when, after King Duncan's death, Macbeth and Thorfinn, Jarl of the Orkneys, shared Scotland between them, and Thorfinn's portion held Buchan, Mar, the Mearns, and Angus. The Scandinavian elements in the Northeast dialect presumably resulted largely from the commercial and political intercourse of the Middle Ages.
8 W. S. Bruce, *The Nor' East*, 2nd ed. (London, 1915), p. 55.
9 G. Skene Keith, *The Agriculture of Aberdeenshire*, p. 154.
10 John Stuart, ed., 'The Woodrow Papers', *Miscellany of the Spalding Club*, ii, 147–74; these papers 'illustrate the ecclesiastical history of the north-eastern shires of Scotland'; D. Macmillan, *The Aberdeen Doctors* (London, 1909); G. D. Henderson, *Religious Life in Seventeenth Century Scotland* (Cambridge, 1937), pp. 232–8; W. Douglas Simpson, *The Earldom of Mar*, p. 94; William Alexander, *Notes and Sketches Illustrative of Northern Rural Life in the Eighteenth Century*, p. 210; Skene Keith, p. 156.
11 David Daiches, however, in *The Paradox of Scottish Culture* (Oxford, 1964), sees the Northeast as the region 'where the sophis-

tication of mediaeval Scottish culture lingered longest after the Union of the Crowns'. He links the local husbanding of the old traditions in courtly music and written literature to the ethos of Episcopalianism (pp. 11–12, 53–5).

12 Dickinson, p. 241; Hume Brown, pp. 193–4; Agnes Mure Mackenzie, *An Historical Survey of Scottish Literature to 1714* (London, 1933), pp. 169, 179; J. W. Baxter, *William Dunbar* (Edinburgh, 1952), pp. 184–6.

Chapter 3   The Agricultural Society (Pages 17 to 27)

1 Wilgus, *Anglo-American Folksong Scholarship since 1898*, pp. 336–43; Alan Dundes, ed., *The Study of Folklore*, pp. 277–336, esp. William Bascom, 'Four Functions of Folklore', pp. 279–98. One of Milman Parry's aims was to initiate 'a comparative study of oral poetry which sought to see how the way of life of a people gives rise to poetry of a given kind and a given degree of excellence' (Lord, *The Singer of Tales*, p. 3). I have adopted the terminological distinction advocated by Dundes, p. 3, between *folklore* (the materials) and *folkloristics* (the study of the materials).

2 P. 20.

3 *British Popular Ballads*, p. 49; see also pp. 43–50; Entwistle, *European Balladry*, pp. 1–9, 30; Hodgart, *The Ballads*, pp. 131–9.

4 Pp. 91, 9.

5 Cosmo Innes, *Lectures on Scotch Legal Antiquities* (Edinburgh, 1872), pp. 241–2, 254, 271–3; Grant, *The Social and Economic Development of Scotland before 1603*, pp. 43–7; G. W. S. Barrow, 'Rural Settlement in Central and Eastern Scotland: The Mediaeval Evidence', *SS*, vi (1962), 123–44.

6 Henry Hamilton, ed., *Selections from the Monymusk Papers 1713–1755*, pp. xxv–xxvi, xx–xxi.

7 Alexander Garden of Troup, Letter of 1683, *Collections for a History of the Shires of Aberdeen and Banff*, ed. Joseph Robertson (Aberdeen, 1843), pp. 97–107; James Anderson, *A General View of the Agriculture and Rural Economy of the County of Aberdeen*, pp. 54–7; Skene Keith, *The Agriculture of Aberdeenshire*, pp. 171–2, 231–42.

8 Hamilton, *Monymusk Papers*, pp. 38, 24, 195.

9 James E. Handley, *Scottish Farming in the Eighteenth Century* (London, 1953), p. 49.

10 Hamilton, *Monymusk Papers*, pp. 145–7.

11 Grant, *Dev. Scot.*, pp. 102–6.

12 Hamilton, *Monymusk Papers*, pp. 29–30. The farmers were seldom happy over the services due to the mill. Because of the practice of thirlage, whereby the tenants were obliged to have their corn ground at a particular mill, not necessarily the nearest, the millers exercised lucrative monopolies. The miller could easily become a petty tyrant: 'there is not in this island, such a compleat remain of feudal

despotism, as in the practice respecting mills in Aberdeenshire: and the millers, in many cases, exercise their power with the most wanton insolence; . . . so that I have myself seen poor farmers, by vexation and despair, reduced to tears to supplicate what they ought to have commanded from him' (Anderson, pp. 47–8; see also Alexander, *Notes and Sketches Illustrative of Northern Rural Life in the Eighteenth Century*, pp. 146–53). As late as 1935, a thirled farmer was sued by a miller in Aberdeenshire for not taking his corn to the mill within whose sucken he fell (J. A. Symon, *Scottish Farming, Past and Present*, Edinburgh, 1959, p. 152). These conditions go a long way to explaining why the miller in folksong is often a highly unpopular character.

13 *Rent Roll of Estates of William, 7th. Baron Forbes, for year 1552*, pp. 6, 18–19, 12, 18.

14 See the Journal for 1749–50 kept by Sir Archibald Grant's overseer, Robert Leitch, in Henry Hamilton, ed., *Life and Labour on an Aberdeenshire Estate, 1735–1750*, pp. 80–130.

15 Alexander, p. 143; James Wilson, 'Farming in Aberdeenshire, Ancient and Modern', *Transactions of the Highland and Agricultural Society*, xiv (1902), 81. The practice of enlivening the harvest with a piper is also referred to in the poem by Robert Sempill of Beltrees, 'The Life and Death of Habbie Simson, the Piper of Kilbarchan' (*The Oxford Book of Scottish Verse*, chosen by J. MacQueen and T. Scott, Oxford, 1967, p. 305); Habbie's death occasions the plaint: 'O wha will cause our shearers shear?'

16 Anderson, p. 108; Skene Keith, p. 513.

17 Kenneth Walton, 'Regional Settlement', in *The Northeast of Scotland*, ed, O'Dell and Mackintosh, pp. 87–99. Scotland's paucity of villages resulted largely from the extensive economic monopolies granted the medieval burghs. See Grant, *Dev. Scot.*, pp. 129–33, 366–72; and for the illustrative burgh charter of Aberdeen, Adolphus Ballard, *British Borough Charters 1042–1216* (Cambridge, 1913), pp. 170, 210–11.

18 Compare, in the Forbes Rent Roll, the Highland touns of Abergardin (pp. 12–13) with the Lowland touns in Formartine (pp. 18–20). See also the Gordon Rent Roll, 'The Rentaill of the Lordschipe of Huntlye alias Strathboggie', *Miscellany of the Spalding Club*, ed. Stuart, iv, 261–319; Arthur Geddes and John Forbes, 'Rural Communities of Ferm-Toun and Baile in the Lowlands and Highlands of Aberdeenshire, 1696', *AUR*, xxxii (1948), 98–104.

19 John Stuart, ed., *List of Pollable Persons within the Shire of Aberdeen 1696*, i, 550–2. See also Mabel D. Allardyce, 'The Poll Book of 1696', *Aberdeen University Library Bulletin*, iv (1925–8), 25–35.

20 Alexander, pp. 9, 156–9.

21 Innes, pp. 251–2.

22 Hamilton, *Monymusk Papers*, p. xxxvii; Innes, p. 254.

23 Dickinson, *A New History of Scotland*, pp. 239–51, 'Burgh Life from Burgh Records', *AUR*, xxxi (1946), 214–26, *Early Records*

of the Burgh of Aberdeen 1317, 1398–1407 (Edinburgh, 1957); John Stuart, ed., *Extracts from the Council Register of the Burgh of Aberdeen* 1398–1625 (Aberdeen, 1844–8).

24 Hamilton, *Monymusk Papers*, pp. xxxi–xxxiv, 185–242; Douglas Barron, ed., *The Court Book of the Barony of Urie 1604–1747* (Edinburgh, 1892); J. Maitland Thomson, ed., 'The Forbes Baron Court Book 1659–1678', *Miscellany of the Scottish History Society*, iii (Edinburgh, 1919), 205–321; James Cruikshank, ed., 'The Court Book of the Barony of Fintray, 1711–1726', *Miscellany of the Third Spalding Club*, i (Aberdeen, 1935), 1–66; J. Stuart, ed., 'Extracts from the Court Books of the Baronies of Skene, Leys, and White-haugh, 1613–1687', *Misc. Spalding Club*, v, 215–38, *Selections from the Records of the Kirk Session, Presbytery, and Synod of Aberdeen 1582–1681* (Aberdeen, 1846), *Extracts from the Presbytery Book of Strathbogie 1631–54* (Aberdeen, 1843).

25 Harald Uhlig, 'Some Remarks on Comparative Research in Settlement Structures', *SS*, vi (1962), 182; see also Uhlig, 'Old Hamlets with Infield and Outfield Systems in Western and Central Europe', *Geografiska Annaler*, xliii (1961), 286–313.

26 P. 198.

Chapter 4   The Border Region (Pages 28 to 34)

1 For a study of the process of infeudation in the Northeast, see Simpson, *The Province of Mar*, pp. 107–29.

2 W. C. Dickinson, G. Donaldson, and I. A. Milne, *A Source Book of Scottish History* (Edinburgh, 1958–61), i, 168–70 ; W. C. Dickinson, *A New History of Scotland*, pp. 202–3; Simpson, *The Earldom of Mar*, pp. 49–53; Buchan, 'History and Harlaw', *Journal of the Folklore Institute*, v (1968), 58–67.

3 Simon Fraser, Lord Lovat, 'Letters', *Miscellany of the Spalding Club*, ed. Stuart, ii, 14. See also Dickinson, *Source Book*, iii, 348–52; Sir Walter Scott, *Waverley* (Edinburgh, 1814).

4 General Wade, 'Report, etc., relating to the Highlands, 1724', *Papers Relating to the Jacobite Period 1699–1750*, ed. James Allardyce, i, 133. See also Grant, *The Social and Economic Development of Scotland before 1603*, pp. 524–7.

5 Wade, in Allardyce, p. 134.

6 Stuart, *Misc. Spalding Club*, ii, 85–90; John G. Michie, ed., *The Records of Invercauld 1547–1828*, p. 332.

7 Wade, in Allardyce, pp. 134–5.

8 Allardyce, i, xiv–xvii, 20–3.

9 Alexander, *Notes and Sketches Illustrative of Northern Rural Life in the Eighteenth Century*, p. 67.

10 [?] Duncan Forbes, 'Memoriall anent the true state of the High-lands as to their chieftenries, followings and dependences before the late Rebellion', Allardyce, i, 171–2; Michie, pp. 231–3.

11 iii, 465–7.

12 Michie, p. 231; Allardyce, i, ix–xiii, 170.
13 John Major, *A History of Greater Britain*, p. 49.
14 M. M. Gray, ed., *Scottish Poetry from Barbour to James VI* (London, 1935), p. 243. In the same vein is the Highlander's traditional retort to the slander that he is a thief: 'Steal ane cow, twa cow, tat be common tief. Steal hundred cow, tat be shentleman drover.'
15 For a fuller discussion see Buchan, 'History and Harlaw'.

Chapter 5   The Clannit Society (Pages 35 to 47)

 1 John Stuart, ed., *The Book of Deer* (Aberdeen, 1869); W. Douglas Simpson, 'The Book of Deer', *TBC*, xvii (1954), 27–30; Dickinson, *A New History of Scotland*, pp. 49–50, 60–1, 65–6; T. Bedford Franklin, *A History of Scottish Farming* (London, 1952), p. 7; R. A. Gailey, 'The Evolution of Highland Rural Settlement', *SS*, vi (1962), 155–77; Geddes and Forbes, 'Rural Communities of Ferm-Toun and Baile in the Lowlands and Highlands of Aberdeenshire, 1696', *AUR*, xxxii (1948), 98–104. The word 'davoch' occurs in a number of northeastern place names such as Findochty, or the toun in the Parish of Coldstone that was called simply 'The Daach' (Stuart, ed., *List of Pollable Persons within the Shire of Aberdeen 1696*, i, 23–4). In Joseph Robertson's *Illustrations . . . of Aberdeen and Banff* (Aberdeen, 1847–62), ii, 164, a 1726 MS. states that 'Strathbogie was of old divided into forty-eight davachs, each containing as much as four ploughs (each having four or five yoke of oxen) could till in a year'. This would account for the area's being known, in a phrase that was formerly a common toast, as 'the Aucht-and-forty Dauch of Huntly' (Alexander, *Notes and Sketches Illustrative of Northern Rural Life in the Eighteenth Century*, p. 13).
 2 Grant, *The Social and Economic Development of Scotland before 1603*, pp. 51–2, 522; Dickinson, p. 89; Watt, *A History of Aberdeen and Banff*, p. 75; Ranald G. Nicholson, 'Domesticated Scots and Wild Scots', *Scottish Colloquium Proceedings* (University of Guelph), i (1968), 7–9.
 3 Watt, p. 86.
 4 Stuart, ed., *Miscellany of the Spalding Club*, iv, 261–319; see also the Gordon Papers on pp. 125–261.
 5 Pp. 6, 10.
 6 Allardyce, ed., *Papers Relating to the Jacobite Period 1699–175 0*, i, 8–18, xx.
 7 Hume Brown, ed., *Scotland before 1700 from Contemporary Documents*, p. 171.
 8 'Memoriall', Allardyce, i, 171.
 9 Walter Macfarlane, *Genealogical Collections* (1750–1), ed. James Toshach Clark (Edinburgh, 1900), i, 236.

10 Stuart, *Misc. Spalding Club*, iv, 164.

11 Stuart, *Misc. Spalding Club*, ii, cvi–cvii; iv, 201–2, 217–19. The Farquharson records also provide evidence that these bonds of Manrent were not confined to the Lowlands. A clan tradition that they were descended from the Shaws perhaps accounts for the 'Mutual Bond of Maintainance between the Farquharsons and the Shaws', though the Shaws' provenience—'Inchgaull', the Hebrides —raises doubts about the practical efficacy of such an alliance. The same questions are raised by the 'Bond of Maintainance between Alexander Farquharson of Invercauld and Alexander Macdonald of Glencoe, 1680' (Michie, ed., *The Records of Invercauld 1547–1828*, pp. 230, 252).

12 *Scottish Abbeys and Social Life* (Cambridge, 1933), p. 128. Parallels to the Scottish situation exist in such European regions as the Low Countries, Switzerland, and the independent Italian city-states, where the incidence of war and the consequent development of a militia system are related to a comparatively early political and social freedom.

13 Leslie, in Hume Brown, p. 180.

14 W. C. Dickinson, G. Donaldson, and I. A. Milne, *A Source Book of Scottish History* (Edinburgh, 1958–61), i, 164.

15 *A History of Greater Britain*, p. 158.

16 Hume Brown, p. 178.

17 Major, p. 47. See also Kurt Wittig, *The Scottish Tradition in Literature* (Edinburgh, 1958), pp. 31–2, 51, 53, 94, and especially p. 95, where he writes: 'The democratic element in Scots literature is one of its most striking characteristics. . . . "Democratic" is really not the correct word; it is rather a free manliness, a *saeva indignatio* against oppression, a violent freedom, sometimes an aggressive spirit of independence or egalitarianism.'

18 'The Boundis of Albioun' (1527), Hume Brown, p. 65.

19 P. 48.

20 Stuart, *Misc. Spalding Club*, ii, 152.

21 *Register of the Privy Council of Scotland*, 2nd ser., v, 289–90.

22 Simpson, *The Earldom of Mar*, pp. 60–1, 70–2.

23 John Spalding, *Memorialls of Trubles in Scotland and England 1624–1645*, ed. John Stuart (Aberdeen, 1850–1), i, 75, 94–5. Gilderoy, however, is the subject of a non-traditional song, a first-person, sentimental plaint.

24 *Register of the Privy Council of Scotland*, vii, 509; viii, 271.

25 Simpson, *Earldom*, p. 106.

26 *Register of the Privy Council of Scotland*, 2nd ser., v, 350, 468, 470, 468, 469.

27 Robert Gordon, *A Genealogical History of the Earldom of Sutherland to 1630* (Edinburgh, 1813), i, 236.

28 *Earldom*, p. 68.

29 Axel Olrik, ed., *A Book of Danish Ballads*, trans. E. Smith-Dampier (Oxford, 1939), pp. 14–22.

Chapter 6   Balladry and Oral Poetry (Pages 51 to 61)

1 Archer Taylor, 'Folklore and the Student of Literature', *The Study
   of Folklore*, ed. Dundes, p. 34. One should, however, bear in mind
   the cautionary epigram in the preceding article, William Bascom's
   'Folklore and Anthropology' (p. 28): 'All folklore is orally transmitted, but not all that is orally transmitted is folklore.' (In this
   quotation, of course, 'oral' is being used in the general sense.)
2 C. M. Bowra, *Heroic Poetry* (London, 1952), pp. 355–6.
3 Lord, *The Singer of Tales*, pp. 101, 13.
4 Lord, pp. 30, 54–5, 56, 92, 104.
5 In Dundes, *The Study of Folklore*, pp. 131–41, appears a translation,
   'Epic Laws of Folk Narrative', of the original article 'Epische
   Gesetze der Volksdichtung', *Zeitschrift für Deutsches Altertum*, li
   (1909), 1–12.
6 See the editorial discussion in Dundes, *The Study of Folklore*,
   pp. 129–30.
7 The Chadwicks point out that while 'we must regard . . . strict
   memorisation as exceptional' in oral tradition, it does seem to occur
   with certain kinds of poems: poems 'intended for collective singing'
   (e.g. boatmen's and other occupational songs); poems 'which have
   come to be regarded as sacred' where 'the actual words were
   believed to possess some inherent power' (e.g. the *Rig-veda*);
   poems 'of carefully studied diction, especially panegyrics, and
   perhaps also poems composed for contests in poetry'; and poems
   which have 'complicated metres', *The Growth of Literature*, iii,
   868) This type of memorization, of course, still differs in kind
   from the literate, as it is an auditory rather than a visual process.
8 *Proben der Volksliteratur der türkischen Stämme* (St Petersburg,
   1866–1904), v, xvi–xviii, quoted by Chadwicks, iii, 181–3.
9 Entwistle, *European Balladry*, p. 23.
10 James H. Jones, 'Commonplace and Memorisation in the Oral
   Tradition of the English and Scottish Popular Ballads', *Journal of
   American Folklore*, lxxiv (1961), 97–112. This well-meaning move
   in the right direction drew a somewhat reactionary reply from
   A. B. Friedman (pp. 113–15), who still maintains that 'memorisation
   . . . is the basic vehicle of oral tradition' (p. 114). Neither writer
   distinguishes clearly between oral in the strict sense and oral in
   the general; both seem to have largely literate conceptions of
   'memorization' and 'improvization'.
11 *English and Scottish Popular Ballads*, p. xxiv.
12 *Peter Buchan and Other Papers*, p. 204.
13 For an incisive account of this murky period in ballad criticism,
   see Wilgus, *Anglo-American Folksong Scholarship since 1898*,
   pp. 3–122.
14 *The Ballad of Tradition*, pp. 1, 12.
15 *On the History of the Ballads 1100–1500*, Proceedings of the British
   Academy pamphlet (1909), p. 25.

16 Pp. 10, 12.

17 *Minstrelsy Ancient and Modern*, pp. xi–xii.

18 'The Structural Study of Myth', in *Myth: A Symposium*, ed. Thomas A. Sebeok (Bloomington, Ind., 1958), pp. 81–106, and in Claude Lévi-Strauss, *Structural Anthropology*, pp. 202–28.

19 A paper presented at the Annual Meeting of the American Folklore Society in Boston, 1966.

20 Pp. 35–6.

Chapter 7   The Oral Ballads of Mrs Brown (Pages 62 to 73)

1 i, vii.

2 Harvard University Library, William Tytler Brown MS., Letter from Thomas Gordon to Alexander Fraser Tytler, 19 January 1793.

3 Gordon also possessed a sardonic northeastern sense of humour. On one occasion Gordon had deeply offended the then Professor of Greek, John Leslie, who challenged him to a duel. Gordon accepted, which gave him the choice of weapons: 'Any of the Greek tragedians that you may choose, and if ye dinna beat me in the knowledge of the author, I'll tak the tawse to your hurdies!' Gordon, adds the narrator, 'was well sure that he knew Greek better than the Professor of it' (George Walker, *Aberdeen Awa'*, Aberdeen, 1897, pp. 115–16). At that time the university posts could be gained through influence as well as ability. On one occasion, a navy surgeon married a Principal's daughter and received the Chair of a language whose very alphabet was unknown to him. See Neil Maclean, *Life at a Northern University* (Glasgow, 1874), pp. 47–8.

4 Alex. Walker, *Disblair 1634–1884* (Aberdeen, 1884), pp. 15–17.

5 Harvard University Library, Child MSS., v, 164. In MacFarlane's MS. 'Collection of Scotch Airs' (1740) 'Disblair' is noted as one of the airs' composers; see James Johnson and William Stenhouse, *The Scots Musical Museum* (Hatboro, Penn., 1962), i, lii.

6 Tytler Brown MS., Letter of 19 January 1793.

7 Child MSS., x, 84, Letter of 17 March 1800.

8 Letter from Mrs Brown to Fraser Tytler, 21 April 1800, quoted in a letter from Robert Anderson to Bishop Percy in John Nichols, *Illustrations of the Literary History of the Eighteenth Century*, vii (London, 1848), 179.

9 Lord, *The Singer of Tales*, pp. 130, 138.

10 'Mrs Brown and the Ballad', *California Folklore Quarterly*, iv (1945), 133, 135, 134, 136, 137, 137, 138. It was probably her methods of oral re-creation that misled A. B. Friedman into lumping her with James Hogg and William Laidlaw as 'artful polishers . . . all of whom almost certainly "cooked" their ballads to some extent' (*The Ballad Revival*, p. 243).

11 Letter of 21 April 1800, quoted by Anderson in Nichols, vii, 179.

12 Letter of 14 September 1800, Nichols, vii, 89; Child, i, 455n.

13 Harvard University Library, William Motherwell MS., ii, 676. See also Child, ii, 274.

14 Harvard University Library, Letters and Papers Relating to the Harris MS., article 13. The present doyenne of Scottish ballad singers, Jeannie Robertson, also remarks that she learned her ballads when a young girl. See also Lord, pp. 20–1.

15 Child MSS., x, 85, Letter of 23 December 1800.

16 Harvard University Library, Kinloch MSS., ii, 107.

17 Letters and Papers Relating to the Harris MS., article 9, Letter of 15 September 1873.

18 Harvard University Library, Gibb MS., p. xi, Letter of 2 Sept. 1881.

19 Bowra, *Heroic Poetry* (London, 1952), pp. 216, 371–2.

20 David Daiches, *Robert Burns* (New York, 1950), p. 1; see also Daiches, *The Paradox of Scottish Culture* (Oxford, 1964), esp. pp. 19–23, and David Craig, *Scottish Literature and the Scottish People 1680–1830*, passim.

21 Edwin Muir, *Scott and Scotland* (London, 1936), p. 22.

22 Although the effects of anglicization on Scottish written literature have often been discussed, most notably by Craig, the ways in which literacy contributed to these effects is a subject that merits fuller study.

23 Child MSS., x, 85, Letter of 23 December 1800.

24 Tytler Brown MS., Letter of 19 January 1793.

25 Matthew Gregory Lewis, *Tales of Wonder* (London, 1801).

26 Child MSS., x, 81, Letter of 17 July 1794. See also *Scottish Songs* (1794), 2nd ed. (Glasgow, 1869), i, 77, where he casts doubt on the 'antiquity' of both Herd's and Tytler's ballads. As his selections show, however, Ritson was in the habit of taking the modern for ancient, as well as vice-versa. It is odd, considering Ritson's reputation for meticulousness, that his correct inclusion of 'Young Bekie' in the Tytler MS. contents (i, 77) did not put an early end to the speculation that the 'fifteenth' ballad might be a version of 'Hugh Spencer's Feats in France'.

27 G. L. Kittredge, 'A Lost Manuscript', *Harvard Library Notes*, no. 3 (January 1921), p. 58.

28 W. Montgomerie, 'Scottish Ballad MSS.: i', *Studies in Scottish Literature* iv (1966), 7, 10 n. 2.

29 Child MSS., x, 84, Letter of 17 March 1800. In a letter to Bishop Percy dated 14 September 1800, Robert Anderson expresses some misgivings about the genuineness of Mrs Brown's texts: 'her character places her above the suspicion of literary imposture; but it is wonderful how she should happen to be the depository of so many curious and valuable ballads'. Three months later, however, his doubts were erased by the ballads—'some of them extremely curious, and all of them of considerable antiquity'—in the Fraser Tytler MS. (Nichols, vii, 89–90, 178).

30 Lord, pp. 148–9.

31 Harvard University Library, Jamieson Brown MS., Appendix, pp. viii, xv; see also Child, iv, 86, 238.

32 Child, ii, 221, 87.

33 Jamieson Brown MS., Appendix, Letter of 2 December 1802.
34 Jamieson Brown MS., Appendix, Letter of 9 June 1805.

Chapter 8   The Substance of the Ballads (Pages 74 to 86)

1 Child MSS., x, 85 (first citation of this and other MSS. mentioned
  in this chapter is given in the notes to chapter 7); Child, iv, 309.
2 Jamieson Brown MS., Appendix, Letter of 18 June 1801.
3 See also the conception of 'fiction' in Rhys Carpenter, *Folk Tale,
  Fiction and Saga in the Homeric Epic* (Berkeley, 1946), pp. 22,
  31–2.
4 Havelock, *Preface to Plato*, pp. 62–4; see also William Bascom on
  the normative function of folklore, 'Four Functions of Folklore',
  The Study of Folklore, ed. Dundes, pp. 297–8.
5 Havelock, p. 173; see also Olrik, 'Epic Laws of Folk Narrative',
  trans. in Dundes, *The Study of Folklore*, p. 137.
6 On the use of the birds as 'characters', compare Havelock on
  Greek oral literature: 'The environment becomes a great society
  and the phenomena are represented as members of this society
  who interact upon each other' (p. 168); and again on the use of
  Belly Blin: '. . . the use of the gods in oral saga can be widely
  explained. They constantly provide an apparatus by which causal
  relations can be rendered in a verbal form with which the listener
  can identify. . . . The complexity of the causal chain is simplified;
  the abstract factors are all crystallised as the interposition of powerful
  persons' (p. 170).

Chapter 9   The Structure of the Ballads I (Pages 87 to 104)

1 See Whitman, *Homer and the Heroic Tradition*, pp. 97–101,
  247–59.
2 See chapter 11 for further description of these terms.
3 'Epic Laws of Folk Narrative', trans. in Dundes, *The Study of
  Folklore*, pp. 136–7.

Chapter 10   The Structure of the Ballads II (Pages 105 to 131)

1 J. F. Campbell, *Popular Tales of the West Highlands* (Edinburgh,
  1860–62), iii, 421–38; see also his *Leabhar na Feinne: Heroic
  Gaelic Ballads* (London, 1872), p. 212, and Child, i, 297–8.
2 In the Greenwood version and in the romance his return is precipitated by the Queen's fear that he might become the teind paid
  to Hell by the Fairies every seven years. The teind motif would
  certainly fit into the tenor of the ballad-story, by showing one
  possible result of breaking the taboo against commerce with the
  Otherworld folk, and by giving point to the third prohibition
  through which the Queen keeps him out of the Fairy Host's power.
  On the other hand, it may owe its appearance in these two places
  to the tendency of the Border tradition to conflate the stories of

Thomas and Tam Lin (see Major Hutton's version of 'Tam Lin', 39M).

3 See also Lord, *The Singer of Tales*, p. 219.
4 *The Ballads*, p. 35.
5 Buchan, 'The Maid, the Palmer, and the Cruel Mother', pp. 103–5.
6 P. 68.
7 P. 97.
8 In *Living With Ballads*, pp. 98–100, Willa Muir relates 'Hind Horn' (17) to the 'hero's return after long absence' story.
9 Lord, pp. 169–85.

Chapter 11   The Structure of the Ballads III (Pages 132 to 144)

1 Ed. and trans. A. D. Lindsay (London, 1935), pp. 74–6. See also Havelock, *Preface to Plato*, pp. 20–1.

Chapter 12   The Sound of the Ballads (Pages 145 to 165)

1 See Lord, *The Singer of Tales*, pp. 4, 30.
2 *Minstrelsy, Ancient and Modern*, p. xix.
3 See p. 102.
4 Compare E. K. Chambers, *The English Folk-Play* (Oxford, 1933), p. 10: 'It is interesting to observe, however, how rhyme helps the memory of the folk. A rhyme-pair, or at least a rhyme-sound, often clings, when the sense of the context has been hopelessly perverted.'
5 Tristram Potter Coffin's related concept of the ballad's 'emotional core' in 'Mary Hamilton and the Anglo-American Ballad as an Art Form', *The Critics and the Ballad*, ed. MacEdward Leach and Tristram Potter Coffin, pp. 245–56, applies to the modern rather than the oral transmission of ballad-stories.

Chapter 13   The Oral Ballad: A Summing-up (Pages 166 to 173)

1 *Minstrelsy, Ancient and Modern*, p. xxiv.
2 Lord, *The Singer of Tales*, pp. 65–6.
3 *English Literature: Mediaeval* (Oxford, 1912), p. 161.
4 Thomas C. Rumble, ed., *The Breton Lays in Middle English* (Detroit, 1965), p. vii.
5 See R. F. Lawrence, 'The Formulaic Theory and its Application to English Alliterative Poetry', in *Essays on Style and Language*, ed. Roger Fowler (London, 1966), pp. 166–83.
6 A knowledge of the formulas of the oral technique, however, would at least modify the kind of ingenious criticism that sees in verbal correspondences between medieval poems 'only one explanation'—a commercial scriptorium (R. S. Loomis, *The Development of Arthurian Romance*, London, 1963, p. 137).

Chapter 14   The Revolutions (Pages 177 to 189)

1 For general accounts of this period see R. H. Campbell, *Scotland since 1707* (Oxford, 1965); W. Ferguson, *Scotland 1689 to the*

Present (Edinburgh, 1968); Henry Hamilton, *The Industrial Revolution in Scotland* and *An Economic History of Scotland in the Eighteenth Century*; J. E. Handley, *Scottish Farming in the Eighteenth Century* (London, 1953) and *The Agricultural Revolution in Scotland* (Glasgow, 1963); W. H. Marwick, *Scotland in Modern Times* (London, 1964); G. S. Pryde, *A New History of Scotland*, Vol. II: *From 1603 to the Present Day* (London, 1962).

2 Sir Archibald Grant, 'Description of the Present State of Monymusk' and Memories of the State of the Country in the early part of the eighteenth century', *Miscellany of the Spalding Club*, ed. Stuart, ii 96–7, 99; Anderson, *A General View of the Agriculture and Rural Economy of the County of Aberdeen*, p. 20; James Grant, *Banffshire Roads during the first half of the Eighteenth Century* (Banff, 1905).

3 Skene Keith, *The Agriculture of Aberdeenshire*, pp. 535–9, 543; David Souter, *A General View of the Agriculture of the County of Banff*, p. 278; Hamilton, *Ind. Rev. Scot.*, pp. 239, 244.

4 Hamilton, *Ec. Hist.*, pp. 75–6; I. F. Grant, 'The Social Effects of the Agricultural Reforms and Enclosure Movement in Aberdeenshire', *Economic History*, i (1926), 107.

5 William Barclay, 'A Northern Diary: The Diary of John Allardise, an Aberdeenshire farmer, 1763–1815', *Transactions of the Banffshire Field Club* (1930), pp. 33–4.

6 Alexander, *Notes and Sketches Illustrative of Northern Rural Life in the Eighteenth Century*, p. 62. See also George Robertson, *A General View of the Agriculture of Kincardineshire or the Mearns*, p. 379; Anderson, p. 81; Souter, p. 123; Sir John Sinclair, ed., *The Statistical Account of Scotland*, v (Pitsligo), 100, vi (Montquhitter), 123, xvi (Deer), 473. *The Statistical Account of Scotland* was compiled by Sir John Sinclair from accounts by their respective ministers of all the parishes in Scotland, and published at Edinburgh in twenty volumes between 1791 and 1799; it is hereafter referred to as the *OSA*.

7 See passim the *OSA*, Anderson, Skene Keith, Souter, Robertson, and for detailed documentation on one estate see Hamilton, *Selections from the Monymusk Papers 1713–1755* and *Life and Labour on an Aberdeenshire Estate, 1735–1750*.

8 Hamilton, *Monymusk Papers*, pp. 108–9.

9 James Grant, *Agriculture in Banffshire 150 years ago* (Banff, 1902), p. 12. See also Alexander, pp. 32–40; *OSA*, v (Keith), 416.

10 J. H. Smith, *The Gordon's Mill Farming Club 1758–64* (Edinburgh, 1962), 38–49.

11 Thomas P. Soper, 'Monymusk 1770–1850' (Unpublished Ph.D. Thesis; University of Aberdeen, 1954), p. 58.

12 *OSA*, xii, 496–7; Hamilton, *Monymusk Papers*, pp. 173, 172, lxx; see also pp. lxxii, 84.

13 Grant, *Agri. Banff.*, pp. 21–4; Souter, pp. 72–5; Alexander, pp. 106–7; Anderson, p. 125.

14 *OSA*, vi (Montquhitter), 128; J. Wilson, 'Farming in Aberdeenshire, Ancient and Modern', *Transactions of the Highland and Agricultural Society*, xiv (1902), 84, citing a minute of the Gordon's Mill Farming Club.
15 Anderson, p. 73; Soper, pp. iv, 29.
16 Skene Keith, pp. 155–6; Hamilton, *Ind. Rev. Scot.*, pp. 74–5 and *Monymusk Papers*, p. 143, where a memorandum records Grant's rationale for the enlargement of farms: 'A large farm is the only way of makeing an esteat by husbandry. It is more certain & less casuall or hazardous than any other bussyness, as well as more innocent, pleasant and ingenious. In a small one, the charge & family to subsist upon it eats up the produce, & it wont allow the various attendants materialls & managements requisite to make advantage, which with the usuall whims or gross negligences of gentlemen is the cause of their miscariage, but a large one, reasonably attended and contrived, is able to allow all charges and will not faile to reward the undertaker. In a large one, all the worke & worke people can be under one view at all times, they can better assist each other than a small number, and also excite each other to diligence & care & honesty; & combinations are less practicable or profitable.'
17 'Rules Orders and Regulations of the Farmer Society of Deer' (Aberdeen, 1795), in a bound volume, *Tracts*, in Aberdeen University Library, pp. 3, 17.
18 Robertson, pp. 451–2; *OSA*, xx (Banff), 368–9; Souter, p. 330.
19 Souter, pp. 327, 329.
20 Hamilton, *Monymusk Papers*, pp. lxxiii, 174, 178, 104–5, 143; *OSA*, xvi (Deer), 471, iii (Fordice), 64–5, vi (Fraserburgh), 7; Skene Keith, pp. 514–5, 523; Souter, pp. 322–4; Robertson, pp. 422–3.
21 *OSA*, xii (Kirkmichael), 438. See also Souter, pp. 322–4; Skene Keith, p. 513; Anderson, p. 121; Barclay, pp. 56, 60; *OSA*, iv (Deskford), 366; and C. W. Sleigh, 'Agriculture on Strichen Home Farm, 1793–1797', *TBC*, xiv (1931), 72.
22 Grant, 'Social Effects', pp. 111–13; *OSA*, vi (Tyrie), 145–6.
23 Alexander Skene, *Memorialls for the Government of the Royal Burghs in Scotland* (1685), 2nd ed. (Aberdeen, 1867), p. 103; I. F. Grant, 'An Old Handicraft Industry in the North of Scotland', *SHR*, xviii (1921), 282–6; Watt, *A History of Aberdeen and Banff*, pp. 318–20; Anderson, pp. 36–7, 50; *OSA*, vi (Maryculter), 82.
24 'Hallow Fair', *The Poems of Robert Fergusson*, ed. Mathew P. McDiarmid, ii (Edinburgh, 1950), 90.
25 Anderson, p. 37; Skene Keith, pp. 578–9. See also 'The Farmer's Ingle', *Poems of Robert Fergusson*, ii, 139.
26 Souter, p. 194; Robertson, p. 284; Hamilton, *Ind. Rev. Scot.*, pp. 100–8, and *Life and Labour*, pp. xxxiv–xl, 137–73. The benefits of linen manufacture were not all economic; 'it has', writes the minister at Cairny, 'almost banished the itch' (*OSA*, xii, 129).

27 William Thom, *Rhymes and Recollections of a Hand-Loom Weaver* (1845), ed. W. Skinner (Paisley, 1880), p. 38.
28 Walton, 'Regional Settlement', *The Northeast of Scotland*, ed. O'Dell and Mackintosh, pp. 87–99.

Chapter 15 The New Society (Pages 190 to 201)

1 Carlo M. Cipolla, *Literacy and Development in the West*, pp. 11–37.
2 Lawrence Stone, 'Literacy and Education in England 1640–1900', *Past & Present*, No. 42 (Feb. 1969), pp. 80–1, 120, 121, 126–7, arrives at extravagant figures for Scotland's literacy rate by, again, taking the stipulation for the deed.
3 Ian J. Simpson, *Education in Aberdeenshire before 1872*, p. 20.
4 Simpson, pp. 21, 214; John Mackintosh, 'Schools', *The Northeast of Scotland*, ed. O'Dell and Mackintosh, p. 209; Souter, *A General View of the Agriculture of the County of Banff*, pp. 318–19; Robertson, *A General View of the Agriculture of Kincardineshire or the Mearns*, p. 222.
5 Simpson, p. 10; see pp. 15–16. In addition, the 'mass of the people' in the early eighteenth century 'were apathetic regarding education' (Simpson, p. 214). A writer discussing a criminal trial of the 1740s noted in the Aberdeen Sheriff Court Records mentions incidentally that 'of the eleven witnesses summoned in this case, five, including Invercauld's ground officer, could not write, and several others, judging by their signatures, could do little more than write their names' (Arthur Birnie, 'Some Glimpses of Aberdeenshire Life in the 18th Century', *AUR*, xviii, 1930, 29–30); Invercauld is in the same area of Upper Deeside as Allanaquoich.
6 Cipolla, p. 45.
7 William Walker, *Some Notes on Chap-Books* (Aberdeen, 1931), pp. 1–4.
8 Simpson, pp. 28, 37, 52, 69–117, 138–44, 213–15; Alexander A. Cormack, *Education in the Eighteenth Century: Parish of Peterculter, Aberdeenshire* (Peterculter, 1965), pp. 27, 44; *OSA*, v (Strachan), 376–7; John Allardyce, *Bygone Days in Aberdeenshire* (Aberdeen, 1913), p. 135. In Peterculter, one schoolmaster, the George Skene Keith of the 1811 *General View*, was appointed at the age of fifteen and a half (Cormack, p. 51).
9 Simpson, pp. 216, 26; Laurance J. Saunders, *Scottish Democracy 1815–1840: The Social and Intellectual Background* (Edinburgh, 1950), pp. 288–93; William Paul, *Past and Present of Aberdeenshire* (Aberdeen, 1881), pp. 80–1, 86–8.
10 Paul, p. 81; Simpson, p. 24.
11 *Preface to Plato*, p. 47.
12 *Appendix to the Regulations, List of Members, and Catalogue of Books of Banff Literary Society* (Banff, 1820); Craig, *Scottish Literature and the Scottish People 1680–1830*, pp. 203–8; George Walker, *Aberdeen Awa'* (Aberdeen, 1897) pp. 71–83; John and

Muriel Lough, 'Aberdeen Circulating Libraries in the Eighteenth Century', *AUR*, xxxi (1945), 17–23; Robertson, p. 199.

13 Simpson, p. 205. The *New Statistical Account of Scotland* was compiled by J. Gordon from reports of parish ministers and published in eighteen volumes (Edinburgh, 1843).

14 Souter, p. 319.

15 Skene Keith, *The Agriculture of Aberdeenshire*, pp. 612–13.

16 John Fraser, *The Humorous Chapbooks of Scotland* (New York, 1873), pp. 2–3.

17 Gregor, *An Echo of the Olden Time from the North of Scotland*, pp. 32–3.

18 Skene Keith, p. 516; J. F. and T. M. Flett, 'The Scottish Country Dance. Its Origins and Development: i', *SS*, 11 (1967), 1–11. 'It is . . . not until about 1775 that we have the first real evidence of Country Dances being performed by the ordinary people in Scotland' (Flett, p. 3); see also the Fletts' *Traditional Dancing in Scotland* (London, 1964), pp. 2–6.

19 Skene Keith, p. 613; Simpson, pp. 45–7.

20 *OSA* [see p. 302, n. 6], iii (Fordice), 64; v (Keith), 428; xvi (Peterculter), 371–2.

21 *OSA*, vi, 132.

22 William Barclay, 'A Northern Diary: The Diary of John Allardise, an Aberdeenshire Farmer, 1763–1815', *Transactions of the Banffshire Field Club* (1930), pp. 41, 43.

23 *OSA*, iii (Fordice), 51, 62–3; v (Keith), 428; vi (Montquhitter), 134, (Leochel), 220.

24 See, for example, the tabulated comparison in *OSA*, xx (Banff), 363–5.

25 Skene Keith, p. 516.

26 Robertson, pp. 277, 288; *OSA*, vi (Newhills), 36; iii (Fintray), 237; v (Keith), 417; vi (Tyrie), 139.

27 Robertson, pp. 426, 441; *OSA*, vi (Montquhitter), 126; xvi (Peterculter), 372; xvi (Deer), 479.

28 *OSA*, vi (Foveran), 68; Robertson, p. 426; *OSA*, vi (Ordiquhill), 352.

29 Alexander, *Notes and Sketches Illustrative of Northern Rural Life in the Eighteenth Century*, pp. 10–11; James Colville, 'Aberdeenshire in the Eighteenth Century', *Aberdeen Journal Notes and Queries*, vii (1914), 44; George Kay, 'The Landscape of Improvement; A Case Study of Agricultural Change in North-east Scotland', *Scottish Geographical Magazine*, 78 (1962), 104.

30 *OSA*, iii (Fordice), 48; v (Cruden), 435; xii (Auchindoir), 493; xvi (Deer), 478; vi (Rathen), 16; xx (Banff), 348.

31 Robertson, p. 442; *OSA*, xii (Kirkmichael), 446–7, (Aberdour), 580–1.

32 *OSA*, xii, 469–70.

33 *Rhymes and Recollections of a Hand-Loom Weaver* (1845), ed. W. Skinner (Paisley, 1880), pp. 6–10, 13.

34 Paul, pp. 69–70; Gregor, *Olden Time*, pp. 23, 28; Alexander, pp. 143–4.

Chapter 16   The Peter Buchan Controversy (Pages 205 to 222)

1 *Peter Buchan and Other Papers*, passim, and *Last Leaves*, pp. xix–xxiv.
2 Letter of 3 May 1825, in William Motherwell, *Poems*, with a Memoir by James M'Conechy, 3rd ed. (Glasgow, 1865), p. xxxiii.
3 Letter of 28 April 1825, Harvard University Library, North Country Ballads: Letters from Abbotsford, xiv, 94.
4 Letter of 14 September 1800, Nicols, vii, 90.
5 Harvard University Library, Child MSS. xvi, 133, 135, 137.
6 Letter of 17 February 1897, Aberdeen University Library, Will Walker MSS., Letters from Prof. Child etc. to W. W. 1890–1903 (number 32). The inception of the 1827 MSS., now at Harvard University Library, is referred to by Buchan in a letter to Motherwell, dated 17 January 1826 and now also at Harvard, when he speaks of collecting 'all my fragments and detached pieces of Old Ballads into a volume by themselves'. The Buchan MSS. Child did see were those of 1828, now in the British Museum, which 'are of a different character and value from that of 1827. Their contents consist of transcripts from his earlier MS. of such items as had not been printed in 1828—a considerable number of ballads taken from broadsheets and chapbooks,—with a few which may have been traditional. Most of the songs are traditional, and though not of that worth which Peter in his enthusiastic way believed them to be, are yet genuine remains of north country lilts still sung' (Walker, *Buchan*, pp. 126–7).
7 Walker, *Buchan*, p. 124.
8 Letter of February 1873, Child MSS., i, 82–3.
9 Letter of 5 January 1875, Child MSS., x, 149.
10 Letter of 5 November 1875, Child MSS., x, 144.
11 Edinburgh, 1862, p. 305.
12 *Ancient Danish Ballads*, i (London, 1860), xv. See pp. 7–8 and *Last Leaves*, pp. xxii–xxiv.
13 *The Ballad of Heer Halewijn* (Helsinki, 1958), pp. 297–316. For a full discussion of Nygard's attack on Buchan see D. D. Buchan, 'Lady Isabel and the Whipping Boy', *Southern Folklore Quarterly*, xxxiv (1970), 62–70.
14 Henderson, 'The Green Man of Knowledge', *SS*, ii (1958), 69; see passim. Grosart and Campbell saw the tales in manuscript, but they were eventually published in *TBC*, ix (1908), 128–94, and reprinted as *Ancient Scottish Tales*, ed. John A. Fairley (Peterhead, 1908).
15 Child, ii, 170.
16 Harvard University Library, A Ballad Note-Book 1826–27, p. 157.
17 Harvard University Library, Peter Buchan: A Collection of 17 Letters. For Bell Robertson's notes see Walker, *Buchan*, pp. 59–60, and *Last Leaves*, pp. 279–80.

18 Walker, *Buchan*, p. 59; cf. Scott's portrait of Davie Gellatley in *Waverley* (Edinburgh, 1814).

19 ii, 368; Kittredge and Sargent, eds, *English and Scottish Popular Ballads*, p. xxx; *The Ballad Book*, p. 31.

20 *Buchan*, pp. 10–13.

21 Ed. J. G. Tait and W. M. Parker (Edinburgh, 1950), p. 428. See also Walker, *Buchan*, pp. 48–50, and *Minstrelsy of the Scottish Border*, ed. T. F. Henderson, i, 51–3.

22 Sharpe wrote to Scott in a letter dated only 1828: 'I have had two terrible literary flytes here lately in which I often wished for you to back me, being almost certain of your invincible aid—the first was about Peter Buchan's ballads, which Mr. Secretary Laing hath got to edite—Peter desired the favour of me to look over the proofs,—but when they came I found that Mr. David set up for a poet, for sooth, and altered word and verse—the beauty of the alterations you may guess at knowing the person. I entered my protest, declaring I would have nothing more to do with the matter; if such abominations went on—so after a world of debate, that matter was carried on the side of common sense and propriety' (*Letters from and to Charles Kirkpatrick Sharpe*, ed. Alexander Allardyce, Edinburgh, 1888, ii, 415).

23 Appendix A; see especially pp. 244, 248, 249, 257, 261, 264, 269, 270.

24 Hustvedt, pp. 264, 257, 264, 269, 248, 249, 244, 261, 270.

25 Hustvedt, p. 264.

26 Lord, *The Singer of Tales*, pp. 137, 130.

27 See Walker, *Buchan*, pp. 202–8; Craig, *Scottish Literature and the Scottish People 1680–1830*, pp. 128–9.

28 See Thomas Crawford, 'Scottish Popular Ballads and Lyrics of the Eighteenth and Early Nineteenth Centuries: Some Preliminary Conclusions', *Studies in Scottish Literature*, i (1963), 53.

29 *Poems* (Edinburgh, 1721), p. 80. The touch of the transcriber was not a happy one; the rather peculiar beginning of the broadside version's third stanza originally stood as:

> And Mary's locks are like *the* craw,
> Her *eye* like diamonds glances

30 See the list compiled by J. A. Fairley in Walker, *Buchan*, pp. 151–7.

31 Fraser, *The Humorous Chapbooks of Scotland* (New York, 1873), p. 6.

32 P. 130.

33 From a collection called 'Squibs, Cartoons, Broadsheets and other Fugitive Writings relating to Aberdeen 1785–1890', which was compiled by Will Walker and deposited in Aberdeen Town House.

34 William Bannerman, *The Aberdeen Worthies* (Aberdeen, 1840), p. 91.

35 David Laing minced no words when he returned Buchan's verses on 'May': 'The truth is, if you will excuse me for saying so, that

they are written in bad taste, and as a caution to avoid the use of such words, as you will see are scored under with a pencil, let me request you, at some time or other, to write them over again, in a more simple and natural style' (Walker, *Buchan*, p. 44; see also the letter from Laing on p. 34).

36 As is evident from his own chap publications and his relationship with Keith, Buchan was directly involved in the broadside industry. From a letter to Motherwell dated 17 January 1826 it appears, even allowing for the hyperbole, that he himself had a fair stock of them: 'As to the other old Ballads in my possession . . . I suppose half a dozen of sheets of paper would not contain all their names, many of them collected by myself of the stalls, and from Ballad singers in London, Edinb., Glasgow, etc. I have also travelled much in Aberdeenshire. . . .'

37 By a different route, a study of certain 'Aberdeen Ballads', Gabrielle Humbert reaches a conclusion similar to that reached here in *Literarische Einflüsse in Schottischen Volksballaden* (Halle, 1932), p. 113: 'His versions deserve the place they have in the Child Collection. An objective appraisal will judge his sole failing to have been a lack of genius and will not ascribe to him intentional forgeries made out of a literary vanity.' (Seine Fassungen verdienen die Stellung, die sie im Rahmen der Childschen Sammlung annehmen. Und ein objektives Urteil wird ihm als einzigen Fehler Mängel an Genie, aber nicht absichtliche Fälschungen aus literarischer Eitelkeit zusprechen.)

38 *Buchan*, p. 13.

39 Lord, p. 134.

Chapter 17   The Ballads of James Nicol (Pages 223 to 243)

1 v, 178.

2 Peterhead, 1823; Aberdeen, 1831; Aberdeen, 1832; Aberdeen 1835.

3 Walker, *Peter Buchan and other Papers*, p. 126; Alastair Shanks, 'Strichen School', *AUR*, xlii (1967), 49.

4 Harvard University Library, Peter Buchan: A Collection of 17 Letters.

5 In the *Garland*, four pieces are ascribed to Pitcairn; one ('O! what a Parish!') is unascribed but appears in Pitcairn's MSS.; and one ('The Jolly Hawk and the Tearsel') is taken from a printed source. Nicol must also have furnished the text of 'The Young Laird of Craigstoun', for it turns up again in the 'North Country Ballads'.

6 v, 223.

7 *Letters from and to Charles Kirkpatrick Sharpe*, ed. Alexander Allardyce (Edinburgh, 1888) ii, 309. Scott's 'notices' on the pieces in the 'Second Collection' are printed in Charles Kirkpatrick Sharpe, *A Ballad Book*, ed. David Laing (Edinburgh, 1880), pp. 144–6.

8 The Nicol ballad-texts are distributed among the collectors thus:

	BUCHAN	MOTHERWELL	MAIDMENT	SHARPE	SCOTT
34A	X	X		X	
39D*		X	X	X	
41C	X	X			
65B		X		X	
66A		X	X	X	X
72D		X			
90B		X		X	
110E	X	X			
173M	X		X		
188D	X	X			
196A	X	X	X	X	X
197	X	X		X	
198A	X		X	X	X
221G			X	X	X
223			X	X	X
231D	X		X	X	X
239A	X		X	X	X
246A	X	X		X	
257C		X		X	
259			X	X	X
302	X	X			

* Also in Pitcairn's MSS.

9 Edinburgh, 1824.
10 ii, 173.
11 *The British Traditional Ballad in North America*, pp. 8–16.

Chapter 18   The Ballads of Bell Robertson (Pages 247 to 254)

1 G. M. Fraser, 'An Aberdeenshire Rural Press', *The Lone Shieling* (Aberdeen, 1908), pp. 169–79.
2 Some good examples of slip-songs are to be found in a collection rather misleadingly entitled 'Squibs, Cartoons and other papers connected with the University' deposited in Aberdeen Town House by Will Walker. Items 24 and 26 are composed of slip-songs locally printed in the eighteen-sixties 'for singers at Feeing Markets', and include such songs as 'Paddy's Voyage', 'She's just the thing', 'Last Rose of Summer', 'The Weary Garret', 'Shadey Groves', 'Highland Mary', 'O'er the Muir', 'Gallant Hussar', 'Does your mother know you're out', and 'Buy a Broom'.
3 *Last Leaves*, p. 193. In *FSNE* (article clvi) Greig prints two stanzas of 'The Rantin Laddie' which Keith does not include in *Last Leaves*.
4 *An Echo of the Olden Time from the North of Scotland*, p. 23.
5 Mrs Frank Russell, *Fragments of Auld Lang Syne* (London, 1925), pp. 316–17.

6 *Last Leaves*, pp. 260, 253, 270, 254. All the songs by Bell Robertson referred to in this chapter come from *Last Leaves*.
7 Walker, *Peter Buchan and Other Papers*, p. 60.

Chapter 19 *The Bothy Ballads* (Pages 255 to 270)

1 'The Bothy System', *Essays* (Edinburgh, 1890), pp. 201–2, 201; see also *My Schools and Schoolmasters* (Edinburgh, 1893), pp. 115–17.
2 George Houston, 'Labour Relations in Scottish Agriculture before 1870', *Agricultural History Review*, vi (1958), 34.
3 James Allan, 'Agriculture in Aberdeenshire in the Sixties', *The Deeside Field*, iii (1927), 33.
4 Gwenllian Evans, 'Farm Servants' Unions in Aberdeenshire 1870–1900', *SHR*, xxxi (1952), 29. See also G. H. Kinnear, *Agriculture in the Mearns* (Montrose, 1895), pp. 24–5.
5 P. 205.
6 The Disruption of 1843 in the Church of Scotland can also be seen as a sign of this tension, for the denunciation of patronage by the Free Church reflected a growing dislike of the powers of the landlords; see William Alexander, *Johnny Gibb of Gushetneuk* (Edinburgh, 1871).
7 See the maps given by Robertson, *A General View of the Agriculture of Kincardineshire or the Mearns*, opposite p. 91, and Souter, *A General View of the Agriculture of the County of Banff*, opposite p. 182.
8 Hamilton, *Selections from the Monymusk Papers, 1713–1755*, p. 12.
9 Pp. 33, 32.
10 P. 425.
11 Allan, pp. 32–3.
12 P. 205; see, however, John R. Allan, *Farmer's Boy* (London, 1935), pp. 111–14, 95–100.
13 Harvard University Library, Child MSS., i, 47; Buchan, *Ancient Ballads and Songs of the North of Scotland*, ii, 109–17; *FSNE*, articles lxvii, cxlvi; Ord, *The Bothy Songs and Ballads of Aberdeen, Banff and Moray, Angus and the Mearns*, pp. 480–6.
14 Harvard University Library, Alexander Laing of Brechin MS., 1829–35, p. 23.
15 Fraser, *The Humorous Chapbooks of Scotland* (New York, 1873), pp. 224–5.
16 *FSNE*, p. 43; see also pp. 43–50, and Ord, pp. 1–26.
17 The songs referred to, both here and later in the chapter, are all to be found in *FSNE*; as it has no pagination beyond the introduction, references are to article numbers. See also Ord, pp. 209–85. 'Lamachree and Megrum' differs from the others in that it deals with a succession of farms instead of just one farm.
18 *FSNE*, article xcii.

19 Gale Huntington, *Songs Whalemen Sing* (Barre, Mass., 1964), p. 34;
   E. C. Beck, *They Knew Paul Bunyan* (Ann Arbor, Mich., 1956),
   pp. 120–2.

Chapter 20 Conclusion (Pages 271 to 277)

1 Tristram Potter Coffin.
2 G. Malcolm Laws.
3 Hustvedt, *Ballad Books and Ballad Men*, p. 218 n. 1.
4 The standard collection of ballad music is Bertrand Bronson's *The
   Traditional Tunes of the Child Ballads*.
5 'Stability of Form in Traditional and Cultivated Music', *The Study
   of Folklore*, ed. Dundes, pp. 170–4.
6 'Prolegomena to a Study of the Principal Melodic Families of Folk
   Song', *The Critics and the Ballad*, ed. Leach and Coffin, p. 110.
7 *English Folk Song*, pp. 28, 30.
8 See Gavin Greig's comments, *FSNE*, p. 53, and Bertrand Bronson,
   'The Interdependence of Ballad Tunes and Texts', in Leach and
   Coffin, pp. 100–102.
9 Cipolla, *Literacy and Development in the West*, p. 55.
10 *The Ballad of Tradition*, p. 193.
11 Child MSS., xvi, 143.

A Selected Bibliography

Ballad collections, other than anthologies, which contain Northeast material are listed in the Appendix.

Alexander, William, *Notes and Sketches Illustrative of Northern Rural Life in the Eighteenth Century*, Edinburgh, 1877.

Allan, James, 'Agriculture in Aberdeenshire in the Sixties', *The Deeside Field*, iii (1927), 29–36.

Allan, John R., *North-east Lowlands of Scotland*, London, 1952.

Allardyce, James, ed., *Papers Relating to the Jacobite Period 1699–1750*, 2 vols, Aberdeen, 1895–6.

Anderson, James, *A General View of the Agriculture and Rural Economy of the County of Aberdeen*, Edinburgh, 1794.

Bronson, Bertrand, ed., *The Traditional Tunes of the Child Ballads*, Princeton, N.J., 1959– .

——, 'Mrs. Brown and the Ballad', *California Folklore Quarterly*, iv (1945), 129–40.

Brown, P. Hume, ed., *Scotland before 1700 from Contemporary Documents*, Edinburgh, 1893.

Chadwick, Hector M. and Nora K., *The Growth of Literature*, 3 vols, Cambridge, 1932–40.

Chambers, E. K., *English Literature at the Close of the Middle Ages*, Oxford, 1945.

Child, Francis James, ed., *The English and Scottish Popular Ballads*, 5 vols, Boston, 1882–98.

Cipolla, Carlo M., *Literacy and Development in the West*, London, 1969.

Coffin, Tristram Potter, *The British Traditional Ballad in North America*, rev. ed., Philadelphia, 1963.

Collinson, Francis, *The Traditional and National Music of Scotland*, London, 1966.

Craig, David, *Scottish Literature and the Scottish People 1680–1830*, London, 1961.

Dickinson, William Croft, *From the Earliest Times to 1603*, Vol. I of *A New History of Scotland*, London, 1961.

Dundes, Alan, *The Morphology of North American Indian Folktales*, Helsinki, 1964.

——, ed., *The Study of Folklore*, Englewood Cliffs, N.J., 1965.

Entwistle, William, *European Balladry*, 2nd imp., Oxford, 1951.

Friedman, Albert B., ed., *The Viking Book of Folk Ballads*, New York, 1956.
——, *The Ballad Revival*, Chicago, 1961.
Gerould, Gordon Hall, *The Ballad of Tradition*, Oxford, 1932.
Gordon, J., ed., *New Statistical Account of Scotland*, 18 vols, Edinburgh, 1843.
Grant, Isabel F., *The Social and Economic Development of Scotland before 1603*, Edinburgh, 1930.
Gregor, Walter, *An Echo of the Olden Time from the North of Scotland*, Edinburgh, 1874.
——, *Notes on the Folk-Lore of the North-East of Scotland*, London, 1881.
——, *The Industrial Revolution in Scotland*, Oxford, 1932; new imp. 1966.
——, ed., *Selections from the Monymusk Papers 1713–1755*, Edinburgh, 1945.
——, ed., *Life and Labour on an Aberdeenshire Estate, 1735–1750*, Aberdeen, 1946.
Hamilton, Henry, *An Economic History of Scotland in the Eighteenth Century*, Oxford, 1963.
Havelock, Éric A., *Preface to Plato*, Cambridge, Mass., 1963.
Hodgart, M. J. C., *The Ballads*, 2nd ed., London, 1962.
——, ed., *The Faber Book of Ballads*, London, 1965.
Housman, J. E., ed., *British Popular Ballads*, London, 1952.
Hustvedt, Sigurd B., *Ballad Books and Ballad Men*, Cambridge, Mass., 1930.
Keith, G. Skene, *The Agriculture of Aberdeenshire*, Aberdeen, 1811.
Kittredge, G. L., and Sargent, H. C., eds, *English and Scottish Popular Ballads*, Cambridge, Mass., 1904.
Laws, G. Malcolm, *American Balladry from British Broadsides*, Philadelphia, 1957.
——, *Native American Balladry*, rev. ed., Philadelphia, 1964.
Leach, MacEdward, ed., *The Ballad Book*, New York, 1955.
——, and Coffin, Tristram Potter, eds, *The Critics and the Ballad*, Carbondale, Ill., 1961.
Lévi-Strauss, Claude, *Structural Anthropology*, New York, 1963.
Lord, Albert B., *The Singer of Tales*, Cambridge, Mass., 1960.
McLuhan, Marshall, *The Gutenberg Galaxy*, Toronto, 1962.
McPherson, Joseph M., *Primitive Beliefs in the North-East of Scotland*, London, 1929.
Major, John, *A History of Greater Britain* (1521), trans. A. Constable, Edinburgh, 1892.
Michie, John G., ed., *The Records of Invercauld 1547–1828*, Aberdeen, 1901.
Muir, Willa, *Living With Ballads*, London, 1965.
O'Dell, A. C., and Mackintosh, J., eds, *The Northeast of Scotland*, Aberdeen, 1963.

Propp, Vladimir, *Morphology of the Folktale*, trans. Laurence Scott, ed. Svatava Pirkova-Jakobson, Bloomington, Ind., 1958.

Rent Roll of Estates of William, 7th. Baron Forbes, for year 1552, Banff, 1876.

Robertson, George, *A General View of the Agriculture of Kincardine-shire or the Mearns*, London, 1807.

Sharp, Cecil J., *English Folk Song*, 4th ed., ed. Maud Karpeles, London, 1965.

Simpson, Claude M., *The British Broadside Ballad and its Music*, New Brunswick, N.J., 1966.

Simpson, Ian J., *Education in Aberdeenshire before 1872*, London, 1947.

Simpson, W. Douglas, *The Province of Mar*, Aberdeen, 1943.

——, *The Earldom of Mar*, Aberdeen, 1949.

Sinclair, Sir John, ed., *The Statistical Account of Scotland*, 21 vols, Edinburgh, 1791–9.

Souter, David, *A General View of the Agriculture of the County of Banff*, Edinburgh, 1812.

Stuart, John, ed., *List of Pollable Persons within the Shire of Aberdeen 1696*, 2 vols, Aberdeen, 1844.

——, ed., *Miscellany of the Spalding Club*, 5 vols, Aberdeen, 1841–52.

Walker, William, *Peter Buchan and Other Papers*, Aberdeen, 1915.

Watt, William A., *A History of Aberdeen and Banff*, Edinburgh, 1900.

Whitman, Cedric H., *Homer and the Heroic Tradition*, Cambridge, Mass., 1958.

Wilgus, D. K., *Anglo-American Folksong Scholarship since 1898*, New Brunswick, N.J., 1959.

Index of Ballads, Songs, Poems and Tales

315

General Index

fermtoun 18–27, 35, 184–5, 189, 268, 275
feudalism 29, 35–47
feuding 40–7
Fife 63
Fifteen rebellion 32, 191
Findlay, Rev. William 278
Fintray Press 247
Fionn 115
fishers 197
Fleeman, Jamie 186
Flemings 15
folklore 17, 51, 53, 60, 118
folktales 115, 199, 209
Forbes, Duncan 45
Forbes, Sir John de 42
Forbes, Lillias 62
Forbes, Lord (1690) 32
Forbes,Master of (1587) 33
Forbes, Baillie William 62–3
Forbes lands, depredations of 32
Forbes Rent Roll 22–3, 36
Forbeses 41–3, 45–6, 173
Formartine 24
Forres 44
Forsyth, William 265
Forth and Clyde canal 178
Forty-Five rebellion 32, 45, 177, 179, 191
France 9, 78, 209, 276
Fraser Tytler Brown MS. 65–6, 69–72, 155
Fraserburgh 264

Gaelic culture 8–10, 35, 46–7, 115, 118, 209; *see also* Celts; Highlands
Galloway 13, 210
Garioch, John 249
Garioch, the 13, 43
Gentleman Farmer 193
Georges, Robert 60
German Peasants' War 39
Germany 26–7
Gerould, G. H. 5, 59–60, 276
Gerrard, Gilbert 70
Gibb, James 67, 278
Gibb, Mrs 67

Gibbon, Lewis Grassic 16
Gilderoy 42
Gillespie, Mrs 248
Glaister o' Glack 43
Glasgow 6, 178
Glenbuchat ballads 5, 278
Glenmuick 44
Goldstein, Kenneth 279
Good Neighbourhood 25, 31, 184, 198
Gordon, Duchess of (1691) 37–8
Gordon, Lord Lewis 45
Gordon, Thomas 62–4, 70, 72, 180, 274
Gordon of Knockespock 188
Gordon Rent Roll 36
Gordons 36, 37–8, 40–1, 43–6, 173
Gordons of Newton 41
Gordon's Hospital 199
Gordon's Mill Farming Club, The 62, 180
Gow, Neil 201
Grampians 13
Grant, Sir Archibald 21, 177–9, 181, 184–5
Grant, Lairds of 30, 32–3
Grants 33
Greek culture 192; *see also* Homeric literature; Plato
Gregor, Walter 248
Greig, Gavin 5, 8, 205, 210, 213, 215, 248–54, 261–70, 278, 279
Grosart, A. B. 209
Grundtvig, Svend 7, 212–13

Harlaw, battle of 29–30, 34
Harris, Amelia 67
Harris, Mrs 66, 67
Harvard University 70, 71
Havelock, Eric 132, 192
Henderson, Hamish 209, 211, 279
Henderson, T. F. 279
Herd, David 159, 278, 279
Herzog, George 274
Highlands 6, 28–34, 35–8, 43–4, 46–7; *see also* Celts; Gaelic culture

Picts 13, 15
Pitcairn, Robert 70, 225–6
Plato 132, 192
plays and pageants 16
ploughing matches 258, 265
population, increase in 186
Pound, Louise 3
Presbyterianism 16, 191
Prior, R. C. A. 208, 213
Privy Council 32, 33, 41, 42, 43–4
Propp, Vladimir 60

Radlov, V. V. 56–8
Ramsay, Allan 218, 222
Rankin, James 209–11, 213
Reformation, the 15, 16, 45, 68, 190
regional tradition
  evolution 167–70, 273–4
  historical ballads 7, 29, 33–4, 43–7, 76
  participants 81, 275–6
  supernatural ballads 7, 76
  women 64, 76, 81
reiving 30–4, 47
rents 22–3, 37, 40, 182
Revolutionary Wars 185
Ritson, Joseph 70–1
Robertson, Bell 210–11, 249–54
Robertson, George 259
Robertson, Jeannie 275
Robertson, Joseph 208, 278, 279
Robin Hood 42
Rosenbach, Dr 71
Ross, Earldom of 29
Russell, Mrs Frank 249
Russian bards 68
Ryabinin-Andreev, Peter 68

Scandinavia 7–8, 9, 17, 26–7, 46–7, 115, 208–9, 213
School of Scottish Studies 5, 279
Scott, Jannie 66, 67
Scott, Robert 69–70, 72, 75, 115
Scott, Rev. Robert, of Glenbuchat 278
Scott, Sir Walter 6, 63, 69, 70, 71, 72, 173, 199, 205–6, 207,

212, 225–7, 251, 278, 279
Scottish Lowlands 4, 5–6, 14, 15, 28–9, 46, 187
Scottish Wars of Independence 18, 39
Seafield, Lord (Chancellor) 68, 179
Secret Songs of Silence MS. 211
Seeger, Peggy 280
Sempill, Francis 261
services of tenant 22, 181, 182
settlement pattern 185, 188–9,
Shakespeare 28, 71, 73   [247
Sharp, Cecil 274–5
Sharpe, Charles Kirkpatrick 212, 225–7, 278
Shorter Catechism, the 191, 192
Sim, Adam 70
Simpson, Dr W. Douglas 45
Skene, Sir George 63
Skene, James, of Rubislaw 6, 63, 225, 278
Skinner, John 216, 217
slip-songs 248
Societie of the Boyis 42–3
sorners 37, 40
Spain 17, 46–7, 78
standard of living, rise in 194–8
steelbow tenure 36
Stevenson, John 212
Stevenson, Thomas 279, 280
Stewarts, the 40
Stonehaven 193, 213
Strachan, John, of Lynturk 42
Strathbogie 13, 43, 44
Strathdee 44
Strathspey 33
Strichen 210, 223, 226, 249

tacks 19–23, 25, 36, 181, 182
Tannahill, Robert 199–200, 217, 261
Tascal-Money 32
Telford, Thomas 178
textile industries 186–8, 201, 247, 255
Thistle of Scotland, The 217–18, 227, 248, 279
Thom, William 188, 199–201

325